Human Rights in Islam

By

Jamaal Zarabozo

1435 H - 2014 G

Introduction

Many scholars are quick to point out that human rights has become a, if not *the*, dominant theme of the world today. For example, Ann Kent writes in *Between Freedom and Subsistence: China and Human Rights*, "The problem of human rights lies at the heart of modern political discourse."[1] Some argue that even those countries which are not completely enamored by the human rights concepts go out of their way to demonstrate that their actions do not violate human rights.[2] Indeed, who could possibly be against a concept entitled "human rights"?

With respect to Islam in particular, Khalid Abou El Fadhl wrote, "Of all the moral challenges confronting Islam in the modern age, the problem of human rights is the most formidable."[3] Undoubtedly, Muslim countries, organizations, scholars and individuals feel the necessity of explaining exactly where they stand on the question of human rights. Actually, the situation has gone even beyond that to one of apparent acceptance of the concept as a whole. When many Muslims speak about political issues, such as the Middle East conflict, they speak about it in terms of human rights. In fact, many times in intra-Muslim political debates centering about rights, it is the human rights paradigm that often resonates with the audience regardless of who that audience may be.

However, in this author's view, a number of important questions have gone relatively unanswered. These questions include: Is the human rights doctrine deserving of the amount of respect and admiration that it has received? What, in detail, should be a Muslim's attitude toward the concept of human rights and the contemporary human rights paradigm in particular? Just as importantly, what is the human rights doctrine's attitude toward Islam? For example, does a Muslim truly

---

[1] Quoted by Anthony C. Yu, "Enduring Change: Confucianism and the Prospect of Human Rights," in Elizabeth M. Bucar and Barbra Barnett, eds., *Does Human Rights Need God?* (Grand Rapids, Michigan: William B. Eerdmans Publishing Company, 2005), p. 107.

[2] Cf., Jack Donnelly, *Universal Human Rights in Theory & Practice* (Ithaca: Cornell University Press, 2003), p. 1.

[3] Khaled Abou El Fadhl, "The Human Rights Commitment in Modern Islam," in Joseph Runzo, Nancy M. Martin and Arvind Sharma, eds., *Human Rights and Responsibilities in the World Religions* (Oxford, England: One World, 2003), p. 301.

have the right to practice his religion within the framework of contemporary human rights thought?

Due to the general importance of human rights in today's world, it is important at the outset to state a few important conclusions that this author has reached.

First, in the contemporary world, a situation wherein human rights are generally recognized and respected seems to be far superior to that of a situation in which such rights are trampled upon and denied. This explains the popularity of human rights among the downtrodden and oppressed, including Muslim masses throughout the world. Regrettably but factually, human rights schemes hold out a promise that many have yet to experience and joy.

Second, even though the philosophies behind the rights are different, there are definitely some recognized human rights that are fully supported by Islam and, as such, it becomes incumbent upon Muslims throughout the world to defend and support such rights—as Muslims must always be a people who defend and support the truth while striving against falsehood, oppression and tyranny.

Third, it must be recognized that the contemporary secular human rights scheme is a not a "complete way of life"—a fact admitted by many human rights proponents (as shall be noted later). At the same time, though, human rights schemes many times become "idolatrous" in the sense that their demands sometimes take precedence over any other beliefs or religion (or they demand that their laws take precedence over religion). The contemporary human rights movement is making demands upon Muslims that touches upon some core Islamic beliefs and practices. It is the argument of this author that if human rights proponents want Muslims to change their religion in the light of their demands, they had best present strong reasons and "proofs" that are convincing enough to require such a demand in a Muslim's perspective. If such "proofs" cannot be offered, it is unfair to demand that Muslims change their ways for something unproven and which rests on faulty foundations.

Fourth, when compared to Islam, the stark reality, though, is that the human rights platform has no means for proper guidance of humankind. The most that it can say is that there is a feeling or agreement that humans, for whatever intrinsic reason, are deserving of rights simply because they are human. However, once those rights are formulated and delineated, one finds that they are, in the light of absolute freedoms and rights, illogical and self-contradicting. Thus, even though Muslim authors as a whole, especially those writing in English, have also jumped on the human rights bandwagon, it could be the case that this human rights movement is not much more than another fad like that of the white man's burden, socialism[1] and the like. Indeed, it is the thesis of this author that the approach and the synthesis created by many such authors is, in the long-run, unacceptable from an Islamic perspective. In fact, the compromises that are made in the name of Islam will be equally unacceptable to the human rights proponents as well.

The Author's Understanding of the Proper Islamic Methodology

Before continuing, the author is compelled to explain his understanding of "Islam" or "Islamic methodology." In other words, what he means by "Islam," "Islamic" and so on. The reason this is important and why it must be stated forthrightly at the outset is that much of the writing on Islam and human rights is premised on the claim that there is no "one Islam," instead there are many "Islams" or many types of Muslim. Many contemporary writers, both Muslim and non-Muslim, are arguing that Islam and Muslims are not monolithic.[2] This may be true. However, their conclusion from this that virtually any expression of Islam should be acceptable and, in fact, should be praiseworthy if it is consistent with human rights doctrine is an illogical and unacceptable conclusion.

---

[1] During the high time of socialism/communism, many Muslim authors wrote about how compatible Islam and socialism were, claiming that the Prophet (peace and blessings of Allah be upon him) or some of his Companions were the first real socialists. Today, many are writing that Islam was the first to bring about human rights and that all of the contemporary human rights demands are already captured in Islam.

[2] See, for example, Mayer writes, "A central thesis of this book is that one should not speak of 'Islam' and human rights as if Islam were a monolith or as if there existed one established Islamic human rights philosophy that caused all Muslims to look at rights in a particular way. The precepts of Islam, like those of Christianity, Hinduism, Judaism, and other major religions possessed of long and complex traditions, are susceptible to interpretations that can and do create conflicts between religious doctrine and human rights or that reconcile the two." Ann Elizabeth Mayer, *Islam and Human Rights: Tradition and Politics* (Boulder, CO: Westview Press, 4th Edition, 2007), p. xi; See also Irene Oh, *The Rights of God: Islam, Human Rights, and Comparative Ethics* (Washington, D.C.: Georgetown University Press, 2007), p. 7; Vartan Gregorian, "Islam: A Mosaic, not a Monolith," at www. drsoroush/E-CMO-20021100-Islam-A_Mosaic-Not_a_Monolith.html.

In such a view, the issues of human rights and Islam simply boil down to ensuring that the proper "form" of Islam is applied throughout the Muslim world. Thus, in a work entitled *Religious Fundamentalisms and the Human Rights of Women*, the Algerian Mahnaz Afkhami expresses a not uncommon view in such works of how any understanding of Islam should be equally valid,

The central point in women's human rights is simple. The Islamists always posit the question of women's rights within an Islamist frame of reference. That frame of reference determines the boundaries of my existence as a Muslim woman. The questions I ask are: Why should I, as a mature Muslim woman, not have the right to determine how to organize my personal life? What gives another person the right to interfere in my personal life? Why is it that a Muslim cleric arrogates to himself the right to place me forcibly in a preordained framework? Does he derive his authority from God? Does he derive it from the text? Does he derive it from tradition? I reject all of these claims for his authority. I argue that as a Muslim woman I know in principle as well as any man what God ordains or what the text says. I argue that tradition is no longer a valid source of authority because societies change, cultures change, I change, and I am both willing and able to discuss these points with him.[1]

Somehow, perhaps due to historical reasons, this type of reasoning resonates with many human rights activists, especially the feminists among them. Can there be an honest and frank discussion of human rights and Islam if such a position on Islam is considered tenable?

There are a number of important points that must be made concerning this non-atypical passage.[2] Her only claim to understanding Islam is the fact that she is a "Muslim woman." The question of scholarship, basing one's view on a sound methodology of interpreting the text and so forth seems to be irrelevant. In fact, it

---

[1] Mahnaz Afkhami, "Gender Apartheid and the Discourse of Relativity of Rights in Muslim Societies," in Courtney W. Howland, *Religious Fundamentalisms and the Human Rights of Women* (New York, NY: Palgrave, 2001), p. 72.

[2] One important aspect that shall be ignored for the time being is that Afkhami is attempting to present the picture of the "traditional" understanding of Islam as that of men vis-à-vis her understanding as a woman. The reality is that there are numerous female Muslim scholars who would disagree with Afkhami and find themselves in agreement with the "him" she refers to as long as "his" statements are consistent with the Quran and Sunnah.

seems that she will reject a man's interpretation even if it is derived from the text. In reality, could there be any serious religion which claims to presents God's truth to the world that could open it doors to any interpretation of the faith simply because an individual is a member of that faith or simply because the individual is a human/male/female, regardless of whether one's understanding of the faith is based upon the texts of the religion of the teaching of the original prophet? Even with all of these shortcomings, her writing finds her way into a "scholarly work" on women's human rights. Sadly, her voice is one of the few writings about Islam that actually comes from a Muslim, as most anthologies have at the most one or two Muslim authors.[1]

One other occasions, one finds lavish praise for heretical groups in Islam, such as the Khawarij, Mutazilah and Republican Brothers (of Sudan), as representing brands of Islam that will human rights platforms can coexist with.[2] Furthermore, the most common representation of Islam and human rights in Western works is probably that of a modernist/progressive position.[3]

---

[1] Thus, for example, in a work entitled *Religion and Human Rights: Competing Claims*, the section on Islam was written by a non-Muslim, Elizabeth Ann Mayer. Apparently the one Muslim they could find who was supposed to write a "reply" or comment to Mayer's work was not able to participate. See Carrie Gustafson and Peter Juviler, eds., *Religion and Human Rights: Competing Claims* (Armonk, New York: M. E. Sharpe, 1999), passim.

[2] Examples of this nature shall be given shortly.

[3] Although other religions are often presented in a variety of ways via a variety of writers, in a number of scholarly works or symposiums, Ann Elizabeth Mayer, a non-Muslim, many times discusses the issue with respect to Islam. In fact, other than Khaled Abou El-Fadhl and Abdullahi An-Na'im (the views of those two shall be discussed in detail later), very few "Muslim voices" are represented and if they are they are usually modernist/progressive as well. Note the following works as examples: Elizabeth M. Bucar and Barbra Barnett, eds., *Does Human Rights Need God?* (Grand Rapids, Michigan: William B. Eerdmans Publishing Company, 2005), with Khaled Abou El Fadhl the only Muslim contributor; Hans Kung and Jurgen Moltmann, *The Ethics of World Religions and Human Rights* (London, England: SCM Press, 1990), with Abdullahi An-Na'im representing Islam; Joseph Runza, Nancy M. Martin and Arvind Sharma, eds., *Human Rights and Responsibilities in the World Religions* (Oxford, England: Oneworld Publications, 2003), with articles from both Abdullahi An-Na'im and Khaled Abou El Fadhl—and an additional one from Amir Hussain; John Witte, Jr. and Johan D. van der Vyver, eds., *Religious Human Rights in Global Perspective* (The Hague, Holland: Martinus Nijhoff Publishers, 1996), with an article by Abdullahi An-Na'im and one by Riffat Hassan.

In this work, the author is approaching the issue of Islam and human rights within the framework of "orthodox Sunni Islam."[1] For those who believe in this understanding of Islam, it is actually the only proper manner by which to discuss this topic. It is true that there are many Muslims throughout the world today who do not believe in or agree with such a perspective. However, that does not negate the fact that it is still one of the most dominant views of Islam today and that much of the Islamic revival that has occurred within the Muslim world during the past century has been in the light of this understanding of Islam. Hence, any serious discussion of Islam and human rights has to take this understanding of Islam head on, rather than offering other forms of Islam that may have very little relevance for the majority of Muslims today.

Some of the seminal features of this "orthodox Sunni Islam" worldview include:

(1) The Quran is the Word of God revealed to the Prophet Muhammad (peace and blessings of Allah be upon him) as perpetual guidance for Muslims. Muslims are obligated to live their lives according to the Quran's guidance. As the Quran states about itself, it is a "clear book,"[2] and its general principles and guidance can be understood by all. As for more detailed aspects of its interpretation, its interpretation is based on principles derived from the Quran itself laid down by scholars throughout the ages, including principles related to the Sunnah (words and practice of the Prophet) and Arabic language.[3] Any interpretation of the Quran which violates the guidance of the Prophet (peace and blessings of Allah be upon him) or the principles of the Arabic language would, thus, not be acceptable.

---

[1] Amazingly, there is probably no good term or expression to convey this meaning in English. The word "orthodox" has implications that are not appropriate. Another term commonly used is "traditional Islam." However, if what is meant by that term is simply what Muslims have been traditionally following, that is not what is meant here as those traditions themselves may contradict the Quran or Sunnah. Another popular term nowadays is "fundamentalist Islam." Again, the history of this term's usage in the West does not apply to Islam. Furthermore, it has strong negative connotations.

[2] Allah says, for example, "Indeed, there has come to you from Allah a light and a clear Book" (*al-Maaidah* 15); "These are the Verses of the Book, and a clear Qur'an" (*al-Hijr* 1). Allah also states that the Arabic of the Quran is a clear Arabic (see *al-Nahl* 103 and *al-Shuaraa* 195).

[3] The Quran states that it has been revealed in the Arabic language in *Yoosuf* 2, *al-Raad* 37, *al-Nahl* 103, *Taha* 113 and *al-Shuaraa* 195, and elsewhere.

(2) The Prophet's Sunnah[1] is an ultimate authority in Islam. There are at least fifty verses in the Quran that establish the importance and authority of the Sunnah of the Prophet (peace and blessings of Allah be upon him).[2] Once again, any interpretation or understanding of Islam that stands in clear contradiction to the way of the Prophet (peace and blessings of Allah be upon him) must be rejected.

(3) The Companions were guided by the Prophet (peace and blessings of Allah be upon him), there understanding was approved by him and, hence, they were along the Straight Path. It does not mean that they were perfect or super-human but it does mean that their understandings of the general concepts of what it means to be a Muslim were correct. Furthermore, this does not mean that contemporary Muslims of this understanding yearn to return to some "idealized past,"[3] but it does mean that their examples are to be learned from and emulated.

(4) The consensus (*ijmaa*) of the Muslim Nation is also an authority in Islam.[4] It is the case that consensus is many times difficult to prove. However, there are definitely times in which something is explicitly stated in the Quran or Sunnah and there is a consensus concerning the understanding of said clear text. An example of this nature would be the amputating of the hand as a punishment for the theft. The Quranic verse is clear on this point and all of the scholars of the past agreed with this general fact.

Again, regardless of whether the reader agrees, disagrees, is pleased or is displeased with this view of Islam, it is a reality for a large number of Muslims throughout the world and it is what one must deal with. Writers about Islam and human rights cannot assume that this view will be changed any time soon among the Muslims. This does not mean that other movements among Muslims do not have some footing, such as the modernist movement. However, still, the overall

---

[1] This refers to the Prophet's statements, actions and tacit approvals.

[2] See the "Appendix," in Jamaal al-Din M. Zarabozo, *The Authority and Importance of the Sunnah* (Denver, CO: Al-Basheer Company, 2000), pp. 257-272.

[3] This is a common critique of "fundamentalists" of various religions. See, for example, John Stratton Hawley, "Fundamentalism," in Courtney W. Howland, *Religious Fundamentalisms and the Human Rights of Women* (New York, NY: Palgrave, 2001), p. 3.

[4] The evidence for the authority of consensus may be found in any basic work on Islamic legal theory (*Usool al-fiqh*).

presentation of Islam that resonates the most with the masses is that of the "orthodox Islam" explained above.

Unfortunately, not everyone who writes about Islam and human rights takes this commonly accepted approach. This has probably caused more confusion than added anything positive to the understanding of the relationship between Islam and human rights. Hence, at this time, it is appropriate to review the basic trends in the literature on Islam and human rights.

Contemporary Trends in the Relationship between Human Rights and Islam

In this abridged survey of the literature, examples from the three major trends in the literature will be touched upon and briefly critiqued.[1]

The three approaches may be summarized as follows:

(a)   The first group of authors argue that there is nothing inherently inconsistent between Islam and human rights. In fact, the basic ideas of the human rights movement can be found in Islam. However, the caveat here is that the "traditional" or "orthodox" understanding of Islam must be discarded. This approach can be termed the modernist/progressive approach.

(b)   The second group of authors argues that, in essence, Islam is not compatible with human rights. In fact, the application of Islam—and for many of these authors, the application of any of the known religions[2]—means nothing but violating the international human rights norms. These writers may have some empathy for the writers found in group (a) above but, in general, their tone towards religions in general and Islam in particular is not very positive or is antagonistic. This approach will be referred as the pessimistic approach. It may also be described as the "human rights

---

[1] The author is not claiming that no authors fall outside of the scope of these three trends. These are the major trends that encompass the vast majority of related works on this topic. Thus, for example, Baderin writes, "Halliday has identified at least four classes of Islamic responses to the international human rights debate. The first is that Islam is compatible with international human rights. The second is that true human rights can only be fully realized under Islamic law. The third is that the international human rights objective is an imperialist agenda that must be rejected, and the fourth is that Islam is incompatible with international human rights. There is a fifth noteworthy response omitted by Halliday, which is that the international human rights objective has a hidden anti-religious agenda. Viewed critically, most of these responses are Muslim reactions to what is often described as the double standards of countries at the helm of international human rights promotion. The responses reflect the entrapment of human rights between humanitarianism and international politics rather than actual disagreements with the concept of human rights in Islamic law. We will now evaluate these responses within the perimeter of Islamic law..." Mashood Baderin, *International Human Rights and Islamic Law* (Oxford, England: Oxford University Press, 2003), p. 13.

[2] Oh (p. 10) writes, "Some of the most prominent theories of human rights in the West today dismiss Islam altogether with claims that religion generally presents obstacles to human rights progress." She cites, in particular, Ignatiefff and Donnelly.

extreme" or "human rights fundamentalist" approach or the "human rights dominance paradigm."

(c)　　The third group of authors are those who support and believe in "orthodox" Islam, as described above, and they argue that that Islam does not, in essence, violate human rights norms. At first glance, it would seem that the present author would be part of this group. However, this author feels that the approach of this group is fundamentally flawed as shall be demonstrated throughout this work. Furthermore, the approaches of many of these authors has left them open to valid criticism from the writers found in groups (a) and (b). This will be referred to as the "somewhat faulty" approach. Actually, this approach may best be described as the "apologetic" approach, a non-flattering word that definitely has some important implications for one's understanding of Islam.

The Self-Proclaimed Modernist/Progressive Approach

The self-proclaimed modernist or progressive approach essentially views human rights doctrine as a modern or progressive development. The basic premise of this approach is that the "orthodox" understanding of Islam is, in fact, inconsistent with contemporary human rights law. The "orthodox" teachings of Islam, on the other hand, may have been quite revolutionary or progressive at some point in time in history but they are no longer valid or proper for current times. Hence, the understanding and particularly the practice of the religion of Islam needs to be tweaked, modernized and understood in a new light, virtually discarding what has been traditionally accepted as Islamic understandings. In this way of looking at things, conformity with contemporary human rights thinking is the goal that requires that Islam adjust itself. This view is popular with a number of writers who currently live in the West and teach at various universities. Writers in this group include Khaled Abou El Fadl, Abdolkarim Soroush[1], Abdullahi an-Na'im and others. By simply googling these names, one is bound to come across entries that will describe each of them as the "leading expert on human rights and Islam…" Hence, some aspects of their teachings need to be dealt with in detail here.

---

[1] Examples from the work of An-Na'im and Abou El Fadl shall be presented here. Soroush's views are reviewed in Oh, *passim*.

Abdullahi an-Na'im is originally from Sudan but is currently teaching at Emory University in Georgia. He is a prolific writer and has published in numerous journals and anthologies.[1] An-Na'im is a follower and staunch supporter of Mahmoud Mohamed Taha (1909-1985), a Sudanese "reformer" who propagated what he termed, "the second message of Islam."[2] Eventually, Taha was executed by Gaafar Nimeiry for his outlandish views.[3] An-Na'im's influence on the question of Islam and human rights is great, as he represents Islam in numerous forums and has also influenced a large number of both Muslim and non-Muslim authors.[4]

---

[1] Although this author's approach to Islam varies a great deal with an-Na'im's understanding, it is true that an-Na'im has made some very insightful comments on human rights in his various and numerous publications.

[2] *The Encyclopedia of Islam and the Muslim World* calls him the "leading representative" of the school of Taha. Richard C. Martin, editor in chief, *Encyclopedia of Islam and the Muslim World* (New York: MacMillan Reference USA, 2004), p. 590.

[3] It should be noted that the death penalty for apostasy has rarely been carried out in the history of Islam. However, it was carried out on Muhammad Mahmood Taha. Above anything else, this is a reflection of the extreme that this man went to in his views.

[4] Probably due to the lack of other voices in the West, numerous non-Muslim authors rely on such authors when writing about Islam and human rights. Thus, for example, Bell virtually completely relied upon an-Na'im for his words about Islam. This includes the following interesting statement that has an-Na'im as its source: "In fact, this is an area of dispute within Islamic circles. Some 'progressive' interpreters argue that the injunction against drinking alcohol refers only to certain types of liquor and the obligation not to be inebriated during prayer time, and not a blanket ban on drinking alcohol (conversation with Addullah An-Na'im)." Daniel A. Bell, *East Meets West: Human Rights and Democracy in East Asia* (Princeton, NJ: Princeton University Press, 2000), p. 72. Surprisingly, though, he has also greatly influenced some Muslim writers. Shaheen Ali, for example, was influenced by his writings, as she quotes him throughout Shaheen Sardar Ali, *Gender and Human Rights in Islam and International Law: Equal Before Allah, Unequal Before Man?* (The Hague, Netherlands: Kluwer Law International, 2000). Gokal calls him, "One of the premier scholars of Shariah" [Alison Swicker Gokal, "Human Rights and Shari'a: An Essay on the development and use of Shari'a in Islamic States and its meaning for Women in Iran, a country with a history of criticism from Human Rights groups and the United Nations," (*Hertfordshire Law Journal* 5(1), 86-106), p. 105]. Amir Hussain refers to him by saying, "For Ustadh Abdullahi Ahmed An-Na'im who inspired a generation of us with *Toward an Islamic Reformation*" [Amir Hussain, "'This tremor of Western wisdom': A Muslim response to human rights and the declaration," in Joseph Runzo, Nancy M. Martin and Arvind Sharma, eds., *Human Rights and Responsibilities in the World Religions* (Oxford, England: One World, 2003), p. 176]. At the same time, though, one finds no reference to his writings in the major writings on human rights that are written in Arabic by Muslim scholars.

An-Na'im's premise is that there is a "drastic incompatibility between Shari'a and modern standards of international relations and human rights."[1] Thus, he calls for a "drastic reform" in the public law of the Shariah. He claims that his view would resonate with many Muslim throughout the world who out of fear of speaking or out of ignorance of the implications of the Shariah would oppose Shariah law if they had the means to do so.[2]

The sum of his argument as to why Muslims of today should be free to construct their own version of the Shariah is as follows,

I have shown that Shari'a was in fact *constructed* by Muslim jurists over the first three centuries of Islam. Although derived from the fundamental divine sources of Islam, the Qur'an and Sunna, Shari'a is not divine because it is the product of *human interpretation* of those sources. Moreover, this process of construction through human interpretation took place within a specific historical context which is drastically different from our own. It should therefore be possible for contemporary Muslims to undertake a similar process of interpretation and application of the Qur'an and Sunna in the present historical context to develop an alternative public law of Islam which is appropriate for implementation today.[3]

It is true that humans have had a hand in the development of *fiqh*.[4] It is also true that humans are fallible. Muslim scholars throughout the history of Islam have admitted that and have actually acted on the basis of that premise, thus differing with one another, refuting one another and so on. However, that in itself does not prove that what those scholars developed is incorrect or needs to be redone today. If it is proven that the way they understood the Quran or Sunnah is incorrect and that there is an alternative, equally sustainable and provable understanding of the texts, then humans are free to chose another interpretation. Thus, one would have to prove that the methodology of *fiqh* is completely wrong or on particular points scholars have

---

[1] Abdullahi Ahmed An-Na'im, *Toward an Islamic Reformation: Civil Liberties, Human Rights, and International Law* (Syracuse, NY: Syracuse University Press, 1990), p. 184.

[2] An-Na'im, *Toward*, p. 185. He, of course, can offer no proof for such a claim.

[3] An-Na'im, *Toward*, pp. 185-186.

[4] Note that an-Na'im is misusing the word *Shareeah*, which is most commonly used to specifically refer to the texts of the Quran and Sunnah and which, hence, are not products of humans.

misunderstood the texts of the Quran and Sunnah. An-Na'im does not bother to do either. He simply starts and ends with the proposition that humans are fallible, humans produced fiqh and there that fiqh which they produced may be dispensed with today. Engineers are also humans who are fallible. However, that does not mean that one should do away with all of the building techniques that they developed, ignore their principles and insist on new ones simply because they were fallible human beings. That, though, is the logic of an-Na'im's argument.

The basic flaw of An-Na'im's arguments (and of many of those similar to him) is that he begins with a proposition and then they seek to impose that proposition on their understanding of the revelation from God. For example, when speaking about the rights of women and non-Muslims, An-Na'im writes, "In the case of Islam, for example, one must be able to establish a technique for reinterpreting the basic sources, the Qur'an and Sunna, in a way that would enable us to remove the basis of discrimination against women and non-Muslims."[1] Ignoring the question of such "discrimination," there is a very basic logical flaw in this argument when seen in a religious light (and not simply a contemporary secular light). His approach is the proverbial "putting the cart before the horse." Indeed, what is the purpose of the revelation in the first place if its only purpose is to be consistent with ideas that humans have concluded on their own?[2]

Finally, an-Na'im must be credited with perhaps the most ironic statement of all the writers on Islam and contemporary human rights. He is presented as one of the leading voices of Islam on human rights and many seem to have hope in him that he will truly spark a change. Yet, at the same time, he himself recognized a very important fact: "For instance, Muslims are unlikely to take seriously the advocacy of Islamic reform by a non-Muslim, or a Muslim who is perceived to be a heretic or

---

[1] An-Na'im, *Toward*, p. 163.

[2] One may pose the question: How is it that such works even get published when they contain such faulty propositions? One must recall that the secular academic world of the West, in general, perceives religion as being a product of the human mind and imagination. In other words, when one does not believe that religion is a revelation from God and thus having a source above and beyond human intellect, it is acceptable then to argue that the tenets and texts of the religion must be made to conform with any new position that humans may take.

apostate for going too far in his or her critique of prevalent understandings of Islam."[1] This is ironic because An-Na'im is the leader of an extreme movement itself. As An-Naim stated,

In addition to explaining and documenting the validity of this premise, I have suggested that the reform methodology developed by the late Sudanese Muslim reformer Ustadh Mahmoud Mohamed Taha appears to be the most appropriate means for constructing the modern public law of Islam out of the Qur'an and Sunna as interpreted in the present historical context. Whether this particular methodology is accepted or rejected by contemporary Muslims, the need for drastic reform of the public law of Shari'a is beyond dispute.[2]

Thus, Na'im is the leader[3] of a movement that was considered so outlandish that its founder was one of the few in Islamic history who actually received the death penalty for apostasy. Of course, none of An-Na'im's views are to be rejected simply because he is the follower of such a movement. In fact, when writing about human rights, secularism and other topics, An-Na'im does have some insightful things to say. However, this movement has definitely so colored his vision of Islam that the proposals that he is making concerning human rights and Islam will most likely never resonate with the masses. In fact, Western institutions have invested a lot in An-Na'im but in the long-run it may be all for naught, as he himself alludes to in the passage quoted above.

Khalid Abou El Fald is another highly praised and important figure in Western discussions of Islam and human rights. Apparently, he is a self-proclaimed Mutazili and is even touted as the leading authority on Islamic law in the United States. He currently teaches at the University of California at Los Angeles.

---

[1] Abdullahi An-Na'im, "The Synergy and Interdependence of Human Rights, Religion and Secularism," in Runzo, et al., p. 41.

[2] An-Na'im, *Toward*, p. 186.

[3] John Voll writes, "The leading representative of this school of thought is Abdullahi An-Na_im, one of Taha's students who, as an expatriate, developed Taha's thinking further and became a prominent Muslim scholar in the field of human rights and international law." John Voll, "Republican Brothers," in Richard C. Martin, ed., *Encyclopedia of Islam and the Muslim World* (New York, New York: MacMillan Reference, 2004), vol. 2, p. 590.

As was noted about modernists/progressives, Islam needs to be reformulated and understood in a new light in order for it to be consistent with human rights theory. The following example from Abou El Fadl demonstrates one of the approaches used to justify reinterpreting Islam or questioning established principles of Islam. In the passage quoted below, Abou El Fadl casts doubt upon how Muslims can claim to know with certainly the meaning of a Quranic passage. Actually, his argument goes well beyond that. His argument is that no one can claim to know what any part of the revelation truly means. The implication that he is trying to make is obvious: If one can never be certain what the Quranic passages truly mean, Muslims should then be free to interpret in a variety of ways and, when that is done, there should be no difficulty in interpreting them in the light of contemporary human rights and international law.

The relevant Quranic passage is the following: "Cut off the hand of the thief, male or female, as a recompense for that which they committed, a punishment by way of example from Allah. And Allah is All-Powerful, All-Wise" (*al-Maaidah* 38). Concerning this verse, Abou El Fadl writes,

The Qur'an uses the expression *iqta'u*, from the root word *qata'a*, which could mean to sever or cut off, but it could also mean to deal firmly, to bring to an end, to restrain, or to distance oneself from. Whatever the meaning generated from the text, then, can the human agent claim with absolute certainty that the determination reached is identical to God's?...

This does not mean that the exploration of God's law is pointless; it only means that the interpretations of jurists are potential fulfillments of the divine will, but the laws as codified and implemented by the state cannot be considered as the actual fulfillment of these potentialities.

But the law of the state, regardless of its origins or basis, belongs to the state. It bears emphasis that under this conception there are no religious laws that can or may be enforced by the state. The state may enforce the prevailing subjective commitments of the community (the second school), or it may enforce what the majority believes to be closer to the divine ideal (the first school). But it bears emphasis: in either case, what is being enforced is not God's law. *This means that all laws articulated and applied in a state are thoroughly human, and should be treated as such…*[1]

It does not take a Muslim scholar of great prominence to refute the above presentation from Abou El Fadl. The only way that El Fadl could come to such conclusions and thereby question the understanding of the Shareeah of the whole was by: (1) distorting the context of the verse or actual Arabic construct of the verse and (2) completely ignoring how the Prophet (peace and blessings of Allah be upon him) understood and applied the verse.[2] First, the verse does not say, "Cut him off," but explicitly states, "Cut off their hands."[3] A word in Arabic may be prone to numerous figurative meanings but when used in relationship with specific other terms, no such figurative meanings are known. Thus, this author perused the classical Arabic dictionaries *Lisaan al-Arab, Taaj al-Uroos, Tahdheeb al-Lughah* and *al-Qaamoos al-Muheet* and did not find any hint of the term, "Cut his hand off," ever implying, as Abou El Fadl states, "Deal firmly, to bring to an end, to restrain, or to distance oneself from." Again, such a distortion of the text would probably not escape the sight of many, many Muslims.

Abou El Fadl has a lengthy passage in which he speaks about the historical debate about when a scholar uses personal juristic reasoning (*ijtihaad*) and whether he is always going to be correct or not. Some have held the view that the scholar is always correct—in other words, his view is to be taken as a correct view—while others argued that he will be rewarded for his efforts but he may be mistaken in his

---

[1] Khaled Abou El Fadl, "Islam and the Challenge of Democratic Commitment," in Elizabeth M. Bucar and Barbra Barnett, eds., *Does Human Rights Need God?* (Grand Rapids, Michigan: William B. Eerdmans Publishing Company, 2005), pp. 102-103 (emphasis added). Incidentally, Abou El Fadl took this entire passage from his earlier work (earlier with respect to publication date), Khaled Abou El Fadl, et al., *Islam and the Challenge of Democracy* (Princeton: Princeton University Press, 2004), p. 35.

[2] It would not be surprising if it is the case that Abou El Fadl or others like him simply do not consider the Prophet's implementation or understanding of the Quran as binding or divinely inspired. This is not the proper place to discuss this issue in detail. The interested reader may consult this author's work: Jamaal al-Din Zarabozo, *The Authority and Importance of the Sunnah*, pp. 103-127.

[3] Although one cannot necessarily map from one language into another, one can close equivalents to the above example. If someone says, "He cut him off," it is possible that he physically cut him off from a building although most likely he cut him off while he was talking or driving or cut him off at the pass. However, once one says, "He cut his hands off," the possibility of their being any other meaning is virtually removed.

conclusion. After this discussion, Abou El Fadl tries to argue that concerning either view, one will never truly be able to say what God's law is. This conclusion is very important to him. Based on premise, he can make statements like, "Shari'a encompasses a variety of schools of thought and approaches, all of which are equally valid and equally orthodox."[1] Hence, there can be no exclusion to introducing a new Islamic paradigm consistent—actually built upon—contemporary human rights thinking. However, in all of that discussion, Abou El Fadl has ignored or overlooked a very important point that destroys his entire edifice. The discussion that he presented and the doubt he was able to cast upon finding the truth is only concerned with matters of *ijtihaad* or when personal juristic reasoning is necessary. A well-established principle states that there is to be no *ijtihaad* when the texts of the Quran or Sunnah are definitive and explicit. Many of the laws that El Fadl deals with, including the punishment for the theft in the example given above, a explicit, definitive texts that are not open to *ijtihaad*. This is why no previous scholar ever concluded that there could be any other punishment for theft. The texts were clear, definitive and explicit and hence it was not a question of *ijtihaad*, which is not infallible.

Note that, like An-Na'im, Abou El Fadl's implications are not truly rational, although modernists usually claim to be rational. Simply because some laws may be open to some amount of doubt does not mean that whole project then needs to be shredded and one is free to start from scratch with any interpretation one desires. In law, it is not the case that one needs absolute certainty that one's interpretation is correct, as long as enough of the evidence and proofs point to it, it will be sufficient. The act of casting doubt and thereby permitting completely new interpretations has been a current theme among progressives and modernists (an-Na'im's example about the "shariah" can also apply here) but the implications that they are trying to impose from it are simply extreme and irrational.

Soroush's views are perhaps even more extreme than the two discussed above[2] and, as Oh states, "The discussions by Soroush on democracy, toleration, and

---

[1] Khalid Abou El Fadl, "The Human Rights Commitment in Modern Islam," in Runzo, et al., p. 321.

[2] To this author, it seems that Suroush's views are much less influential in both the West and in the Sunni world and hence much less space will be devoted to him.

human rights stand out as the most compatible with current Western notions of human rights."[1] Mayer summarizes Soroush's main concept of justice in the following statement: "Soroush has dared to maintain publicly that justice preceded Islam and that Islamic law should conform to the criterion of justice."[2] Thus, Soroush has a theory that God's religion must be simply based on the concept of justice and freedom.[3] However, it goes without saying that "justice" and "freedom" are vague terms to say the least and one's person's concept of justice or freedom may be very different than another person's concept of those ideals. In fact, it could be argued that humans do not need Divine guidance if that is the most Divine guidance has to offer.

Expectations Related to This Approach

Although some Western authors seem to place a lot of hope in such Muslim writers and in such an approach to Islam,[4] the simple fact is that such an approach will probably never be accepted by the Muslim world as a whole. Oh notes, "Well-known American scholars, such as Abdullahi An-Na'im and Ann Mayer, have written extensively on human rights, but their influence is felt primarily in North American and Western European audiences."[5] She does not bother to explain why

---

[1] Oh, p. 112.

[2] Mayer, *Islam and Human Rights*, p. 53.

[3] See Oh, pp. 86-87. Abou El Fadl makes virtually the same argument in Runzo, et al., p. 330, where he stated, "In my view, justice and whatever is necessary to achieve justice is the divine law and is what represents the supremacy and sovereignty of the Divine." It is interesting to note that one of his main arguments is that *ijtihaad* based on Quranic texts is "doubtful," yet he seems to propose that "justice" (not based on texts or anything, apparently) will be easier to nail down.

[4] See for example Mayer's praise of an-Na'im and Abou El Fadl in Mayer, *Islam and Human Rights*, p. 58.

[5] Oh, p. 7. An-Na'im recognizes this fact but remains very optimistic of his own possible influence, stating (pp. 186-187), "It may therefore appear presumptuous to expect a book that is written in English and is likely to be banned in some Muslim countries to have any significant impact in the Muslim world. Despite the oppressive nature of most political regimes and the conservative orientation of many societies in the Muslim world, however, I believe that the ideas expressed here will reach the hearts and minds of many Muslims. For one thing, most of these ideas already exist, perhaps in somewhat rudimentary and reticent form, in the hearts and minds of many Muslims, especially the younger generations, who are the more active agents of social change. It is my hope and expectation that this book will act as a catalyst for change in the Muslim world by presenting these ideas in a systematic and comprehensive fashion and

they have virtually no influence elsewhere. It is probably because the Muslim scholars and many of the Muslim masses can easily see that such presentations are seriously flawed. In fact, one often wonders exactly towards whom such writers are writing. One can reasonably ask as to whether they are simply writing for Western academia, which seems willing to accept any new theory about Islam.

There have been other attempts at a "synthesis" between Islam and non-Islam in the past and, for the most part, they met with failure. Noah Feldman, for example, can understand how this approach to develop a different style of Islam is reminiscent of previous failed attempts. Feldman, commenting on Abou El Fadl's work, stated,

Efforts such as Abou El Fadl's to synthesize Islam with democracy recall the medieval Islamic philosophers who sought to integrate Aristotle and Plato with an authentically Islamic worldview. Al-Farabi, Averroes, and Avicenna produced a rich philosophical literature, *but their intellectual influence was greater in the Western world*, and to a lesser extent the Persian-speaking one, than among the Arabs.[1]

It cannot seriously be expected that the writings of such individuals in their professorship chairs in the West is truly going to have a strong influence on the ground in the Muslim world, especially not when their arguments are so flawed. They are simply tweaking Islam "too much" in order to achieve their "human rights results."

The reason such writings may resonate with Western writers and not with Muslims is that many Westerners do not understand how different Islam is from Christianity or Judaism. Although, some in the West seem to be expecting some kind of Martin Luther-like reformation in the Muslim world but that will probably never resonate with the Muslims. The Mutazilah never became the dominant paradigm (even when they held power for a little) and the modernist movement of Abduh-

---

providing them with an Islamic rationale. Moreover, the cultural interdependence of the modern world is making it increasingly difficult to exclude ideas and diminish their impact."

[1] Noah Feldman, "The Best Hope," in Khaled Abou El Fadl, et al., *Islam and the Challenge of Democracy* (Princeton: Princeton University Press, 2004), p. 61. A classic example is that of Averroes (ibn Rushd) who is heralded as such a great Muslim philosopher in the West while S. Maqbul Ahmad writes in the widely acclaimed *The Encyclopedia of Islam*, "Ibn Rushd had few disciples in Islam" (S. Maqbul Ahmad, "Ibn Rushd," in B. Lewis, et al., *The Encyclopaedia of Islam* (Leiden: E. J. Brill, 1986), vol. III, p. 919.)

Afghani has had its influence but it was quickly refuted and seen as faulty. Contemporary modernists may be very influential in the West and in some parts of the Muslim world but it is very difficult to expect that they will ever become the dominant paradigm. There is simply too much up against them. The situation is different in Islam than in Christianity in many ways. For example, there is no oppressing Church to revolt against. Similarly, science has not falsified the Quran in any way as many felt it did with respect to the Bible.

Before moving on, it is important to note that there are also some very troubling points related to the virtual pushing of a modernist theology upon the Muslim world. One should never forget the great deal of bloodshed that took place in Europe as a result of such movements—interacting with various political facts. One need only read Norman Housley's *Religious Warfare in Europe 1400-1536* and Richard Dunn's *The Age of Religious Wars 1559-1715* to realize that one is speaking about centuries of "religious wars" internally among Christians in Europe due to such reformations in the Church, which one could argue were needed in Christianity due to its own particular history. With the brute force of contemporary warfare and the fact that the world has become a "global village," it is hard to imagine that one would want something of that nature to be unleashed in the Muslim world today. However, sadly, it is hard to expect that anything other than that will occur when people are forced to accept views of their own religion that they simply did not believe in or agree with. Without convincing the Muslims first, with sound Islamic arguments, that such changes are acceptable and needed from an Islamic perspective, violence is a most likely result. The contemporary modernists, in this author's view, have failed to present any compelling Islamic arguments and, as such, forcing their views, in the name of "human rights" or any other platform, is most likely to lead to more harm than good.

The Pessimistic Approach

The pessimistic approach, in essence, sees Islam (perhaps, religion as a whole) as more of a hindrance than a help when it comes to implementing human rights throughout the world. In particular, this approach has no patience for what has been termed here "orthodox" Islam—although they will more likely use the term "fundamentalist Islam." This view revolves around three major points:

(1)   The contemporary human rights scheme is proper and must be applied. Thus, there is no room for any religion to violate human rights.

(2)   Muslim states must abide by the documents that they have signed. If Muslim states make reservations to the documents, their reservations are to be rejected and, in essence, ignored, if those reservations virtually negate the spirit and intent of the document.

(3)   Human rights have become part of international norms and laws today. Thus, even if Muslim states have not signed onto certain documents, they are obligated by law to abide by such international standards. Indeed, some authors clearly argue that it is high time that the international community uses all of the means available to it to force Muslim states to abide by such international norms.

Although a number of authors may be placed in this category, due to space limitations, a limited number will be discussed in detail here.

One work that deserves some special attention is Ann Elizabeth Mayer's *Islam and Human Rights: Tradition and Politics.* Its fourth edition has just been published. It is used as a textbook in many university courses throughout the United States. Additionally, in a number of anthologies about human rights, it is Mayer who is chosen to write about the relationship between Islam and human rights, not to speak of the numerous conferences that she has attended while representing the authority on Islam and human rights.

Mayer is a strong proponent of the universality of human rights. This belief means that every human is deserving of the same set of human rights and, as such, no religious or cultural practice may interfere with the acceptance of such human rights. In fact, she refutes the concept of cultural relativism at length and on numerous occasions makes it clear that Muslims should be free to have the right to practice their religion *as long as it does not violate said human rights*. Thus, she wrote, "Believing that international human rights law is universally applicable, I naturally also believe that Muslims are entitled to the full measure of human rights protections offered under international law."[1] This rather innocuous statement—and

---

[1] Mayer, *Islam and Human Rights*, p. xv.

here this author is using the type of language that Mayer uses when commenting on Islamic human rights schemes—implies a great deal more than what first may come to the mind of the reader. More than anything else, she is actually speaking about Muslim having the human right to follow laws that violate the religion of Islam.

Mayer is one of those many who argue that Islam is not a out, Muslims throughout the world have varying views on the relationship between Islam and human rights—some outwardly rejecting the concept while others completely embracing it. Here, she is correct, as no one can doubt the existence of these viewpoints among contemporary Muslims. However, one cannot jump from this fact and the claim that Islam is not a "monolith" to the conclusion that there are numerous acceptable versions of "Islam." In the following passage, Mayer admits that she is an outsider writing about Islam and cannot truly tell Muslims what version of Islam they should ultimately accept. She states,

I welcome the emergence of principled human rights advocacy in Middle Eastern countries and the growing tendency to interpret Islamic sources in ways that harmonize Islamic law and international human rights. However, I recognize at all times that I am an outside observer commenting on developments in another tradition, one in which my views can have no normative or prescriptive value. Therefore, I do not endorse any particular reading of Islamic doctrine, nor do I presume to signal which interpretations Muslims should deem authoritative.[1]

It is possible to accept her statement, "nor do I presume to signal which interpretations Muslims should deem authoritative," yet at the same time her book is mostly dedicated to showing how the "orthodox" understanding of Islam undercuts human rights and therefore cannot be accepted from an international perspective.[2] Seen in an international law perspective, she may not be "signaling" to Muslims what they may believe in but she certainly does seem to be *demanding* that those views of Islam incompatible with contemporary human rights schemes not be tolerated.

---

[1] Mayer, *Islam and Human Rights*, p. xv.

[2] For example, on p. 3 she writes: "On the contrary, Islamic human rights schemes, such as the one promoted by the Organization of the Islamic Conference, have consistently used distinctive Islamic criteria to cut back on the rights and freedoms guaranteed by international law, as if the latter were excessive."

Mayer claims that she believes in freedom of religion, as all good human rights proponents would also claim. However, it is very clear that Mayer's understanding of what it means to be believing in and practicing a religion is a secular or very restricted understanding of the term. She makes it very clear that religion only has to do with private beliefs and is not allowed to interfere with politics or law. Thus, she writes,

Muslims may have the sincere conviction that their religious tradition requires deviations from international law, and *such private beliefs must be respected.* However, the situation becomes different when beliefs that Islamic rules should supersede human rights are marshaled to promote campaigns or measures for stripping others of rights to which they are entitled under international law or when such beliefs are cited to buttress governmental policies and laws that violate the International Bill of Rights. The resulting curbs on rights and freedoms go well beyond the realm of protected private beliefs and enter the domains of politics and law.[1]

In this passage, Mayer has clearly gone from declaring freedom of religion to declaring what types of religion will be free to exist and put into practice. Her statement is reminiscent of Henry Ford's famous statement, "You can have the Model-T in any color you like as long as it is black."

On more than one occasion, Mayer overtly does try to demonstrate what "versions" of Islam should be encouraged and supported and this leads her to some very strange conclusions. She actually sings the praises the Khawarij and Mutazilah, due to a bias that runs throughout the human rights paradigm: a stress on individualism and rationalism (which shall be discussed in more detail later). After

---

[1] Ann Elizabeth Mayer, *Islam and Human Rights* (Boulder, CO: Westview Press, 1999), p. xv, emphasis added. In the newer edition of her book, she changed this passage a little, writing (p. xiv): "[E]ven though I understand that individual Muslims may freely decide to accept the authority of interpretations of Islamic sources that place Islamic law at odds with international human rights law. Muslims' right to have such private beliefs must be respected. However, the situation becomes different when claims that Islamic rules should supersede human rights are made in a context where they are used to strip people of human rights that they aspire to enjoy and to which they are entitled under international law. Here one is not talking about personal religious beliefs but programs affecting the domains of politics and law."

supposedly critiquing the "orthodox view" on rights, Mayer then turns her attention to the Khawarij. She writes,

These characteristics of Islamic thought inhibited the growth of concepts of individual rights that could be asserted against infringements by governments but never totally eclipsed other currents in Islamic thought that were hospitable to rights ideals. One can identify humanistic currents beginning in the early stages of Islamic thought and continuing to the present. In addition, early Islamic thought includes precursors of the idea of political freedom. Concepts of democracy very much like those in modern political systems can be found in the earliest period in Islamic history in the ideas of the Kharijite sect, which broke off from mainstream Islam in the seventh century over the latter's refusal to agree to the Kharijite tenet that the successors to the Prophet Muhammad must be elected by the community. Kharijites have been castigated for their unorthodox views, and their literature is not familiar to most other Muslims; but it still might be said that the Islamic tradition from the outset has included ideas that anticipated some of the democratic principles that underlie modern human rights norms.[1]

It is nothing short of amazing that this proponent of human rights feels no shame to extol the virtues of the Kharijites. Of course, she does not mention that the Kharijites were probably the most violent of all of the sects known to Islam and are virtually unanimously looked upon as true extremists. In fact, their "democratic" view of life led them to declare virtually all Muslims outside of their fold as disbelievers and it was considered permissible to spill the blood of those non-Kharijite Muslims.[2] In this day and age of extremism, terrorism and violence, one cannot seriously argue that Muslims should look back to the Kharijites for inspiration.

As for the Mutazilah, she fails to mention that when they actually held sway in the Muslim world, they tried to force their beliefs upon the Muslim scholars and masses, thereby not demonstrating much respect for freedom of belief. More than one Muslim scholar was imprisoned when they refused to bow down to their pressure. The

---

[1] Mayer, *Islam and Human Rights*, p. 53.

[2] Perhaps Ms. Mayer is right on another point that demonstrates how modern the Kharijite were: Like contemporary proponents of democracy, freedom and human rights, the Kharijites were not averse to resorting to force to enforce such freedoms.

famous story of Ahmad ibn Hanbal need not be recounted here. Yet, curiously enough, this is whom the contemporary Muslims should be looking up to concerning freedom and human rights. In reality, perhaps this is not so curious. In the name of freedom, human rights and rationality, Mayer is actually calling for, in not so obvious terms, the end of "traditional, orthodox" Islam, at least on a public level.

Mayer's attitude is made even clearer in an article she wrote in a work entitled *Women's Rights Human Rights: International Feminist Perspectives*.[1] In this article, Meyer delineated some of what she objects to concerning the traditional understanding of Islam. The reader who is familiar with Islam will readily note how many of objections deal with laws that are clearly and unequivocally stated in the Quran or Sunnah,

Laws [in the Muslim Middle East] commonly provide that the wife must obey her husband, that wives are not allowed to work outside the home without their husbands' permission, that men may take up to four wives, that a Muslim woman may not marry outside the faith, and that women are entitled to only one-half the inheritance share that men inherit in the same capacity. Depending on the country involved, one may find that women are compelled to wear concealing garments in public… that their testimony in court is excluded or valued at one-half the weight of a man's, that they are not allowed to travel without the permission of a male relative or unless accompanied by a male relative… Obviously it would be hard to justify the retention of such laws if one took seriously international norms such as Article 2 of CEDAW [Convention on the Elimination of all Forms of Discrimination Against Women, in force since 1918], requiring all states "to pursue all appropriate means and without delay a policy of eliminating discrimination against women."[2]

---

[1] This is one of many examples in which Mayer is called upon as an expert to deal with the issue of Islam and human rights.

[2] Ann Elizabeth Mayer, "Cultural Particularism as a Bar to Women's Rights: Reflections on the Middle Eastern Experience," in Julie Peters and Andrea Wolper, eds., *Women's Rights Human Rights: International Feminist Perspectives* (New York: Routledge, 1995), p. 177.

It should be noted that few Muslim countries have ratified the CEDAW and among those that have, they entered reservations on some of its points. Mayer, however, argues that such reservations are not valid because they are "incompatible with the object and purpose of the treaty or convention involved."[1]

Actually, Mayer believes that human rights law has to be obeyed regardless of whether or not a country has accepted or ratified such laws. Thus, this proponent of "rights and freedoms," has written,

Although the patterns of ratification of international human rights conventions have been uneven and there is much that remains controversial about international human rights law, there is sufficient consensus to justify the claim that many human rights have come to be part of customary international law and are therefore binding on all countries regardless of the status of their ratifications.[2]

This is a curious statement to say the least. It starts with admitting that not all human rights conventions have been ratified to then mention that there is a difference of opinion over international human rights law to then concluding that nonetheless all nations must abide by such laws regardless of whether they assent to them or not.

This last point is deserving of further comment here, as it has far-reaching implications. It means that once something becomes part of accepted human rights norms, such as the possible future acceptance of homosexual marriage or the unlimited right to abortion, they will then become part of international law. Although

---

[1] Mayer, "Cultural," p. 178. Here Mayer has only presented one possibility as to what to do when a reservation seems to go against the intent of the document. From an international law and international relations perspective, the resolution to such a conflict is not as simple as Mayer presents it and what she calls for is not the only possibility. See, for example, a study of Saudi Arabia's reservation to the CEDAW and what are possible resolutions to such an impasse: Sarah Helaoui, "Cultural Relativism and Reservations to Human Rights Treaties: The Legal Effects of the Saudi Reservation to CEDAW" (Master's Thesis, Faculty of Law, University of Lund, 2004). Here is part of her conclusion (p. 65): "This conclusion is unfortunate. The universality versus integrity dilemma surfaces; is it better to 'keep' the reserving State at the cost of the integrity of the treaty than to invalidate the treaty ratification at the cost of universality? I answer in affirmative, however, with great dissatisfaction. A consistent, even automatic, use of severability on incompatible reservations is definitely the preferable solution as it would be a triumph both for the universality and the integrity of treaties. At the same time, however, severability would be a drawback for State sovereignty."

[2] Mayer, *Islam and Human Rights*, p. 49.

there is some debate as to how much "binding" is international law[1], the goal that they are working towards is very clear. Once these are signed off on, every government is expected to comply completely. As D'Amato wrote,

International law doctrine now goes beyond the state duty not to interfere with international human rights, to hold states accountable for not acting positively to ensure rights. Moreover,… international law now obligates states to use due diligence to prevent, investigate, and punish systematic and egregious human rights violations between private actors.[2]

Not just governments are effected, but they want to stretch their hands into non-governmental bodies. Henry J. Steiner and Philip Alston wrote,

The rights declared in the [International] Covenant [on Civil and Political Rights] are not by their terms restricted to rights against *governmental* interference. That is, interference by non-governmental, private actors (the rapist, say) could as destructively impair the right to "security of person" (Article 9). The state's duty to provide effective remedies can than be read to attach to conduct (rape) that was initially non-governmental.[3]

Most importantly, this means that no religion or tradition can stand in its way and they plan on making those who ratify such things live up to it—even if it were under a former government as Mayer noted,

Countries are not permitted to opt out of their international legal obligations at will or on pretexts of their own devising… [D]erogation from international human rights standards is permitted only under specific, narrow conditions, which do not include denying people human rights by appeal to the standards of any particular religion.[4]

---

[1] Cf., Anthony D'Amato, "Is International Law Really 'Law'?" 79 *Northwestern U.L. Rev.* 1293 (1985); Jonathan I. Charney, "Universal International Law," 87 *American J. International L.* 529 (1993).

[2] Rebecca J. Cook,"Women's International Human Rights Law:The Way Forward," in *Human Rights of Women: National and International Perspectives* 3, 6-7 (Rebecca J. Cook, ed., 1994). Quoted in Michael J. Perry, *The Idea of Human Rights: Four Inquiries* (New York: Oxford University Press, 1998), p. 44.

[3] Henry J. Steiner and Philip Alston, *International Human Rights in Context: Law, Politics, Morals* (Oxford, England: Oxford University Press, 1996).

[4] Mayer, *Islam and Human Rights*, p. 12.

The danger or threat of this reality can be very great. Once something is part of international law, international organizations and human rights bodies can use their pressure, boycott and maybe even intervene in the name of violating human rights. Even if the government should change, they will still be held responsible for these international law agreements.

There are a couple of more points that need to be made with respect to Mayer such that these leanings or (perhaps) biases of this expert on human rights and Islam are well understood, as these leanings obviously influence her comments on Islam. In a world in which "Islamicists" and "fundamentalists" are too often criticized for being "extreme," the extremists of other movements' platforms should also be pointed out.

In what can be called an extreme view and seemingly utopian vision of human rights, Mayer makes some rather outlandish claims on behalf of the human rights platform. Mayer continually criticizes Muslim scholars for claiming specific human rights as being accepted by Islam and then noting when Islamic Law has some reservations to the overall right. This is, in reality, rather disingenuous on her part. At some places, she notes that international human rights laws allows for some exceptions but at the same time, especially when critiquing Islamic approaches, she makes it appear as if the rights granted by international agreements are absolute and not open to any form of restriction. For example, while critiquing Islamic laws on marriage that restrict who a Muslim man or woman who marry, Mayer states, "In international law the freedom to marry is unqualified."[1] This is recognized by all states not to be true. Thus, each state lays down numerous conditions on marriage, including same-sex restrictions and age restrictions.[2] What Mayer meant to say is that the freedom to marry is unqualified when it comes to religion, race and nationality but she chose not to state it in that fashion.

---

[1] Mayer, *Islam and Human Rights*, p. 123.

[2] In fact, in the 2008 state elections in California, Proposition 8 dealt with same-sex marriages. Very few, if any, during the discussions made the claim that restricting same-sex marriage would be a violation of international human rights laws. (It was interesting to watch the demonstrations that took place after the proposition banning same-sex laws was banned. Many same-sex marriage proponents are also adamant supporters of democracy. However, it is often recognized that democracy itself must be sacrificed if other, greater issues are involved.)

The following example is even more illustrative and important. Mayer writes,

International human rights law allows no constraints on a person's religious beliefs: Freedom of religion is an unqualified freedom. One of the most influential statements of this freedom is in Article 18 of the Universal Declaration of Human Rights (UDHR). Article 18 states: "Everyone has the right to freedom of thought, conscience and religion; this right includes freedom to change his religion or belief, and freedom, either alone or in community with others and in public or private, to manifest his religion or belief in teaching, practice, worship and observance."[1]

Elsewhere, Mayer speaks about religious persecution of minorities in Iran and once states, "Iran's religious persecutions clash with the principle of freedom of religion, which in international law is a freedom not subject to any constraints."[2]

Is it possibly true, as she claims and as is stated in Article 18 of the UDHR, that human rights law "allows no constraints on a person's religious beliefs" or the "freedom of religion"? In fact, this is a remarkable claim in the midst of a book whose ultimate claim is that some "versions" of Islam violate international human rights law and, as such, their implementation in the real world cannot be tolerated. What has happened to that unqualified freedom "either alone or in community with others and in public or private"? The stark reality is that the above passage itself points to one of the fundamental flaws of contemporary international human rights law. One cannot have things both ways: One cannot say that some practices should not be tolerated while at the same time claiming that everyone is free to believe and practice as they wish.

Another writer of this category who has touched upon the subject of Islam and human rights (in particular women's rights) is Courtney Howland. Although Mayer speaks mostly about Islam, Howland spreads her critique more generally over any brand of "fundamentalist" religion.

Howland continues in the same vein as Mayer but is arguably more explicit in her conclusions. She concludes that the laws of Islam concerning the internal structure

---

[1] Mayer, *Islam and Human Rights*, pp. 168-169. Incidentally, Article 9 of the European Convention on Human Rights (ECHR, 1950) states virtually the same.

[2] Mayer, *Competing Claims*, p. 192

of the family, woman's dress, marriage laws, inheritance and so on are all violations of women's human rights as recognized by the UN. For example, she writes, "[M]any religious fundamentalist systems of marriage and divorce require women to submit to their husbands, and even obey their husbands. These laws conflict with two areas of protection in the Universal Declaration: liberty rights and equality rights."[1] She then shows that there is no legitimate argument to defend such religious practices. She further argues that states have a responsibility, therefore, to work against any such laws and against any such parties that may try to impose such laws. She states, for example, "A state would be permitted, and indeed may have a duty, to outlaw religious practices that are systematically violative of women's liberty and equal rights. Under this approach, it is arguable that states with strong religious fundamentalist movements, including, for example, Japan, Italy, Sri Lanka, and the United States, may have a duty to pass laws prohibiting the practice of requiring wives to be obedient."[2] Finally, she argues that the other member states of the UN must take punitive actions against those countries that have allowed religious-fundamentalist laws to be part of their corpus of laws. As she states it, "All enforcement mechanisms at the community's disposal should be used to coerce these pariah states to cease violating articles 55 and 56. It is time for the international community to live up to the standards of the Charter and the Universal Declaration."[3]

It is very difficult to imagine how an approach like this is supposed to resonate with the Muslim masses—indeed, it is even difficult to imagine how human rights activists claim to have the right to insist upon this approach. First they make the claim that they are representing an absolute freedom of religion. In reality, though, among Muslims they are actually saying that they are bringing the rights to women, non-Muslims and even apostates. Everyone, that is, except for those who believe in fundamentalist, traditional, orthodox Islam are free to practice their "form" of Islam. Thus, in the name of freedom of religion and human rights, the human rights platforms are going to decide what form of religion people are "free" to choose.

---

[1] Howland, p. 187. Note that Howland was not writing about Islam alone but also Judaism, Christianity, Buddhism and Hinduism. In particular, the targets of her arguments are those that she describes as "fundamentalists" among these different religions.

[2] Howland, p. 198.

[3] Howland, p. 201.

Perhaps most importantly for many Muslims who believe that the Quran and Sunnah have truly been revealed from God is that this human rights approach strips God of aspects of His Divinity, or what is known as *al-Haakimiyyah*. They are literally saying that God does not have the right to lay down laws for humanity. Certainly, or even more so, He does not have that exclusive right. In other words, their approach to Islam is "offensive" to many Muslims concerning a vital aspect of Muslim belief, not simply some trivial matter that one could or may expect Muslims to overlook.

This approach of theirs demonstrates a fundamental flaw and logical inconsistency when it comes to rights and freedoms. There is no such thing as absolute rights and freedoms because eventually those rights and freedoms will trample upon the rights and freedoms of others. Thus, there is inevitably going to be some trade-off. The ultimate question will eventually boil down to who has the right to determine what trade-offs are going to be accepted. Mayer explicitly understands this reality, however she argues that at no time may religion be the reason for such an exception to the general rights and freedoms. Again, as quoted earlier, she stated,

Countries are not permitted to opt out of their international legal obligations at will or on pretexts of their own devising... [D]erogation from international human rights standards is permitted only under specific, narrow conditions, which do not include denying people human rights by appeal to the standards of any particular religion.[1]

It is true that there are numerous human rights advocates that seem to have a more balanced approach to human rights than those discussed above. To some extent, Jack Donnelly may be considered more moderate. There is also the approach of McGoldrick who has observed that:

The presence of experts from different legal systems can assist the HRC in its consideration of reports under article 40. For example, during consideration of the report of Morocco it was useful to have members of the HRC who were conversant with Islamic laws. The provision in article 31(2) can give States parties the confidence that their approach will at least be understood even if disagreed with...[2]

---

[1] Mayer, *Islam and Human Rights*, p. 12.

[2] Quoted in Baderin, p. 221.

However, there are plenty examples of the more demanding view, such as Mayer and Howland above. Note the following explicit and eye-opening comment:

For example, one advocate of the unilateral approach, while answering the question 'How should international law respond to the incompatibility of claims based on Shari'a with international human rights norms?', submitted that: 'international law norms must not be compromised, and that it may be desirable for Muslim scholars to explore alternative interpretations of Islamic sources under which Shari'a can be reconciled with developments in international human rights law'.[1]

One is reminded of the feminist human rights proponent Simone de Beauvoir who once stated about women being allowed to stay at home as housewives or mothers,

No, we don't believe that any woman should have this choice. No woman should be authorized to stay at home to raise children. Society should be totally different. Women should not have that choice, precisely because if there is such a choice, too many women will make that one.[2]

When one reads these kinds of statements coming from the proponents of human rights, one readily recognizes that they are, in fact, just as dogmatic and zealous as any religious extremist or fundamentalist. Of course, they would probably argue that their position, though, is not simply a matter of blind faith[3] but a well-thought out, reasonable view of the world. The question of what this view is truly founded upon shall be left for later chapters.

---

[1] Nanda, V.P., "Islam and International Human Rights Law: Selected Aspects," *American Society of International Law Proceedings*, (1993), p. 331. Quoted in Baderin, p. 222.

[2] Quoted in Christina Hoff Sommers, *Who Stole Feminism?* (New York, Simon and Schuster, 1994), pp. 256-257.

[3] Since many of these proponents come from the West, they probably view religion as a matter of blind faith, as many Christians emphasize that such is what faith is all about. However, this view of religious belief does not hold in Islam. The belief of a Muslim should be built upon reasoning and thought, as throughout the Quran humankind is directed to ponder and consider the realities of this existence.

The Optimistic but "Apologetic" and Faulty Approach

A third approach has been labeled here as optimistic but apologetic and faulty. The basic premise or general tenor of this approach is that there is no real conflict between contemporary human rights reasoning and Islam. In fact, it is not uncommon for such Muslim authors (in general, these will be Muslim authors) to claim that human rights were first promoted by Islam.[1]

This category may be broken into two important subcategories:

(a) One group basically agues that if one were only to appreciate the justice, equity and wisdom of Islamic Law, one would recognize that, in fact, Islam and human rights are completely compatible with one another.

(b) Another group of authors argues that when one realizes that there is room for interpretation and a margin of appreciation within human rights law and with some re-understanding of some Islamic practices, one will find that, in reality, there is no incompatibility between Islam and human rights.

In many critics' view, this third approach is one that comes across as a rather apologetic presentation of the relationship between human rights and Islam. As stated above, the goal seems to be to demonstrate that there is no conflict between the contemporary human rights schemes and Islam. However, in order to achieve this goal, the Islamic laws that seem to contradict contemporary international human rights standards must be "explained away." Although the defense of many "controversial" Islamic laws is often times correct and defensible, this will only seem obvious to the believing Muslim. In other words, for many non-Muslims the rhetoric and arguments used are nothing but an attempt to hide the conflict between Islam and human rights. Sadly, for these defenders of the Islamic version of human rights, the end result is probably more harmful than beneficial as these works are easily critiqued and virtually ridiculed by some non-Muslim writers, as shall be noted below.[2] In fact, as shall be noted below, sometimes the same aspects that the

---

[1] For a presentation of such claims, see Donnelly, p. 72; Mayer, *Islam and Human Rights*, pp. 58ff.

[2] For example, for a critique of some of the apologetic responses concerning women and "fundamentalist Islam," see Howland, in Bucar and Barnett, pp. 169-172.

writers of this approach praise as proper for humans is the exact aspect that is critiqued[1] as violating human rights.

In reality, there is a relatively large number of works that could be placed in this category. Many of these writings list and discuss all of the various rights that Islam has to offer humans. Some of them are probably more useful as introductions to Islam rather than works on human rights, in the sense that they cover virtually every aspect of the religion and attempt to demonstrate all the rights that Islam has given, everything from the right of privacy of the spouses to the rights of parents and so on.[2] At the same time, though, they also discuss when and why there seems to be some variance between the general human rights statements and the views of Islam on certain issues.

A typical work that attempts to demonstrate that there is no real conflict between human rights thought and Islam is Abdullah ibn Baih's *Hawaar an Bu'd Haul Huqooq al-Insaan fi al-Islaam*. He begins by refuting those who say that Islam does not recognize any concept of human rights. He then goes on to argue that it is the materialistic, secular Western civilization that has prostituted and abused women.[3]

---

[1] In particular, by authors like Mayer, Howland and others.

[2] The following topics, for example, were covered in a typical book of this nature entitled, *In Pursuit of Justice: The Jurisprudence of Human Rights in Islam*: Sanctity of Life, Freedom of Speech, Freedom of Religion, The Status of Women, Non-Muslims, Property Rights, Citizenship, Freedom of Association, Freedom of Movement, Children, Security of Person, Slavery and Social Services. Cf., Hathout, Maher with Uzma Jamil, Gasser Hathout and Nayyer Ali, *In Pursuit of Justice: The Jurisprudence of Human Rights in Islam* (Los Angeles, CA: Muslim Public Affairs Council, 2006). In Marwaan al-Qaisi's *Mausooah Huqooq al-Insaan fi al-Islaam* ("Encyclopedia of Human Rights in Islam"), everything from a spouse's wife to privacy to the rights of the deceased is covered.

[3] Abdullah ibn Baih, *Hawaar an Bu'd Haul Huqooq al-Insaan fi al-Islaam* (Riyadh: Maktabah al-Ubaikaan, 2007), pp. 15ff. Many Muslims who write about Islam and human rights emphasize the rights that Islam gave women over and above what was given to women in numerous pre-Islamic cultures. [See, for example, virtually the entire chapter devoted to this discussion in *Conferences of Riyad, Paris, Vatican City, Geneva and Strassbourg on Moslem Doctrine and Human Rights in Islam between Saudi Canonists and Eminent European Jurists and Intellectuals* (Riyadh, Saudi Arabia: Ministry of Justice, n.d.), pp. 155-190.] Although no unbiased person can doubt what Islam did for women at that time, these writers seem to miss the point that all of that is irrelevant. The feminists, for example, argue that women have been oppressed in all earlier societies, including Muslim societies, and what they have achieved and what they continue to achieve is the contemporary standard that one must speak about.

When discussing the position of women in Islam, though, ibn Baih simply offers what is found in most such works on human rights in Islam.[1] After critiquing some of the more recent developments in the feminist movement (for a page or two) and speaking about how this movement is a threat to the family, he then speaks about how Islam views the two sexes as complementary to each other, taking into consideration what Allah has bestowed upon each particular sex. He then says that Islam seeks tranquility and mercy in the relationship between the spouses. He says that this is something that Islam introduced to the world and that the woman had never known before.[2] He then goes on to speak about how Islam is a revelation from Allah and was a type of revolution for the woman. This was especially true for the Arabs who would become very displeased when they learned that their wives had given birth to females. Furthermore, women were not allowed to inherit and there was no limit to the number of wives a male could have.[3]

He moves from there to state that differences in laws concerning men and women in Islam does not mean that their honor or dignity differs from an Islamic perspective, wherein he quotes, for example, the verse, "Whoever works righteousness, whether male or female, while he (or she) is a true believer (of Islaamic Monotheism) verily, to him We will give a good life (in this world with respect, contentment and lawful provision), and We shall pay them certainly a reward in proportion to the best of what they used to do (i.e. Paradise in the Hereafter)" (*al-Nahl* 97).

Then he states, "However, it is imperative that one discusses the particular responsibilities that are appropriate based on the nature [of each sex]. Distributing roles and responsibilities and prioritize rights and jobs is not an issue of inferiority."[4] Thus, he says, one will once again note the complementary relationship between the two sexes. This, he says, explains why the inheritance is sometimes different for a man and woman, as the woman is never financially responsible for herself, either being under the responsibility of a husband, father, other male relative or the state.

---

[1] See ibn Baih, pp. 49-59.

[2] ibn Baih, p. 51.

[3] Ibn Baih, p. 52.

[4] Ibn Baih, p. 53.

He then cites of examples of women participating in actions outside of the home during the time of the Prophet (peace and blessings of Allah be upon him). He then goes on to discuss the difference of opinion as to whether women are allowed to be judges, rulers and so on. Again he states that Islam was a revolution for women's rights.[1] In sum, he states that the rights of women are protected in Islam. However, the principle of leadership of men is a principle stated in the Quran which is irreproachable: "Men are the protectors and maintainers of women, because Allah has made one of them to excel the other" (*al-Nisaa* 34). But then he is quick to say,

But this leadership is for the benefit of woman before anything else and for the benefit of the household and the family, as the man fulfills the responsibility of maintenance and as the woman has responsibilities and obligations within the household… What is meant by leadership, though, is not dictatorship, tyranny, oppression or persecution…[2]

Although there are some points that ibn Baih made that are open to critique, overall what he stated is correct and sound from an Islamic perspective. However, this kind of reasoning does not resonate with the proponents of human rights. His writing is fine when "preaching to the choir," that is, when speaking to people who already believe in Islam as a divinely revealed religion, but it does very little to make people understand where Islam is coming from on the question of human rights.

The shortcomings of this approach demonstrates the difficulty of trying to explain to "the other" what is the basis of one's human rights. It is reminiscent of Donnelly's discussion of the challenges facing natural law proponents. Donnelly states,

Natural law theories today face much the same problem. John Finnis's Natural Law and Natural Rights (1980) is a brilliant account of the implications of neo-Thomist natural law for questions of natural (human) rights. To those of us outside of that tradition, the "foundational" appeals to nature and reason are more or less attractive, interesting, or persuasive. For Finnis, though, operating within that tradition, they are definitively compelling. Having accepted Finnis's starting point

---

[1] Ibn Baih, p. 57.

[2] Ibn Baih, p. 58.

we may be rationally compelled to accept his conclusions about natural rights. But a skeptic cannot be compelled by reason alone to start there.[1]

In fact, ironically, the very same points that ibn Baih praises as part of the beauty, greatness and perfection of Islam are those characteristics that human rights activists argue are violations of international human rights laws or that are nothing more than distorted twists on what human rights is supposed to be. For example, Mayer critiques Maudoodi's view on specific rights of women that Maudoodi had mentioned, writing similarly to ibn Baih's writings. Mayer responds by saying,

Other "rights" that have been derived from Islamic sources include the right of women not to be surprised by male family members of the household walking in on them unannounced. When one thinks about the implications of protecting women from surprise intrusions, one realizes that, far from affording protection for freedoms, it contains implicit restrictions on women's rights. There is an assumption that the world is sexually segregated and that women stay at home in seclusion from men. This segregation is so extensive that even male family members should never intrude on women's quarters without giving women warning so that they can cover themselves in a suitably modest manner. The provision implies that even in the home there will be female seclusion and veiling, which in turn is connected with a woman's duty to avoid indecency. Thus, the "right" is linked not with any meaningful human right but with women's traditional duty under the shari'a to stay segregated, secluded, and veiled.[2]

The seemingly rather eclectic choice of rights to be fully accepted and those grossly modified is also a source of criticism. Mayer is one of the leading critiques of these attempts to present an Islamic declaration of human rights. She rightly noted,

For the most part, Islamic human rights turn out to involve rights that are borrowed from international law and then qualified or distorted in some fashion. The misleading "equality" formulations already mentioned are perfect illustrations. These Islamic human rights initiatives represent hybrids of international rights principles and incongruous Islamic features. The borrowed rights are subject to supposedly "Islamic"

---

[1] Donnelly, p. 19.

[2] Mayer, *Islam and Human Rights*, p. 68.

limitations. For example, Article 24 says: "All the rights and freedoms stipulated in this Declaration are subject to the Islamic shari'a." Imposing such Islamic conditions is an exercise in vacuity so long as specific definitions of what these Islamic conditions entail are not forthcoming. The authors obviously have no wish to be explicit as to how they intend to circumscribe rights, preferring to equivocate and thereby accord governments the freedom to interpret Islamic limits as broadly as they please. Since modem civil and political rights are typically designed to protect the rights of the individual against the state. Allowing the state complete discretion to define the scope of rights and freedoms renders them illusory.[1]

In sum, it can be argued that what Muslim writers speak about as "human rights" are very different from what is proposed by the contemporary human rights embodied in proponents such as Mayer and numerous others. One can actually conclude that there is a complete disjoint between the "Islamic" discussions of these "apologists" and the demands and understandings of the human rights movement. This has led Mayer to make the following conclusion concerning "Islamic human rights" documents:

After examining the vague and confused concepts that the authors of Islamic human rights include in their agendas, one sees that they have no sure grasp of what the concerns of human rights really are. They include provisions that would be totally out of place in a scheme that shared common philosophical premises with those of international human rights.[2]

Although many Muslim authors may not be pleased with the harsh critique that Mayer gives of the "Islamic human rights schemes,"[3] there is no question that, when viewed in the light of the understanding of numerous contemporary human rights proponents, there is much validity to what she is saying.

One is actually left with quite an impasse here. In the same way that the approach of Abou El Fadhl and Naim will not resonate with the masses of the

---

[1] Mayer, *Competing Claims,* p. 182, see also Mayer, *Islam and Human Rights,* p. xii (although that passage contains many overgeneralizations itself, for the most part its critique is noteworthy). Many of Mayer's statements about Muslim writings on human rights are also open to various criticisms.

[2] Mayer's conclusion, *Islam and Human Rights,* pp. 69-70

[3] See, in particular, Mayer, *Islam and Human Rights,* pp. 193-6.

Muslims, the apologetic approach does not resonate with the Western human rights scholars.

Mashood Baderin is one author who has gone beyond others in trying to bridge this obvious impasse. His work has some unique features to it, in that he explicitly tries to incorporate specific aspects of "Western" human rights legal theory with particular aspects of Islamic legal theory. Hence, his book, which stems from his Ph.D. dissertation, deserves some attention here. Baderin is perhaps the best example of the second approach of this category, described above as recognizing room for maneuvering within both human rights law and Islamic law.

Baderin himself explains how his approach differs from that of others:

The approach in most previous works has been generally monological, and reflects what Watson has described as the presumption that the current interpretations of international human rights law are impeccable with everything else being adjusted to maintain that assumption. The argument has often been that when Muslim States ratify international human rights treaties they are bound by the international law rule that a State Party to a treaty 'may not invoke the provisions of its internal law as justification for its failure to perform a treaty'. In practice however, Muslim States… often argue not against the letter of the law but against some interpretation of international human rights law which, they contend, does not take Islamic values into consideration… [T] here is need for a synthesis between two extremes and provision of an alternative perspective to the relationship between international human rights law and Islamic law. Using evidence from Islamic jurisprudence and international human rights practice, this book challenges the argument that the observance of international human rights law is impossible within an Islamic legal dispensation. It theoretically engages international human rights practice in dialogue with Islamic jurisprudence. It develops a dialogical perspective to the issues. A dialogical approach demands a culture of tolerance and persuasion and the abandonment of a culture of parochialism, violence and rivalry. It requires capacity to listen, respect, accommodate and exchange.[1]

---

[1] Baderin, pp. 4-5.

Baderin admits that there are "differences of scope" between the Shareeah and international human rights law. He argues that there is room for discussion rather than opposition. However, again, he states that there has to be adjustments on both sides of the issue. Here is his explanation of what he is calling for:

Applying the justificatory principle, a paradigm shift is sought from traditional hardline interpretations of the Shari'ah and also from exclusionist interpretations of international human rights law. The Islamic legal doctrine of *maslahah* (welfare) and the European human rights 'margin of appreciation' doctrine are explored in establishing the arguments herein.[1]

This is not merely a theoretical stance on his part but is the result of his comparison with human rights documents—both secular and Islamic. As he states towards the end of his work,

The detailed examination of both the ICCPR and the ICESCR in the light of Islamic law demonstrates the possibility of constructive harmonization of international human rights norms with Islamic law. This however requires good faith and the abandonment of prejudice between Islamic law and international human rights scholars and advocates.[2]

He concludes that seeing Islam as being compatible with human rights is the most appropriate approach. He argues that this is not via an apologetic approach but by recognizing certain aspects of Islamic Law, such as principles of good government, respect for justice and human welfare and so on.[3] In particular, Baderin argues that human rights is first and foremost about the dignity of human rights which is what Islamic law is all about.[4] (However, as shall be noted later, the concept of "human dignity" is much too vague to lead to any type of concordance except in the most general of concepts.)

---

[1] Baderin, p. 6. He elaborates on this further toward the end of his work, see pp. 220ff. Concerning the margin of appreciation, Baderin writes, "The margin of appreciation doctrine exists within the European human rights regime and it has been defined as 'the line at which international supervision should give way to a State Party's discretion in enacting or enforcing its laws'." Baderin, p. 231.

[2] Baderin, p. 219.

[3] Baderin, p. 13.

[4] Baderin, p. 14.

The genesis of his argument with respect to how Islamic law should change in reaction to human rights has been explained by Baderin himself:

The scope of international human rights can be positively enhanced in the Muslim world through moderate, dynamic, and constructive interpretations of the Shari'ah rather than through hardline and static interpretations of it. This is particularly so in respect of women's rights, minority rights, and the application of Islamic criminal punishments. We have shown by reference to the different schools of Islamic jurisprudence and classical juristic views that even the early Islamic jurists and scholars emphasized the importance of moderation and had adopted constructive views that can be relied upon today greatly to enhance the realization of international human rights norms within the dispensation of Islamic law. The Qur'an described the Muslim Ummah as 'justly balanced', a description signifying moderation. This Islamic legal analysis of the two international human rights Covenants establishes the need for review of some traditional interpretations of the Shari'ah, in the light of equally valid moderate opinions that had existed even from the time of the earliest Islamic jurists, for the full realization of the rights contained in them within the application of Islamic law. The rules of Islamic jurisprudence do actually encourage interpretations of the Shari'ah that promote the benevolent nature of Islam, especially where the reasoning for such interpretations is commensurate with prevalent needs of social justice and human well-being.[1]

In many cases, one can argue that Baderin's conclusions are within the scope of generally accepted fiqh conclusions. For example, with respect to the woman's dress, he states that it would be best if the state were to leave the choice open to the woman as to whether she would cover herself completely or display her face and hands.[2] At the same time, though, it would be hard to imagine that human rights proponents like Mayer would accept the idea that there is a special dress code for women only. In fact, Baderin himself quotes the Committee's comments on human rights conventions as saying,

---

[1] Baderin, pp 219-220.
[2] See Baderin, pp. 63-66.

Inequality in the enjoyment of rights by women throughout the world is deeply embedded in tradition, history and culture, including religious attitudes… States parties should ensure that traditional, historical, religious or cultural attitudes are not used to justify violations of women's right to equality before the law and to equal enjoyment of all Covenant rights. States parties should furnish appropriate information on those aspects of tradition, history, cultural practices and religious attitudes which jeopardize, or may jeopardize, compliance with article 3, and indicate what measures they have taken or intend to take to overcome such factors.[1]

Baderin seems to be missing the point that what he supports as part of Islamic law cannot be considered equality and hence some will have the right to argue that it does violate international law. In fact, his own words perhaps demonstrate more than anything else how his approach to rapprochement is not bound to be accepted:

Although males and females are regarded as equal, that may not imply equivalence or a total identity in roles, especially within the family. Muhammad Qutb has observed that while the demand for equality between man and woman as human beings is both natural and reasonable, this should not extend to a transformation of roles and functions. This creates instances of differentiation in gender roles under Islamic law that may amount to discrimination by the threshold of international human rights law. Although the UN annotations on the draft of Article 3 on equal rights of men and women recorded an appreciation of the drafters that '[i]t was difficult to share the assumption that legal systems and traditions could be overridden, that conditions which were inherent in the nature and growth of families and organized societies could be immediately changed, or that articles of faith and religion could be altered, merely by treaty legislations', the HRC now seems convinced that 'in the light of the experience it has gathered in its activities over the last 20 years', it intends to push through a universal standard of complete gender equality under the Covenant aimed at changing traditional, cultural, and religious attitudes that subordinate women universally.[2]

---

[1] Baderin, p. 59.

[2] Baderin, pp. 39-40.

On other occasions, Baderin's proposes the acceptance of what must be considered more minority opinions among scholars through the ages. Before giving examples from Baderin, it is important to mention a very important point related to Islamic law that Baderin fails to take into consideration in his exuberance to try to reconcile Islam with contemporary human rights law. Simply because an opinion is stated by a Muslim scholar, this does not mean that it is to be given weight from a Shariah perspective. The ultimate question is whether something can be justified from the point of the view of the Shariah and not simply whether any Muslim had ever held a certain opinion. What is obligatory upon a Muslim scholar (or, in reality, any Muslim for that matter) is to follow the "truth," which is defined as that which is supported by the Quran and Sunnah. Choosing an opinion simply because it is more "politically correct" even if it seemingly or clearly contradicts the Quran or Sunnah cannot be considered justifiable. Furthermore, there seems to be something very troubling to lean toward particular views simply because they are in accord with the world's dominant paradigm today.

On the question of apostasy, Baderin wrote,

The interpretation of the right to freedom of thought, conscience, and religion to include freedom to change one's religion or even to adopt atheistic views has not been without controversy among Islamic scholars in relation to the question of apostasy under Islamic law. The different views will be analysed below. However, the trend among contemporary Islamic scholars on the issue of religious freedom under Islamic law has mostly been towards emphasizing the Qur'anic provision which states that: There is no compulsion in religion: truth stands out clear from error…[1]

He then goes on to quote Ismail al-Faruqi's and Fathi Uthman's opinions on this issue. Invoking classical scholars, Baderin then goes into a rather irrelevant discussion of how non-Muslim wives of Muslim may not be compelled to embrace Islam.[2]

---

[1] Baderin, p. 120.

[2] Baderin, pp. 121f. He also, perhaps for the sake of "completeness," also points out ibn Hazm's extreme view on this question.

With respect to a husband's right to divorce, while discussing the HRC comment that states that "grounds for divorce and annulment should be the same for men and women," Baderin argues that "the judicial control of marriage dissolution by the State can as well be justified under the doctrine of public welfare (*maslahah*)."[1] He further argues that such a control over divorce could also be considered part of the doctrine of *hisbah*, wherein the state is required to order the good and eradicate evil. To further support this innovative approach, Baderin argues, "Since dissolution by Judicial Order (*faskh*) is a method sanctioned already by Islamic law, this will not amount to making any new law but the removal of a procedural advantage which has been generally subjected to abuse." Baderin then notes that this will obviously face great opposition. He writes,

However, Khallaf considered such abrogation of men's right of Unilateral Repudiation and vesting dissolution of marriages entirely in the courts as dubious and non-genuine welfare (that is, *maslahah wahmiyyah*). One could disagree with this view of Khallaf, on the grounds that the approach does not violate or come in conflict with any direct Qur'anic verse on Unilateral Repudiation (*talaq*). The approach is consistent with the Prophet's Tradition which states that: "There should be no harming nor should any harm be remedied with another harm." That approach will remove genuine hardship from women without placing any consequential hardship on men, since it does not totally block every avenue to divorce for men, but only ensures that they divorce for justifiable reasons.[2]

If Baderin's argument here is taken to its logical conclusion, it would mean that if the Islamic state felt that men were not going to abuse the right of divorce (*talaq*), this right would be returned to them. However, this would be a violation of the human rights mandate, as it would give unequal rights to divorce between men and women. Hence, Baderin's argument here is fallacious. He cannot claim that the "Law" can be made consistent with human rights demands except under exceptional circumstances of men abusing this right. Once that no longer occurs, one once again has the conflict between Islamic Law and "human rights" demands.

---

[1] Baderin, p. 151.

[2] Baderin, p. 151.

Furthermore, there are some cases in which Baderin states that Muslims cannot be "flexible" and, as such, it becomes incumbent to invoke the margin of appreciation concept in international law and accept the special circumstances of Muslims due to their religious faith. Thus, for example, he argues against the acceptance of abortion simply upon the grounds that the pregnancy was unwanted.[1] Similarly, concerning "illegitimate children" he writes,

The problem areas concern mainly the issues of women in employment and the concepts of the family and of children out of wedlock. While the issue of women in employment in most Muslim States has been circumscribed by custom rather than Islamic law per se, the issue of the family and children out of wedlock is strictly dictated by the Islamic religion and regulated by Islamic law… the question of the family and children out of wedlock involves an Islamic religio-moral principle and requires the recognition of some margin of appreciation for Muslim States as is further elaborated in Chapter 5.[2]

In sum, the first part of Baderin's thesis has to do with tweaking the international approach to human rights. The second part of his thesis has to do with taking a fresh look at Islamic Law. One part of his thesis relies greatly on the concept of "margin of appreciation." Another part of his thesis has to do with the Islamic concepts of public welfare (*maslahah*) and the goals of Islamic Law (*maqaasid al-shareeah*). Both of these points are definitely open to criticism, at least in the manner that he presented them.

With respect to the margin of appreciation, it is important to note that it has not been a widely accepted concept in the human rights movement. In fact, Baderin himself noted: "In practice, the UN Human Rights Committee has not formally adopted the margin of appreciation doctrine but has alluded to it only on one occasion in Hertzberg and Others v. Finland."[3] In fact, as Baderin himself notes, on other occasions the HRC explicitly rejected the concept of "margin of appreciation" and

---

[1] Cf., Baderin, p. 74.

[2] Baderin, p. 218.

[3] Baderin, p. 231. This was a relevant issue, as it had to do with censuring of homosexual display on the media. It shall be referred to later. It should also be noted that even in that case, the embrace of a concept of margin of appreciation was very far from explicit.

stated that the individual state was bound to the conditions of the relevant article of the international convention.[1] There is a fear that the margin of appreciation approach will lead to cultural relativism and the denial of human rights on that basis. Hence, this means that Baderin is basing his theory of reconciliation on a theory that is not yet respected as part of the law or interpretation of international human rights law, even given the prominent status of Europe when it comes to understanding human rights.

Baderin's approach to Islamic Law also needs to be questioned. It is interesting to note that Baderin agrees with Mayer that some bygone approaches to Islam need to be revived in order for Islam and human rights to be made more compatible. After quoting a passage from Mayer in which she refers to "many philosophical concepts, humanistic values, and moral principles" found in the "premodern Islamic intellectual heritage," Baderin writes, "It is those Islamic humanistic concepts and values of the Shari'ah that need to be fully revived for the realization of international human rights within the application of Islamic law in Muslim States."[2] Unfortunately, Baderin does not elaborate on this point. One can only hope that he, like Mayer, does not offer praise for the Mutazilah and Khawarij or hopes to revive their methodologies.

With respect to Islamic Law, Baderin argues against a "static" interpretation of Islamic Law and, as noted above, he emphasizes the importance of *maslahah* and *maqaasid al-shareeah*.[3] Here is his explanation of his approach:

Against the background of the nature and evolution of Islamic law established above, the doctrine of *maslahah* is thus advocated in this study as a veritable Islamic legal doctrine for the realization of international human rights within the dispensation of Islamic law. This is based on the understanding earlier expounded that international human rights has a universal humanitarian objective for the protection of individuals against the misuse of state authority and for the enhancement of human dignity. We will rely on the doctrine of *maslahah* within the ample scope of the *Shari'ah* in deriving legal benefits and averting hardship to the human person, as endorsed by the

---

[1] Baderin, p. 232.

[2] Baderin, p. 31.

[3] See Baderin, pp. 40f. He defines *maqaasid al-Shareeah* as, "the object and purpose of the Shari'ah" and *maslahah* as "promotion of human welfare and prevention of harm."

Qur'anic verse that: 'He [God] has not imposed any hardships upon you [humans] in religion.'

This utilization of *maslahah* in relation to the *maqasid al-shari'ah* will accommodate the principle of *takhayyur* (eclectic choice), to facilitate movement within the principal schools of Islamic jurisprudence as well as consideration of the views of individual Islamic jurists to support alternative arguments advanced on topical issues in this book.[1]

These are two very important and useful concepts that are undoubtedly generally accepted within the framework of "orthodox" Islamic legal theory. However, the problem with these two tools is that they are easily abused. Furthermore, it is one thing to override earlier established fiqh conclusions in the name of these two principles and it is quite another to override clear and definite texts of either the Quran or the Sunnah in the name of these two principles. The former could be easily argued while the latter is many times very problematic or totally unacceptable.

Another principle that Baderin invokes is, "Legal rulings may change with the change in time." He states that this applies mostly to matters "concerning human interactions."[2] This is obviously a very important principle that facilitates change in Islamic fiqh. Yet, at no time does he mention the fact that this principle only applies to laws and rules that are not explicitly decreed in the Quran or Sunnah. This is a very important point that people sometimes neglect when invoking that principle.

Baderin also emphasizes the differences between the "traditionalist" /"hardline" and "evolutionist" approach to Islamic Law. He clearly favors what he has called the "evolutionist" approach, stating,

The 'evolutionists' are those who, while identifying with the classical jurisprudence and methods of Islamic law, seek to make it relevant to contemporary times. They believe in the continual evolution of Islamic law and argue that if the Shari'ah must really cope meaningfully with modern developments and be applicable for all time, then such modern developments must be taken into

---

[1] Baderin, pp. 43-44.

[2] Baderin, p. 46.

consideration in the interpretation of the Shari'ah. They are also referred to as Islamic liberals or moderates. They adopt a 'back and forward looking' approach in their interpretations of the Shari'ah and a contextual application of classical Islamic jurisprudence. The scope of harmonization between Islamic law and international human rights law depends largely upon whether a hardline or moderate approach is adopted in the interpretation of the Shari'ah and the application of classical Islamic jurisprudence.[1]

His dichotomy between "hardliners" and "liberals" may resonate with many Western ears but, in reality, it is a bogus dichotomy that has been forced upon the discussion of Islam in recent years for many political reasons. The reality is that the "traditionalist" elements must be "flexible" in their application of Islamic Law as such was the example set forth by the Prophet (peace and blessings of Allah be upon him) himself and his followers. However, that flexibility is within well-defined limits of the Shariah. The liberal approach has not been accepted by many "traditionalist" scholars because it seeks to go beyond those limits, they would argue, in such ways that cannot be justified by a reading of the Quran and Sunnah.

At first glance, Baderin's thesis seems to be a fresh approach and attempts to strike a happy accord between some modern interpretations of human rights thinking and some aspects already found in Islamic legal theory. The following important conclusions can be made concerning Baderin's work:

(1)   Baderin does argue that there are certain issues in which Islamic Law cannot be compromised and that on those points the views of Islamic Law will simply have to be respected. Furthermore, on other points, he consistently falls short of the modernist/progressive extreme in that he does not call for a completely new understanding of the laws but, instead, he looks for views that have been held by some scholar(s) of the past. This will make his conclusions resonate much better with the Muslim masses. However, on this point, he has neglected the fact that the real issue for fiqh is not simply whether someone in the past, no matter how respected, has held a particular opinion but whether that opinion can be adequately substantiated in the light of the Quran and Sunnah.

---

[1] Baderin, p. 44.

(2)   Although he calls for those on the human rights side of the issue to resort to invoking the "margin of appreciation," it is hard to imagine that some of his conclusions would be acceptable by some of the more hardline human rights proponents, such as Mayer, Howland, feminists in general and so on. In this manner, some of his reasoning and interpretations do not differ from the other somewhat "apologetic" writings on human rights.

(3)   One must question the relevance of invoking *maslahah* and other tools of Islamic Law in order to make one's fiqh consistent with the contemporary human rights platforms. First, one must ask whether this is an acceptable manner of invoking *maslahah*. Second, one must also question why Islamic Law need be forced to comply with contemporary human rights thinking. This is the biggest question that Baderin essentially sidesteps. However, it is a question that will play a major role in the remainder of this work.

One final point that needs to be made concerning Baderin is his invoking of the concept of *maqaasid al-shareeah* or the overall goals and priorities of Islamic Law. The reality is, as shall be demonstrated later, that if there is anything that demonstrates that the goals, ideology and reality of Islam is different from that of the human rights movement it is the goals of the Shareeah. The primary goals of the Shareeah around which virtually all Islamic laws revolve are five—the founding, preserving and promoting of religion, life, familial ties (and honor), wealth and human intellect. These goals are very different from the goals of the human rights activists, especially when one takes into consideration the ultimate emphasis placed on religion. Thus, for example, one law that human rights have a great deal of difficulty accepting is the Islamic law of apostasy. However, if any law is consistent with the goals and purposes of the Shareeah it is this law that is meant to protect and preserve the ultimate goal of religion itself. Thus, in reality, invoking *maqaasid al-shareeah* does not, in the long-run, bolster Baderin's case.

Baderin's work was discussed in some detail here because it seemed that he was offering something different: a real synthesis between Islamic Law and Human Rights Law. He attempted to accomplish this by incorporating not only some aspects of Islamic Law, which is the typical approach by many in this more apologetic category, but also incorporating alternative in human rights law. However, in the long-run, his attempt falls somewhat short. As shall be demonstrated throughout the remainder of this work, it is not a surprise that this attempt, like all the other attempts, has seemingly failed. There is definitely some root cause for the impasse that continues to occur between proponents of Islamic Law and proponents of the contemporary human rights movement.

Where to Go from Here?

In this chapter, many pages have been dedicated to a review of current approaches to Islam and human rights. The reason such detail was given to this review is that it captures how this topic is currently being dealt with and puts the contemporary discussion in its contemporary frameworks.[1] Two of three approaches basically call for the abandoning of the religion of Islam as it has been understood and practiced for centuries. The third approach seeks a very unimpressive combination of Islam and human rights. In fact, this author very much agrees with Ignatieff's view when he wrote,

There have been recurrent attempts, including Islamic Declarations of Human Rights, to reconcile Islamic and Western traditions by putting more emphasis on family duty and religious devotion, and by drawing on distinctively Islamic traditions of religious and ethnic toleration. But these attempts at syncretic fusion between Islam and the West have never been entirely successful: agreement by the parties actually trades away what is vital to each side. The resulting consensus is bland and unconvincing.[2]

The author's approach here is that Islam is something completely independent of the contemporary human rights movement. The sources and foundations for each are completely different and independent. Thus, it is unreasonable to expect that one

---

[1] There are others who may not fall within the different categories described in this chapter. For example, Abu Ala Mawdudi's *Human Rights in Islam* (Leicester, England: the Islamic Foundation, 1976) is distinct in a number of ways from the works reviewed here. However, as Mayer pointed out, even though Maudoodi sees a fundamental conflict between human rights and Islam, he does go out of his way to demonstrate that Islam originally provided human rights and so on. Cf., Mayer, *Islam and Human Rights*, pp. 73f.

[2] Michael Ignatiefff, *Human Rights as Politics and Religion* (with commentary by K. Anthony Appiah, David A. Hollinger, Thomas W. Laqueur, Diane F. Orentlicher) (Princeton, NJ: Princeton University Press, 2001), p. 59.

will somehow be completely compatible with the other. Furthermore, even comparing the two is very difficult because one is virtually comparing the proverbial oranges and apples (although some effort of comparison will be made here).

It is very important for both sides of the issue to understand exactly what the other side is. The reality is that the human rights movement makes some very great and bold claims for itself. Islam also makes some very great and bold claims for itself. Many times these claims are about the same issues but the conclusions are very different, if not completely contradictory. In this day and age, one has to be honest and open about such philosophical differences.

It will be shown that the philosophy and premises of the human rights movement differ from that of Islam. This brings up a very simple point: Why would Muslims try to fit Islam into a system that is not Islam? Certainly Muslim scholars do not do this with Christianity and Judaism—they do not try to prove that the two of them are completely compatible. However, perhaps due to some inferiority complex that started when Western nations colonized much of the Western world, many Muslims have bought into this idea that human rights—like Western civilization and Western science previously—are a godsend and they feel that they must prove that there is no conflict between human rights and Islam.

The argument here is not one of cultural relativism but it is in fact questioning the very basis of the human rights platform.Even from a secular perspective this critique is valid and crucial. It questions what this movement has to offer to Islam. This does not mean that everything that human rights proponents argue for is unacceptable. Indeed, Islam does endorse and support many of the same concepts, as shall be touched upon later. However, Islam must never be confused with the secular, manmade philosophy /ideology that constitutes the contemporary human rights movement.

In fact, this author can even state his premise in stronger terms. In the preceding pages, the difficulties of completely reconciling the current theories of human rights with Islamic Law have been expounded. In all three approaches, Islamic Law is somehow requested to come up to the standards or at least be acceptable in the light of contemporary human rights theory. However, a key question has not yet been addressed: Why must Islam be held accountable to the claims of human rights theory? In other words, what is there in human rights theory that makes it so strong or such an unquestionable purveyor of truth that even religions are demanded to come up to its standards? Is there something so "right" about human rights theory that this is not even an acceptable question to ask? Or, is this simply a repeat of the "white man's burden" in which the people of the West feel they have to rescue the Muslims?[1]

This work will take a very different approach to the current issue. It will demonstrate that Islam is not in need of the human rights ideology. This will be concluded not in some arrogant fashion by simply saying that Islam is the guidance from God and that human thinking can never reach the greatness of God's system—although that is definitely what a Muslim believes. Here the approach **shall** be different. Herein, the critique at which the human rights movement projects at Islam will be used to demonstrate that the human rights platform is actually flawed, self-contradictory and logically inconsistent.

This does not mean that Islam is opposed to "human rights." Indeed, Islam supports and defends numerous "human rights," as shall be noted. Neither does this mean that there is nothing good or important about the human rights platform. However, it does mean that, like all other man-made systems, the human rights platform as it is currently envisioned by so many today cannot bring to humankind what the true religion of God can bring.

---

[1] Oh (p. 3) states that human rights advocates must appreciate the ex-colonial environment that many Muslim states have or are experiencing, making them very suspicious of any "ideology" that is demanded of them from the West. Bricmont (p. 10) writes, "[W]hen the first Europeans arrived in distant lands, they discovered 'barbarous customs': human sacrifices, cruel punishments, binding of women's feet, and so on. Violations of human rights, the absence of democracy or the fate of women in Muslim countries are the contemporary version of those barbarous customs." Bricmont (p. 20) also discusses how this human rights discourse is used as justifying military intervention in other parts of the world, while previously the excuses where those of the white man's burden, spreading Christianity and the like. In fact, Bricmont stated (p. 29), "Whenever dictators, monarchs, bosses, aristocrats, bureaucrats, or colonialists exercise power over others, they need a justifying ideology. That justification almost always comes down to the same formula: when A exercises power over B, he does so for B's 'own good.' In short, power habitually presents itself as altruistic." Bricmont then goes on to give numerous examples to justify this claim. See Jean Bricmont, *Humanitarian Imperialism: Using Human Rights to Sell War* (New York: Monthly Review Press, 2006).

The History of the "Human Rights" Are Human Rights a "Western, Modern" Concept?

Views vary widely concerning the inception and history of human rights. For example, Mayer writes, "Concepts of human rights are just one part of a cluster of institutions transplanted since the nineteenth century from the West."[1] J. Donnelly is one of the most adamant in denying that any other civilization (including the pre-modern West) had any concept coming close to the contemporary concept of human rights. He wrote, for example,

Most non-western cultural and political traditions lack not only the practice of human rights but the very concept. As a matter of historical fact, the concept of human rights is an artifact of modern western civilization.[2]

Elsewhere, Donnelly unequivocally reiterated this when he said, "I argue that non-Western cultural and political traditions, like the premodern West, lacked not only the practice of human rights but also the very concept."[3]

On the other hand, Yogindra Khushalani claims that "the concept of human rights can be traced to the origin of the human race itself."[4] Perhaps more realistically, the *Encyclopedia Britannica* states,

Most students of human rights trace the historical origins of the concept [of human rights] back to ancient Greece and Rome, where it was closely tied to the premodern natural law doctrines of Greek Stoicism (the school of philosophy founded by Zeno of Citium, which held that a universal working force pervades all creation and that human conduct therefore should be judged according to, and brought into harmony with, the law of nature).[5]

---

[1] Ann Elizabeth Mayer, *Islam and Human Rights* (Boulder, CO: Westview Press, 1999), p. 9.

[2] J. Donnelly, "Human Rights and Dignity: An Analytic Critique of Non-Western Human Rights Conceptions" *American Political Science Review* (1982, 76), p. 303. Quoted in Ali, p. 17.

[3] Jack Donnelly, *Universal Human Rights in Theory & Practice* (Ithaca: Cornell University Press, 2003), p. 71. Concerning the pre-modern West, Donnelly writes (p. 76), "I want to turn immediately to the premodern West, where it is equally clear that the idea and practice of human rights were utterly foreign."

[4] Quoted in Donnelly, *Universal*, p. 71. Donnelly calls this claim "patently absurd."

[5] "Human rights," *Encyclopædia Britannica: Ultimate Reference Suite* (Chicago: Encyclopædia Britannica, 2009). An interesting and detailed discussion of "human rights" or related concept in Roman times is Richard A. Bauman, *Human Rights in Ancient Rome* (Routledge: London, 2000). One concludes from this work, as Bauman did (p. 130), that the current system owes it debt to Roman times.

Additionally, as noted earlier, some Muslim authors imply that the idea of human rights began with the coming of Islam. Commenting on this phenomenon, Donnelly writes,

In almost all contemporary Arab literature on this subject [human rights], we find a listing of the basic rights established by modern conventions and declarations, and then a serious attempt to trace them back to Koranic texts (Zakaria 228). Many authors (e.g., Tabandeh 1970:1,85) even argue that contemporary human rights doctrines merely replicate 1400-year-old Islamic ideas. The standard argument in this now extensive literature is that "Islam has laid down some universal fundamental rights for humanity as a whole, which are to be observed and respected under all circumstances … fundamental rights for every man by virtue of his status as a human being" (Mawdudi 1976:10). "The basic concepts and principles of human rights [have] from the very beginning been embodied in Islamic law."[1]

(Incidentally, Donnelly ends that passage by expressing his views toward such claims, "Such claims, however, are almost entirely baseless."[2])

Ishay highlights the fact that the origin of human rights is a politically charged question wherein some privilege will be given to a particular value system against any challenges to that original orthodoxy.[3] Thus, one can find such various claims about the origins of human rights.

The most obvious question that arises now is: How could these researchers come to such different conclusions concerning the history and origins of human rights? The answer to that question is actually remarkably simple. With all the talk about the importance of human rights today, the sometimes unmentioned fact is that various people have very different understandings of what human rights is actually all about. Hence, some can argue that "human rights" can be traced back to ancient history while others can argue that it is a "modern, western" invention.

---

[1] Donnelly, p. 72.

[2] Donnelly, p. 72.

[3] Micheline R. Ishay, *The History of Human Rights: From Ancient Times to the Globalization Era* (Berkeley, CA: University of California Press, 2004), p. 6.

It is hard to conceive that earlier civilizations had no recognition of certain "rights" that every individual human possessed. Rights such as the right to form a family, freedom of movement and so on were more or less—just as nowadays many rights are "more or less"[1]—accepted and respected without having such things spelled out as "human rights." This was particularly true in Islamic Law wherein there is a general principle that states that all things are considered permissible unless there is a stated prohibition against it.[2] In other words, in essence, every individual has the right or the freedom to do any or all things that have not been prohibited by the law. This was probably never stated as a "right" as such since that terminology was not in vogue in earlier times.

At the same time, it is very important to recognize that there is a current conception of "human rights" that can be rightly claimed to be recent and Western origin. Donnelly highlights how this conception has to do with the rights of humans and has virtually nothing to do with the obligations of humans, the latter being an aspect found in other and earlier societies. In his words,

"Traditional" societies—Western and non-Western alike—typically have had elaborate systems of duties. Many of those duties even correspond to values and obligations that we associate with human rights today. But such societies had conceptions of justice, political legitimacy, and human flourishing that sought to realize human dignity, flourishing, or well-being entirely independent of human rights. These institutions and practices are alternatives to, rather than different formulations of, human rights.[3]

---

[1] Many of those rights were restricted to certain classes of society or were not completely available to non-citizens. In reality, in the world of nation states today, that process continues. Sometimes people are dealt with in a very different fashion simply because they are non-citizens. In the United States, for example, a born citizen born outside of the United States does not have the right to become President of the United States.

[2] Allah says in the Quran, "What is prohibited for you has been expounded in detail" (*al-Anaam* 119). Beyond the basic harmful aspects that have been prohibited, humans are free to act and pursue any adventures they wish. For a discussion of this principle see Abdullah al-Judai, *Taiseer Ilm Usool al-Fiqh* (Beirut: Muassasah al-Rayyaan, 1997), pp. 48f.

[3] Donnelly, p. 71.

Although the difference between obligation and rights can be overblown, the fact is that there is something truly modern, Western-grown in the contemporary view of human rights that sets it apart from other conceptions that may seem, outwardly, to be similar to the human rights conception. The unique aspects of this history have colored the current conception of human rights, as this history reflects a revolt against various types of authority, in particular the authority of the church and the kings. It has been this struggle that has led to the emphasis on "rights" only and not on obligations or duties.[1] That is probably why there is no such thing as the "universal declaration of human obligations" coming from these Western-derived bodies. In reality, individual "obligation," as opposed to "right," is virtually the antithesis of what this struggle has been all about and this historic reality has steered the discussion that has followed.

In sum, the claim that the concept of human rights is Western has some validity to it—in the sense that the contemporary human rights schemes as proposed by many human rights activists is indeed Western and modern in its nature. It is therefore of some importance to understand the background of the development of current human rights thinking as that background to this day still greatly affects many of the contemporary proponents of human rights. Incidentally, this history and development also sheds some light on the question of whether the contemporary human rights platform can deservedly be called "universal" in nature.

---

[1] Donnelly claims that rights are "tools given to the oppressed" while duties are nothing but "obligations of the privileged." However, "With this distinction in mind, rights nonetheless lack significance if no one accepts the duty to aid those whose rights have been violated. The rights of the oppressed, although they can always be claimed, cannot be realized or restored unless those who are in a position to help believe that they have a duty to do so" (Oh, p. 25). In many ways, the differences between rights and obligations may be overblown or the dichotomy may be overemphasized. If rights do not correspond to some type of obligation upon others—even the obligation just to let the other be—it is a right that can never truly be fulfilled. Furthermore, if people do not accept the obligations that are upon them, attaining rights will always be a struggle, which is something clearly reflected in the contemporary human rights movement. Abu El Fadl in Bucar and Barnett, pp. 88-91, has a lengthy refutation of those who imply that the idea of rights never existed in previous cultures or in Islamic culture in particular. He begins his discussion by saying, "To argue that the juristic tradition did not develop the idea of fundamental or basic individual rights does not mean that tradition was oblivious to the notion. In fact, the juristic tradition tended to sympathize with individuals who were unjustly executed for their beliefs or those who died fighting against injustice…" See also Oh, pp. 26-27.

Brief History of the Current Human Rights Movement

The contemporary human rights movement is closely related to the unique history of Europe. Obviously, the entire world did not experience the same kind of history as the West did, part of which shall be described below. At the outset, then, one could argue that it will be difficult to imagine that concepts born out of such a unique history will necessarily be suitable for the remainder of earth's inhabitants who did not suffer a similar fate of history.

The ideas of freedom and equality were born out of environments in Europe wherein freedom and equality were restricted. For the most part, they were restricted by religion and government—these two bodies were actually closely entangled in the theory of the "divine right of kings."

The historical process is well and succinctly described in the following passage from the *Encyclopedia Britannica*,

The scientific and intellectual achievements of the 17th century--the discoveries of Galileo and Sir Isaac Newton, the materialism of Thomas Hobbes, the rationalism of René Descartes and Gottfried Wilhelm Leibniz, the pantheism of Benedict de Spinoza, the empiricism of Francis Bacon and John Locke--encouraged a belief in natural law and universal order; and during the 18th century, the so-called Age of Enlightenment, a growing confidence in human reason and in the perfectability of human affairs led to its more comprehensive expression. Particularly to be noted are the writings of the 17th-century English philosopher John Locke--arguably the most important natural law theorist of modern times--and the works of the 18th-century Philosophers centred mainly in Paris, including Montesquieu, Voltaire, and Jean-Jacques Rousseau. Locke argued in detail, mainly in writings associated with the Revolution of 1688 (the Glorious Revolution), that certain rights self-evidently pertain to individuals as human beings (because they existed in "the state of nature" before humankind entered civil society); that chief among them are the rights to life, liberty (freedom from arbitrary rule), and property; that, upon entering civil society (pursuant to a "social contract"), humankind surrendered to the state only the right to enforce these natural rights, not the rights themselves; and that the state's failure to secure these reserved natural rights (the state itself being under contract to safeguard the interests of its members) gives rise to a right to responsible, popular revolution. The Philosophers, building on Locke and others and embracing many and varied currents of thought with a common supreme faith in reason, vigorously attacked religious and scientific dogmatism, intolerance, censorship, and social-economic restraints. They sought to discover and act upon universally valid principles harmoniously governing nature, humanity, and society, including the theory of the inalienable "rights of Man" that became their fundamental ethical and social gospel.[1]

It is interesting to note, though, that this early "human rights movement," which greatly influenced the American and French constitutions, did eventually, to some extent, weaken. It weakened mostly because it was lacking any firm basis. As many of the theories of the Renaissance and Enlightenment began to be questioned, the question of natural law and similarly other theories were more or less discarded, leading to a very large vacuum and decay in the progress of human rights.

Furthermore, it should be noted that the development of such human rights thinking in the West is hardly anything to "boast" about, as it has most to do with failures and extremes that existed in the West.[2] The extremes of the church and the rulers led to human rights demands (in the same way that the extremes and atrocities of the Western nations in World War I and World War II as well as via colonialism also led to human rights demands). This is been aptly summarized by the *Encyclopedia Britannica* in the following passage:

In sum, the idea of human rights, called by another name, played a key role in the late 18th- and early 19th-century struggles against political absolutism. It was, indeed, the failure of rulers to respect the principles of freedom and equality, which had been central to natural law philosophy almost from the beginning, that was responsible for this development. In the words of Maurice Cranston, a leading

---

[1] "Human rights," *Encyclopædia Britannica: Ultimate Reference Suite* (Chicago: Encyclopædia Britannica, 2009).

[2] It seems that Donnely recognizes this reality but it is not willing to state it in such blatant terms. Hence, he states (p. 62), "This historical priority, of course, reflects no special Western virtue or merit. The characteristic indignities and injustices of modern markets and modern states simply happen to have been experienced first in the West."

student of human rights, " . . . absolutism prompted man to claim [human, or natural] rights precisely because it denied them."[1]

Ignatieff's discussion on this point is also very enlightening. He wrote,

The Declaration may still be a child of the Enlightenment, but it was written when faith in the Enlightenment faced its deepest crisis of confidence. In this sense, human rights is not so much the declaration of the superiority of European civilization as a warning by Europeans that the rest of the world should not seek to reproduce its mistakes.[2]

In fact, human rights thinking was partially a reaction in Europe to a time in which there was virtually no freedom of religion. The state would declare its religion and, for the most part, people were not free to practice and perhaps even accept any religion other than the State's. Ishay describes part of this dark history of Europe— the likes of which the rest of the world has probably never seen:

Yet the battle for religious freedom was far from over. In France, an important advance in that struggle had been the Edict of Nantes (1598), in which Henry IV had sought to end the French wars of religion by guaranteeing religious freedom to French Protestants (or Huguenots). In 1658, however, Louis XIV revoked the edict, depriving the Huguenots of all civil and religious liberties. In England, the Parliament passed the Tolerant Act in 1689, which, though allowing some dissenters to practice their religion, continued to exclude Jewish and Catholic worship.[3]

Ishay makes the developments in Europe sound very logical and rationally drawn out, when she writes,

Yet if a series of long-lasting religious wars eroded the initial aspirations of Christendom, the international nature of the wars incited the development of a new

---

[1] "Human rights," *Encyclopædia Britannica: Ultimate Reference Suite* (Chicago: Encyclopædia Britannica, 2009). See also Ishay, p. 64.

[2] Ignatieff, p. 65. In the same book, he also wrote (p. 4), "Calling the global diffusion of Western human rights a sign of moral progress may seem Eurocentric. Yet the human rights instruments created after 1945 were not a triumphant expression of European imperial self-confidence but a war-weary generation's reflection on European nihilism and its consequences."

[3] Ishay, p. 77.

vision of world unity based on rational thinking rather than on revealed truth—principles that had shown their divisive nature during the wars of religion. By asserting individual responsibility in matters of salvation and in seeking happiness on earth, the Protestant influence helped advance a new credo relying on individual choice and rights. The belief in the value of individuals and their capacity to reason was further strengthened by a burst of scientific breakthroughs.[1]

However, that rosy picture of the development of "rational thinking" may not be sound at all. In fact, the process by which Europe developed new understandings about life were not necessarily "rational" and well-thought out. In other words, the changes that occurred in Europe were brought about as a reaction to European civilization's and religion's own shortcomings and weaknesses. For example, a typical contemporary European view of "religion" is not necessarily rational but more emotional in its roots. As McGoldrick noted concerning the French approach to religion and secularism:

The modern French approach to religion was not arrived at after principled and philosophical reflection on the importance and value of religious freedom. Rather, it was reached after centuries of bitter, and often violent, state-church conflict. France has a long history of religious hostility and conflict including Religious Wars from 1562-98. In much of that conflict the Catholic Church played a dominant political role. Indeed, one of the objectives of the French Revolution (1789-95) was to diminish the political power and the social and cultural influences of the Roman Catholic Church. In 1789 the Constituent Assembly declared that Catholic Church property would henceforth be at the disposal of the nation. In 1790 a Decree was made which dissolved all monastic vows and a Civil Constitution of the Clergy was adopted. Thousands of Catholic priests were murdered or deported.[2]

It is very important to understand and realize this background of the human rights movement because it still has a strong influence on the movement today. There is a clear movement away from the authority of any type of religion to the

---

[1] Ishay, p. 71.

[2] Dominic McGoldrick, *Human Rights and Religion: The Islamic Headscarf Debate in Europe* (Portland, OR: Hart Publishing, 2006), p. 34. He goes on to discuss more of the anti-clerical feelings in French history, see pp. 34ff.

authority of what is innocently called "human reasoning," "freedom" and the like. In fact, they are fighting against dogmatism or the belief that a principle or rule is fixed and remains so. This is given up in the name of the authority of human reasoning which no longer accepted the beliefs of the Christian Church, especially with respect to the physical world.[1] In fact, one of the messages of the Enlightenment, this major root of the contemporary human rights movement, is that everything is about "man." As Rasmussen noted:

This Enlightenment narrative understood humanity as a species apart, just as it conceived the rest of nature in Cartesian and Kantian terms. Kant himself was utterly clear: "Animals are not self-conscious and are there merely as a means to an end. That end is man." "Nature," "natural rights," and "natural law" are, to be sure, serious moral, religious, and metaphysical subjects and key terms in Enlightenment rights discourse. The appeals of Locke, Rousseau, Jefferson, Paine, and other such champions of this good cause rest here. But the attention is anthropocentric without qualification… The theocentric universe of medieval cosmology, with all nature alive as an ocean of symbols linking earth to heaven, is thoroughly secularized in the same broad movement that set the thinking, judging human self at the center of rights discourse and ethical theory. God, and nature as a fecund expression of divine emanations, are discarded in favor of morally self-sufficient humans set over against mechanistic and passive nature. For better or worse, then, rights language arises within and inhabits a moral world that is neither theocentric nor biocentric, but anthropocentric.[2]

The following passage sums up the important points on the history of the modern rights movement—it is a passage in which Mayer admits some important aspects concerning human rights that once again demonstrates that freedom of belief and religion cannot possibly be part of the overall contemporary human rights platform. Mayer writes,

---

[1] However, Muslim critics have noted that "human reasoning" many times is not much different from "human wants and desires" or *ahwaa*, especially when it is freed from the constraints of religion and even morality.

[2] Larry Rasmussen, "*Human Environmental Rights and/or Biotic Rights,*" in Gustafson and Juviler, pp. 37-38.

The human rights formulations utilized in international law are relatively recent, although one can find ideas that anticipate human rights concepts in ancient times. Certainly, the development of the intellectual foundations of human rights was given an impetus by the Renaissance in Europe and by the associated growth of rationalist and humanistic thought, which led to an important turning point in Western intellectual history: the abandonment of the premodern doctrines of the duties of man and the adoption of the view that the rights of man should be central in political theory, During the European Enlightenment, the rights of man became a preoccupation of political philosophy, and the intellectual groundwork for modern human rights theory was laid…

It was on these Western traditions of individualism, humanism, and rationalism and on legal principles protecting individual rights that twentieth-century international law on civil and political rights ultimately rested. Rejecting individualism, humanism, and rationalism is tantamount to rejecting the premises of modern human rights.[1]

It is amazing that such a history of the current human rights movement—and such characteristics of it must be recognized—and yet the questioning of the universality of such human rights is considered virtually "blasphemous." Among the writers in the West who are willing to recognize and comment on this fact is Stackhouse who wrote,

To be sure, some of the purported defenders of human rights leave themselves open to critique and the unwitting discrediting of the human rights ideas they wish to defend. For instance, Rhoda E. Howard and Jack Donnely argue that the idea of human rights "is rooted in structural changes that began to emerge in the late medieval and early modem Europe." However, if it is so that such ideas are little more than a by-product of a particular historical and social context, it becomes very difficult to argue that they ought to be taken as governing principles when the context has changed substantially, or is not contiguous with other areas of the world. Of course, we may believe that some inexorable logic of universal history moves toward ever fuller and fuller actualization of rights and autonomy everywhere, along

---

[1] Mayer, *Islam and Human Rights*, pp. 47-48, emphasis added.

with social, political, and economic change. But such a quasi-religious conviction is beyond the evidence and beyond most people's confidence in history's logic. History does not seem to warrant a rollicking confidence in an innate drive to do good once life is liberated from all religious and social constraint, as some thinkers of the Enlightenment wanted so much to be the case. Nor is it obvious that autonomy should be the highest moral purpose.[1]

The Formalization of Human Rights and Contemporary Human Rights Doctrines

It can be rightly argued that the largest transformations in the formalization of human rights took place after World Wars I and II. Between World War I and World War II, wherein the "savage treatment of individuals and groups," once again predominantly in the West led to calls for more rights for more people. In particular, there was concern for minority groups in Central and Eastern Europe. This is part of what led to the Covenant of the League of Nations. In fact, in 1929, an international private body called the Institute of International Law adopted the non-binding Declaration of the Rights of Man.[2]

The horrors of over fifty million people dying in the second "world war"— rooted once again in Europe—led many to the conclusion that something had to be done. After the failure of the earlier League of Nations, the United Nations, which still exists today, was created. The United Nations was created via a treaty that emphasized "universal respect for, and observance of, human rights and fundamental freedoms for all without distinction as to race, sex, language, or religion." This international body with member states spanning the entire world was the first organization of its kind that could seriously discuss the question of "universal" human rights, spreading beyond nation states to each individual of every state. It took on this task very early in its history, drawing up the Universal Declaration of Human Rights (UDHR) by 1948.[3]

---

[1] Max Stackhouse, "Why Human Rights Needs God: A Christian Perspective," in Bucar and Barnett, p. 13.

[2] Cf., Baderin, pp. 1718.

[3] A copy of this document is provided in the Appendix.

A short history of the drafting of this document is definitely called for here. The original drafting of the UDHR was prepared under by a commission spearheaded by Eleanor Roosevelt, the widow of the late President Franklin Roosevelt. This commission had eighteen members from various parts of the world, including Australia, Belgium, Byelorussia, Chile, China, Egypt, France, India, Iran, Lebanon, Panama, the Philippines, Ukraine, the United Kingdom, the United States, Uruguay, the USSR, and Yugoslavia. In the formulation process, a questionnaire had been distributed enquiring into the rights traditions of various cultures, including the Chinese, Islamic and Hindu cultures. After receiving a number of responses from throughout the world, the commission felt that they had enough of a consensus concerning primary human rights to move forward.

For a year and a half work continued on the final preparation of the document. Along with Mrs. Roosevelt, the final formulating committee consisted of commission co-chairman Chinese philosopher Pen-Chung Chang, Lebanese existentialist philosopher Charles Malik and French legal scholar Rene Cassin. Hence, it can definitely be argued that a number of broad perspectives were actually involved in the original drafting of the document.

Even at that early stage, it was clear that the drafting of a universal set of rights that would span the entire world with equal respect and application was not that easy of a task—and if simply the drafting were problematic, there is no question that the application would be even more so problematic. The following passage demonstrates some of the tensions that occurred, in particular between the "Socialist Eastern bloc" and the "Western" representatives:

Illustrative of such intrinsic ideological and philosophical differences was the first major argument during the first session of the human rights commission, in which the definition of human nature was discussed. Malik's provocative questions—"Is man merely a social being? Is he merely an animal? Is he merely an economic being?"—generated a heated debate between advocates of individual and collective rights. Warning against the danger of collectivism that ultimately absorbed "the human person in his individuality and ultimately inviolability," Malik asserted the centrality of a person's mind and consciousness, the sanctity of individual property rights, and individual protection against religious, state, and other forms of external coercion. His position prompted reactions from communist representatives like Yugoslav Vladislav Ribnikar (1900-1955) and the Russian representative Valentin Tepliakov, In the words of Ribnikar, "ITlhe psychology of individualism has been used by the ruling class in most countries to preserve its own privileges; a modern declaration of rights should not only consider the rights favored by the ruling class." How can one understand individual rights and obligations apart from those of one's own community, asked Tepliakov.

The Soviet representatives, unsurprisingly, gave priority to social and economic rights and equivalent civic duties, while American representatives favored political and civil rights. Central to this controversy was a face-off between proponents of central planning and advocates of programs that provided some room for the "invisible hand" to operate. This unleashed tempestuous accusations on each side; for instance, in response to American accusations of civil and political human rights abuses in the Soviet republic, Soviet delegates would point out that aside from making "slanderous allegations," the United States was "hypocritically" maintaining segregation in its own country, depriving Southern blacks of their fundamental civil, political, and economic rights.[1]

Note that some of the problems highlighted in the above passage have yet to be resolved and the same kinds of accusations are continually (and rightfully) cast today.

Eventually, when it came to adopting the declaration, the Soviet bloc abstained and the declaration was "adopted." The fact that an entire section of countries abstained from voting on this declaration is rarely explicitly mentioned by those who support human rights today and argue that it must be considered universal. Similarly, the make-up of the UN at that time is also rarely discussed. Ishay provides some of the details of the final passing:

When this important, albeit non-binding, document was put to a vote, the UN had only fifty-eight member states. Fifty ratified the declaration, while Byelorussia, Czechoslovakia, Poland, Saudi Arabia, South Africa, Ukraine, the Soviet Union, and Yugoslavia abstained. Those countries worried that this document, predominantly

---

[1] Micheline R. Ishay, *The History of Human Rights: From Ancient Times to the Globalization Era* (Berkeley, CA: University of California Press, 2004), p. 221.

"individualist" in its selected category of rights, would challenge the sanctity of domestic jurisdiction guaranteed by the legally binding UN charter. These fears proved warranted, as state practice, and regular invocations of the declaration over time, turned the document into respected customary international law. More importantly, human rights commissioners knew that the declaration was but a first step toward the development of a more specific legally binding covenant of human rights.[1]

It would be years later before any covenants of full legal force would be approved by the UN. These two documents were the International Covenant on Economic, Social and Cultural Rights (ICESCR) and the International Covenant on Civil and Political Rights (ICCPR).[2] These were adopted by the General Assembly of the United Nations in 1966 and were to enter into full force and effect in 1976. These two covenants along the UDHR constitute the International Bill of Rights.

It is important to highlight another aspect of the debate that occurred during that time that still has great ramifications today. There are different "types" of rights that are recognized in these various documents. They are usually described as civil and political rights as one category and economic and social rights as another.[3] The West, under the leadership of the United States and with its ultimate belief in free market capitalism, has always been reluctant to recognize the economic and social rights. In fact, the United States has clearly stated that the economic, social and cultural rights are merely "societal goals" rather than "human rights."[4] (This rather selective way of looking at human rights shall be commented upon later when discussing Islam's compatibility with "human rights.")

The Role of Muslims in the Formulation of the UDHR

Authors like Mayer and Donnely have emphasized and reminded their readers that Muslim states were signatories to the UDHR and took an active role in its final drafting. Mayer argues, "All in all, it is inaccurate to claim that when the foundations of the modern UN human rights system were being laid, Muslim

---

[1] Ishay, p. 223.

[2] The texts of both are provided in the Appendix.

[3] Civil and political rights are also known as "first generation rights" while economic, social and cultural rights are known as "second general rights."

[4] Cf., Baderin, p. 21.

countries were foes of human rights universality."[1] Mayer, in particular, seems to be very happy and pleased to find Susan Waltz' article "Universal Human Rights: The Contribution of Muslim States."[2] The manner in which Mayer and Donnelly refer to these facts gives one the feeling that they are trying to say that Muslims have no room to argue or complain today because, in reality, they were part of the process and agreed to the concept of international human rights law.

However, especially coming from authors like Mayer and Donnelly, the points that they are trying to make are weak if not downright deceiving. Mayer discusses this issue for several pages but in the end there are no points that she was trying to make that have any validity to them. This is so for the following reasons:

(1)   People like Donnelly and Mayer argue that Islam is not a monolith. Hence, just because they found a sector of Muslims—most likely, the elite, many times Western educated—who bought into this movement and signed onto it, then, according to their own thesis, one cannot assume that all the other Muslims (perhaps the majority) agree with it or are in line with it.
This important point did not escape Oh 21-22 who wrote,

Although the international scale of the human rights project demonstrates that the instigators of the UDHR earnestly attempted to include non-Western voices, they were nonetheless products of their time. The majority of the leaders of the human rights effort in the late 1940s were Western-educated white men of privilege from Europe and the United States. They guided an effort that remained in its overall structure a product of their beliefs and imagination, even if along the way they sought input from delegates of non-Western nations.[3]

---

[1] Mayer, *Islam and Human Rights*, p. 15.

[2] Cf., Mayer, *Islam and Human Rights*, pp. 12ff. She begins her discussion by stating, "Indeed, *in a welcome development,* a number of recent studies on the genesis of the international human rights system have amplified our appreciation of how input from representatives of Muslim countries influenced foundational UN human rights instruments. The studies document the relatively minor role played by Western powers such as the United States and highlight the significant contributions made by representatives of countries outside the North Atlantic region—including several Muslim countries" (Mayer, *Islam and Human Rights*, p. 12, emphasis added). Waltz' article is *Human Rights Quarterly* (vol. 26, 2004, pp. 799-844).

[3] Oh, pp. 21-22.

Her view was echoed by Renteln who noted "that all the eighteen drafts considered for the UDHR 'came from the democratic West and that all but two were in English'." She concluded thus that "(t)he fact that there were no dissenting votes should not be taken to mean that complete value consensus had been achieved."[1]

(2)   Mayer[2] argues that the Muslims involved in the original human rights documents did not object to the document based on Islamic grounds. It seems that they did not see any problem with these documents from an Islamic perspective. At the same time, though, Mayer admits elsewhere that Islamic scholars did not take up the issue of human rights until the Islamic revival in the 70s, after the Arab-Israeli wars.[3] In fact, the most-conservative Saudi Arabia's representative to the original was a Lebanese Christian.[4] How then can she argue that Muslims were truly involved when she realizes the fact that from an Islamic perspective this issue was never taken up until much later? Indeed, she goes beyond that and admits that for the most part, Islam was simply ignored or not taken seriously by the developers of human rights law. Here is what she herself wrote,

The learned literature on international human rights produced by academic specialists has traditionally shown an indifference to the Islamic tradition. Until recently, Islamic law was only occasionally mentioned in scholarly writing on international human rights, and then it was treated as a marginal, exotic phenomenon. Behind this lay an assumption about the authority of international law and its associated institutions and a belief in the relative backwardness of any Islamic models with which international law might conflict. The critiques offered by Muslims who object to international human rights law on religious grounds did not provoke much consternation or interest on the part of Western scholars of

---

[1] Baderin, p. 25.

[2] Mayer, *Islam and Human Rights*, p. 13.

[3] Mayer fully recognizes the changes that have taken among Muslims. She herself wrote (p. xiv), "What currently distinguishes Muslims' approaches to rights is their frequent recourse to interpretations of religious sources to develop positions supporting or condemning rights…"

[4] Mayer, *Islam and Human Rights*, p. 13. Interestingly, Mayer does not seem to find this ironic or a sign of a lack of preparation on the part of Muslim authors at that time. *Mayer, Islam and Human Rights*, p. 11, also wrote, "Muslims since the 1980s have produced a large literature trying to define where Islam stands on human rights and comparing Islamic and international human rights."

international law, for the latter did not feel that the legitimacy of international law was in any way jeopardized by assertions that it clashed with Islamic rules.[1]

(3)   There is no mandate/vote involved. Some today argue that Muslims throughout the world do not have a chance to vote on implementing Islam and that if they were allowed to cast such a vote, they would reject Islam. Interestingly enough, there has never been any type of vote by the masses on human rights declarations. In particular, when the first documents were passed, the Muslim states were post-colonial states, many times run by ex-colonial officers or dictatorships. Hence, one cannot claim that they represent any kind of will of the people or Islam itself. In fact, many were socialists, capitalists, areligious and so on.

(4)   When one reviews the articles that were objected to during the development of the UDHR, Muslims at that time, according to Mayer,[2] were objecting to some of the same issues that the Muslim scholars are objecting to today, such as issues related to marriage and family.[3] In other words, instead of proving her point that Muslims should not complain about the human rights documents since they had a hand in the original documents, she has to admit that Muslims have been objecting to some of the same issues since the inception of the human rights movement.

There is no need to delve into the Muslim role in the history of the early human rights documents any further than what was stated above. What authors like Mayer and Donnelly are trying to substantiate is meaningless and, in reality, simply not there. Their discussion are extremely weak if they are trying to imply in any way that Muslims today should not object to human rights documents because somehow some other Muslims or Muslim governments were involved in the original designing of such documents.

---

[1] Mayer, *Islam and Human Rights*, p. 49.

[2] Mayer, *Islam and Human Rights*, p. 14.

[3] Mayer, *Islam and Human Rights*, p. 14. Mayer also stated, "It was not only Muslim countries that quibbled; the United States, where states at the time had laws criminalizing interracial marriage, objected to a proposal for prohibiting limitations on marriage based on race, nationality, or religion. Significantly, such an objection, which showed that the United States was unwilling to accommodate one of the most basic human rights ideals, has rarely been highlighted in accounts of the work leading up to the UDHR."

Actually, Mayer herself highlights one of the differences between an Islamic view of human rights and a Western view of human rights, saying,

It is often overlooked that the package of rights in the International Bill includes economic and social rights. Muslim countries generally endorsed the ideas of economic and social rights, which the United States has always opposed as being antithetical to its capitalist ethos. When demands were made that, instead of preparing a single covenant elaborating on the rights set forth in the UDHR, economic and social rights should be set forth in a separate covenant. Muslim countries opposed the splitting of the domain of human rights. Their position ultimately proved to be a losing one, but in recent years, supporters of human rights have tended to see human rights as being mutually reinforcing, concluding that splitting the UDHR into two separate covenants was misguided and harmful for rights. Thus, the position of Muslim delegates, the more progressive position, has belatedly won some vindication.[1]

In fact, she goes even further and demonstrates another great divide between the "Western" approach and the approach held by Muslims:

Muslim countries' positions on self-determination and the wrongs of colonialism were emphatically endorsed by a majority of UN members and became enshrined in many international human rights documents. At the same time, Western countries did not always take the stances that are associated with a pro-human rights philosophy and sometimes joined those opposing minority rights, measures to ensure effective implementation of human rights, and bans on discrimination.[2]

Finally, regardless of what role Muslim states may have had in the development of some of the first human rights documents, there is no question that the trend in human rights thinking and documents since that time has been dominated by Western representatives and a "Western" perspective, a point that Mayer never made in her work. Baderin notes,

Joseph, Schultz, and Castan have however observed that 'a Western representative bias can be detected in recent years, with over half of the [Human

---

[1] Mayer, *Islam and Human Rights*, p. 16.

[2] Mayer, *Islam and Human Rights*, p. 16.

Rights Commission] members serving from 1998 to 2000 coming from the United States, Canada, Australia, the United Kingdom, France, Italy, Israel, Finland, Germany and Poland'. Thus the need for the reflection of a more 'equitable distribution of membership' not only of the HRC but of all the UN human rights treaty bodies cannot be overemphasized.[1]

More Recent Developments: Cairo, Beijing and Related Matters

In more recent years, the demand for respect of human rights has continued. At the same time, the scope and gamut of human rights has also expanded and become much more specific. General statements of earlier documents are made more precise and particular groups (such as women and children) have been targeted. Later documents stemming from the UN, which were not as widely ratified as some of the earlier documents, include:

Convention on the Elimination of All Forms of Discrimination Against Women (December 1979)

Convention Against Torture and Other Cruel, Inhuman or Degrading Treatment or Punishment (December 1984)

Convention on the Rights of the Child (December 1992)

In particular, mostly due to Western liberal influences, the demands for sexual freedoms and alternative lifestyle rights have dominated much of the discussion. In 1994, Cairo hosted the World Population Conference. Among the issues emphasized at that conference were "the advancement and empowerment of women, the elimination of all kinds of violence against women and women's right to control their own fertility."[2] In 1995, the Beijing Conference on Women was held. It made new demands for the sake of women. In the words of Desai,

The most significant new addition to the document is the acknowledgment of a kind of right to sexuality: "The human rights of women include their rights to have control over and decide freely and responsibly on matters related to their sexuality

---

[1] Baderin, p. 221, quoting from Joseph, S., Schultz, J., and Castan, M., *The International Covenant on Civil and Political Rights, Cases, Materials, and Commentary* (2000) p. 10.

[2] Quoted in Kausar, p. 7.

including sexual and reproductive health, free of coercion, discrimination, and violence."[1]

The Document fell short of explicitly declaring lesbianism, for example, as a human right. That was a contentious part of the debate surrounding the Platform. Needless to say, numerous religious groups oppose that type of "right." Hence, Beijing concluded with the above vague statement that actually could be interpreted to imply that such must be accepted as a human right.[2]

In addition, the tone and conclusion was much bolder. Again, Desai writes,

As one workshop organizer observed: "In Nairobi we were tentative, the emphasis was on that governments should support the international human rights treaties; in Beijing the demand is: governments must comply."[3]

These types of "rights" are now being demanded while other explicitly agreed upon rights continued to be, more or less, ignored. Nowadays, human rights are classified into various categories by subject, object or "generation." The major emphasis is still on civil and political rights. As Baderin notes, these rights are the "favourites of Western States, some of whom considered them as the only true human rights."[4] Economic, social and cultural rights are referred to as "second generation" rights. They may be favored by a number of developing nations but, as of yet, there is not a strong support for them in the overall human rights movement. This is interesting because the rights that are perhaps most needed for the protection of "human dignity" is given less attention by human rights programs. Again, Baderin notes, "Despite their inevitability for the sustenance of human dignity, the economic, social, and cultural rights are often considered as 'utopian aspirations', non-legal and non-justiciable."[5] Jeane Kirkpatrick, Reagan's US ambassador to the United

---

[1] Manisha Desai, "Women's Rights," in James R. Lewis and Carl Skutsch, *The Human Rights Encyclopedia* (Armonk, New York: Sharpe Reference, 2001), vol. 3, p. 949.

[2] For a complete discussion of the various debates and controversies surrounding the Beijing Conference, see Zeenath Kausar, *Woman's Empowerment and Islam: The UN Beijing Document Platform for Action* (Selangor, Malaysia: Ilmiah Publishers, 2002), *passim*.

[3] Desai, p. 948.

[4] Baderin, p. 21.

[5] Baderin, pp. 21-22. They are some authors, such as Henry Shue, who argue that the rich have, from a human rights perspective, a great responsibility toward those living in poverty throughout the world.

Nations, described these rights as, "a letter to Santa Claus."[1] Bricmont noted that her statement did not get much response from the press and intellectuals. He wondered what would have been the response if someone were to have called the civil and political rights "a letter to Santa Claus."[2]

The third generation of rights refers to collective rights and not individual rights. This third generation of rights includes the "right to peace"[3] and the "right to development." These are the most recent concepts and have received the least amount of overall attention.

Although the UN General Assembly has asserted that all human rights are indivisible and interdependent, the practice of human rights has been very different. Thus, when international organizations present their lists of major human rights violators, the violations are mostly concerned with the "first generation" rights and very little attention is given to all of the other varied rights. This bias concerning the emphasis of the human rights movement is one of the reasons that Islam and other religions are targeted as being at variance with hguman rights while entire social

---

See Henry Shue, *Basic Rights: Subsistence, Affluence and U.S. Foreign Policy* (Princeton University Press, 1980). However, voices like that are sadly very few and far between in the contemporary human rights literature.

[1] Quoted in Bricmont, p. 83.

[2] Bricomon, pp. 83-84. Bricmont is obviously very left leaning but he makes an interesting point about Cuba. On p. 84, he writes, "For some time now, the European left has largely taken up the demand for democratization of Cuba. Let us admit, for the sake of argument, that the Cuban regime is as "totalitarian" as our media claim. Nevertheless, it is perfectly clear that in the rest of Latin America, where the sort of democracy Cuba is exhorted to install already exists, both health care and education are of a notably lower quality and less accessible for the poor majority of the population. If the Cuban public health policy were adopted elsewhere in Latin America, hundreds of thousands of human lives would undoubtedly be saved. It should also be noted that Cuban efforts to provide public health care and education have continued long after the island ceased being "subsidized" by the Soviet Union, and despite being subjected to a severe embargo and countless acts of sabotage caused by the North American superpower, which obviously obliged the Cuban government to allot extra resources to defense, counterespionage, and so on." Incidentally, Donnelly is adamant in his rejection of this perception of the Western world concerning these types of rights. He says that the welfare states of Europe and the United States are sufficient to demonstrate that the West has always taken these rights seriously. See his full discussion in Donnelly, pp. 49ff.

[3] In 1984, the UN General Assembly issued the "Declaration on the Right of Peoples to Peace."

systems that pay little attention to the needs of the poor, for example, are not highlighted and blasted in the media.[1]

In sum, regardless of the history and original foundations of human rights and regardless of whether each society has had its own vision of human rights, there is definitely a Western bias in the contemporary human rights movement. The rest of the world is viewed in the light of a Western yardstick. This has led to a very paradoxical situation in which in the name of human rights and freedom other societies and cultures are expected to mimic and imitate these norms of the West. Incidentally, this does not bode well for the human rights movement itself, as more and more voices have been raised to challenge its view of the world and individual societies.

Given the overall "consensus" that many authors point to concerning the acceptance and authority of human rights, there is still a great deal of difference concerning which rights are indeed human rights and, concerning human rights that are agreed upon, how such human rights are to be implemented. Even in the nations of the West, the self-proclaimed leaders of the human rights crusade, there are still great variances in how these human rights are put into law and practice.

---

[1] There are some who try to highlight this discrepancy and call for change in the perspectives on human rights, such as the contributors to Anuradha Mittal and Peter Rosset, *America* Needs *Human Rights* (Oakland, CA: Food First Books, 1999), *passim.* Articles in that work include: "Hunger in the Land of Plenty," "How the US Economy Creates Poverty and Inequality," "The War on the Poor," and "Welfare Reform Violates Human Rights." One could argue that the current debate and resistance to the Obama Administration's health care reform is an overall reflection of the rejection of such social "human rights" in American society. In fact, even Donnelly (p. 33) wrote, "As an American, I want to note explicitly that this includes the United States, where economic and social rights are systematically violated in significant measure because they still are seen as not really matters of rights (entitlement) but as considerations of justice, charity, or utility."

Fundamental Issues Regarding the Contemporary Human Rights Paradigm

In this chapter, some of the fundamental issues regarding the contemporary human rights paradigm shall be discussed. These are issues that should influence one's attitude toward the contemporary human rights paradigm. These fundamental issues include the following:

(1)   The justification of HR

(2)   How can something be determined to be a "human right."

(3)   The paradox of the human rights paradigm.

(4)   Human rights between theory and practice.

The Justification for Human Rights

When reading books on human rights, it seems clear that some human rights advocates expect all societies and religions to bow down to their demands and implement the contemporary human rights schemes. This is quite a hefty demand upon Muslims, for example, who believe that they possess a divine revelation from God—a belief that entails that they do not have the right to deviate from what God has revealed.

If human rights advocates are serious in their demands upon others, they, at the very least, should have an extremely sound basis or justification for what they are claiming for themselves and demanding of others. This leads to the inevitable question of the very foundation of human rights. On what is the belief in human rights based on?

Perhaps even human rights advocates will admit that on this issue comes the first chink in the armor of the human rights movement. In fact, this question was often "dealt with" by simply avoiding it. It is admitted by many that it is simply too controversial, divisive and confusing an issue to ask about the foundations of human rights. It is easiest and best simply to accept the theory and to ensure that every human is granted these rights. However, more and more theorists are questioning such a blind approach and raising questions concerning the foundations of human rights. More and more are realizing that somehow this question must be answered and it must be answered satisfactorily. In the words of An-Na'im, a pro-human rights writer, "But more than fifty years later [after the UDHR], the question of the moral or philosophical foundation of human rights remains both difficult to answer and critical for the practical implementation of these rights."[1]

As noted, when making demands on all of human society, one would hope that there would be something truly substantial behind those demands. If not, then, it could be argued, it is nothing but bigotry, fanaticism and arrogance that would lead such advocates to demand that the entire world follow along their path.

History of the Question: Sidestepped by the UDHR

Undoubtedly, one of the greatest causes for differences of opinion concerning human rights relates to the issue of the very foundation of human rights. This fundamental question influences important issues such as what constitutes a human right and how is human rights law to be manifested.

In an attempt to get universal agreement of the original drafting of the Universal Declaration of Human Rights back in the 1940s, the framers intentionally decided to sidestep this fundamental question. As Bucar and Barnett write,

UDHR had a limited goal, to articulate the specific human rights that member states could agree upon. The limited nature of this project is reflected in French Catholic philosopher Jacques Maritain's comment on the debates preceding its drafting: "We agree on these rights, providing we are not asked why. With the 'why,' the dispute begins." The text of the UDHR follows Maritain's advice, intentionally remaining vague and general on the "why" of human rights. The UDHR affirms that "the inherent dignity [of and] the equal and inalienable rights of all members of the human family is the foundation of freedom, justice and peace in the world," but bases these rights on an unnamed, unspecified, ungrounded "common understanding."[2]

---

[1] Abdullahi An-Na'im, "The Synergy and Interdependence of Human Rights, Religion and Secularism," in Runzo, et al., p. 28.

[2] Elizabeth M. Bucar and Barbra Barnett, "Introduction: The 'Why' of Human Rights," in Elizabeth M. Bucar and Barbra Barnett, eds., *Does Human Rights Need God?* (Grand Rapids, Michigan: William B. Eerdmans Publishing Company, 2005), pp. 1-2.

This strategy on their part might have been considered very clever at that time, in order to derive some initial agreement on an innovated topic. However, the reality is that it was a flaw. Sadly, though, in general, this flaw has not been dealt with in an honest manner since. As Bucar and Barnnett stated immediately after the above quote:

Following this early attempt to bracket any rationale for human rights, the world community has simply continued to agree to disagree, fearing perhaps that any discussion of the differences among the various rationales for human rights might undermine the consensus manifested in the UDHR.[1]

In many circles, this attitude continues until today. Although at some general level there may be widespread agreement, the fact is that on substantial issues there are great differences of opinion, as Weston noted,

[T]o say that there is widespread acceptance of the principle of human rights on the domestic and international plane is not to say that there is complete agreement about the nature of such rights or their substantive scope.[2]

One must keep in mind that the contemporary human rights movement is about much more than simply some rights that must be guaranteed or laws that need to be passed. It has to do with an entire view of humans and it makes demands upon every society on earth. Furthermore, it makes great claims, such as, "Humans must have the right to X and Y." This should lead to the following question that must be answered: Is there something so sacred or special about humans that each and everyone is deserving a special list of rights simply for being human?

The argument made here is that fundamental questions can no longer be ignored. Indeed, many of the concerns surrounding the contemporary human rights movement are founded upon core issues that have heretofore been left unanswered. Fortunately, more and more scholars are also recognizing this point and realizing that it may very lie at the crux of the issue of the success or failure of the human rights movement. The basis for these claims about humans cannot simply be assumed away or ignored. Gutman was definitely hitting the point when he wrote,

---

[1] Bucar and Barnett, "Introduction: The 'Why' of Human Rights," in Bucar and Barnett, p. 2.

[2] Quoted in Baderin, pp. 1-2.

What, pragmatically minded people might ask with some incredulity is at stake in the equally heated—and quite common--arguments about the metaphysical and moral foundations of human rights? These arguments—for example, about human agency, dignity, and natural law—tend to be quite abstract, and it may therefore be tempting to assume that not much of practical importance is at stake. But such an assumption would be rash. What is at stake in determining the foundations of human rights is often the very legitimacy of human rights talk in the international arena. If human rights necessarily rest on a moral or metaphysical foundation that is not in any meaningful sense universal or publicly defensible in the international arena, if human rights are based on exclusively Eurocentric ideas, as many critics have (quite persistently) claimed, and these Eurocentric ideas are biased against non-Western countries and cultures, then the political legitimacy of human rights talk, human rights covenants, and human rights enforcement is called into question.[1]

Chris Brown perceptively takes the discussion much further than Gutman did. He stated,

Virtually everything encompassed by the notion of "human rights" is the subject of controversy.… The idea that individuals have, or should have, "rights" is itself contentious, and the idea that rights could be attached to individuals by virtue solely of their common humanity is particularly subject to penetrating criticism.[2]

This is a reality that human rights proponents must admit and face. They cannot hide behind beautiful sounding terms—like "human rights"—while in reality what they are proclaiming is nothing but a mere myth with no foundation to it whatsoever. The question of the foundation of human rights must be brought to the forefront if people around the world are actually expected to change their societies and even religion based on the human rights mandate.

In response to very fundamental questions, a number of theories have developed in order to justify the mere existence of a human rights platform. For example, in Orend's introductory work on human rights, Chapter 3 is devoted to the question of the justification of human rights. Orend covers moral convention,

---

[1] Gutman, p. xvii.

[2] Quoted in Donnelly, p. 20.

personal prudence, Rawls' renowned method, dignity, consequentialism, inference, vital needs and the duty not to harm.[1] Actually, one does not even need to read the chapter to understand that these arguments are not very impressive—one can see that simply by their descriptions.

Orend's own option is that of "pluralism" in the justification for human rights.[2] This view virtually recognizes that no one justification is sufficient and complete enough to justify the human rights argument, as each argument in itself has some defect to it. Hence, a combination of deficient arguments are accepted as justification with the expectation that by putting them all together the sum will be much greater than the rather weak total, like a lawyer presenting partial arguments to a jury to convince them of a entire picture.[3] Again, one must never lose sight, though, of the entire picture and long-run goals of the human rights movement. Entire religions and ways of life are being adjusted or modified in the name of this movement. Certainly, something more powerful than an analogy of a lawyer with perhaps circumstantial evidence should be demanded of the human rights proponents.

(Some have actually questioned whether there is any need to justify human rights. The demand for a convincing justification should be an even greater concern for the human rights advocates themselves. If they truly wish to have others follow their lead—without mere coercion, military threats, economic boycotts and the like, all of which make humans suffer more than they benefit humans[4]—they should or must prevent some convincing argument for their stand. Given all that is at risk, a failure to do so only points to the weakness of their claims.)

---

[1] Brian Orend, *Human Rights: Concept and Context* (Broadview Press, 2002).

[2] Cf., Orend, pp. 69-70.

[3] Orend, p. 70.

[4] Note what Orend wrote (p. 71), "[T]hat is why it is ultimately the use of force, and the threat of coercive punishment and rectification, which stands as the most effective and reliable guarantee against human rights violation. When human rights violators fail to respond to other appeals, we respond with force, and rightfully so. Rights, to be real, need to be enforced." Can there be any clearer way of saying: "If those people cannot be convinced to believe in the human rights platform and to respect what they do not believe in, we will just use force against them."

Human Rights as a Compound Term: The Nature of a Human vis-à-vis Human Rights

In order to further illustrate how important it is to understand a basis for human rights, the phrase "human rights" itself shall be analyzed as a compound term. The perception that one has of the terms "human" and "right" affects the overall perception of the concept. As Orend noted, "Usually, in moral and political debate, these premises will involve some conception of human nature and some understanding of a foremost requirement of morality and justice."[1]

For the sake of brevity, only the first term, "human," shall be discussed here. (The latter term, "right," is a legal term that probably has corresponding realities throughout different societies.)

One's conception of a "human" has many ramifications for one's overall view of human rights. It also will have great ramifications for whether or not others should even accept the concept of human rights or not.

Peoples throughout the world have varying views of what humans are. In fact, this question regarding the nature of humans was something that was debated in the lead up to the UHDR. As Ishay notes,

Illustrative of such intrinsic ideological and philosophical differences was the first major argument during the first session of the human rights commission, in which the definition of human nature was discussed. Malik's provocative questions—"Is man merely a social being? Is he merely an animal? Is he merely an economic being?"—generated a heated debate between advocates of individual and collective rights. Warning against the danger of collectivism that ultimately absorbed "the human person in his individuality and ultimately inviolability," Malik asserted the centrality of a person's mind and consciousness, the sanctity of individual property rights, and individual protection against religious, state, and other forms of external coercion. His position prompted reactions from communist representatives like Yugoslav Vladislav Ribnikar (1900-1955) and the Russian representative Valentin Tepliakov. In the words of Ribnikar, "ITlhe psychology of individualism

---

[1] Orend, p. 69.

has been used by the ruling class in most countries to preserve its own privileges; a modern declaration of rights should not only consider the rights favored by the ruling class." How can one understand individual rights and obligations apart from those of one's own community, asked Tepliakov.[1]

Beyond the question of animal or not, societal or not, religion, obviously, influences a person's view of what it means to be "human."[2] Some people view their own particular people as God's chosen people, putting all others in a category of subhuman. Furthermore, due to their conception of God and the relationship between God and humans, they are some Christians who are diametrically opposed to the concept of "human rights," considering it blasphemous that humans would possess any rights independent of God along bestowing those rights upon them.[3] Concerning Eastern Orthodox Christianity, Guroian states explicitly, "Human rights thinking is alien to Orthodoxy."[4] Some non-Eastern Orthodox Christians also definitely held the view that Christianity has nothing to do with human rights. For example, Guroian quotes the famed Dietrich Bonhoeffer who wrote,

The Church's word to the world can be no other than God's word to the world. This word is Jesus Christ and salvation in His name. It is in Jesus Christ that God's relation to the world is defined.... In other words, the proper relation of the Church to the world cannot be deduced from natural law or rational law or from universal human rights, but only from the gospel of Jesus Christ.[5]

Others see religion as one of the main driving forces behind the implementation and respect for human rights in the first place.[6] One could argue that by sidestepping any religious aspect, it actually makes it difficult to claim human rights because what is there then about humans that make them deserving of such

---

[1] Ishay, p. 221

[2] Islamic perspectives shall be dealt with later.

[3] In fact, if the "flesh" is evil, as many Christians have traditionally held, it is difficult to imagine that that evil "flesh" is deserving of a great multitude of "human rights."

[4] Vigen Guroian, "Human Rights and Modern Western Faith: An Orthodox Christian Assessment," in Bucar and Barnett, p. 42.

[5] Quoted in Guorian p. 45.

[6] This is a theme that runs throughout the work Joseph Runzo, Nancy M. Martin and Arvind Sharma, eds., *Human Rights and Responsibilities in the World Religions* (Oxford, England: One World, 2003).

grand and important rights. This point, in itself, has led theorists such as Max Stackhouse and Michael Perry to argue that the idea of human rights is "grounded in the idea of God" or "ineliminably religious." Perry argues that the very idea of human rights is based on the idea that every human is "sacred," that is, "each and every human being is 'inviolable,' has 'inherent dignity and worth'" and so on.[1] In comparing between Dworkin (who claimed that one could have a secular belief about the sacredness of humans) and Tawney (who claimed that such a belief has to be a religious one), Perry wrote,

For reasons I develop in this chapter, I conclude that Tawney is right and Dworkin, wrong: There is no intelligible (much less persuasive) secular version of the conviction that every human being is sacred; the only intelligible versions are religious.[2]

Many see one of the goals of the human rights movement as restraining humans in their behavior towards others—or making humans treat other humans as they deserved to be treated. On this point, as well, some have argued that this facet demands "religion." Ignatieff notes,

It is unsurprising, therefore, that in the wake of the Holocaust human rights should face an enduring intellectual challenge from a range of religious sources, Catholic, Protestant, and Jewish, all of whom make the same essential point: that if the purpose of human rights is to restrain the human use of power, then the only authority capable of doing so must lie beyond humanity itself, in some religious source of authority.[3]

Ignatieff, who is writing from a humanist's perspective, recognizes the perplexity of "human rights" simply for the sake of "human rights," without believing something special about humans. He wrote,

If idolatry consists in elevating any purely human principle into an unquestioned absolute, surely human rights looks like an idolatry. To be sure,

---

[1] Michael J. Perry, *The Idea of Human Rights: Four Inquiries* (New York: Oxford University Press, 1998), p. 5.

[2] Perry, p. 11.

[3] Ignateif, pp. 81-82. It is interesting to see that in this passage, Ignatieff does not mention Muslim scholars who make the same argument although he comments on Islam and Muslims throughout the work.

humanists do not literally worship human rights, but we use the language to say that there is something inviolate about the dignity of each human being. This is a worshipful attitude. What is implied in the metaphor of worship is a cult-like credulity, an inability to subject humanist premises to the same critical inquiry to which humanist rationalism subjects religious belief. The core of the charge is that humanism is simply inconsistent. It criticizes all forms of worship, except its own.[1]

The only possible reply that humanists may give is historical: This is the language that humans created as a form of defense against oppression.[2]

However, many of the most vocal human rights proponents approach the question of human rights from a purely secular perspective, attempting to take God or religion out of the picture. Orend, for example, argues that religious justifications for human rights are "too controversial and exclusionary."[3] There is definitely some truth to what he is saying but avoiding a difficult issue does not necessarily solve anything.

Frankly, leaving God/religion out of the picture may not necessarily be the best approach for a foundation of human rights. "Secular" thinking in the past the present does not paint a rosy picture for the treatment of humans.[4] For example, Darwinian thinking, wherein humans are simply evolved animals, certainly did not or should not lead to any sense of human dignity or human rights. Mamdani highlighted some of the past points of this way of thinking:

Herbert Spencer wrote in *Social Statics* (1850), "The forces which are working out the great scheme of perfect happiness, taking no account of incidental suffering, exterminate such sections of mankind as stand in their way." This is a train of thought Charles Lyell had pursued twenty years earlier in *Principles of Geology*: if "the most significant and diminutive of species ... have each slaughtered their thousands, why should not we, the lords of creation, do the same?" His student, Charles Darwin, confirmed in *The Descent of Man* (1871) that "at some future period not very distant as measured in centuries, the civilized races of man will

---

[1] Ignatieff, p. 83.

[2] Ignatieff, p. 83.

[3] Orend, p. 73.

[4] Secularism, of course, is also a dominant paradigm in the world today. It is another "ideology" that Muslims are being impressed upon to accept.

almost certainly exterminate and replace throughout the world the savage races." "After Darwin," comments Sven Lindqvist in his survey of European thought on genocide, "it became accepted to shrug your shoulders at genocide. If you were upset, you were just showing your lack of education."[1]

Max Stackhouse is adamant in his view that secular human rights is not going to be a reality. He wrote,

From the recent explosion of literature on this topic, I would like to draw attention to the current "Special Communications" of the Journal of the American Medical Association. In a series of articles it shows that "the most advanced centers of medical and legal research (all working on post- or anti-theological bases) were among the most energetic legitimators of the most grotesque travesties." They drew from Hume, Rousseau, Darwin, and Ploetz, all of whom developed the idea of "racial hygiene" and fostered the notion of "eugenics." The lead article also points to a Dr. Leo Alexander, who offered in the Nuremberg Doctors Trial the testimony that a combination of Hegelian theories of historicist development and notions of "rational utility" were the guiding principles of the recent dictatorships, and that these had displaced "moral, ethical, and religious" values. All the decisive theorists thought that one or another form of post-theological theory could supply the foundations for modem thought, politics, law, and morality without the need for anything beyond "nature" and "history," "culture" and 'human creativity," anything such as "God.""[2]

Gustafson and Juviler also note, in the introduction to the provocatively entitled *Religion and Human Rights: Competing Claims,*

The authors of the essays in this collection are fully aware that our experience of our neighbors in this twentieth century, especially in our politics, has left us anything but confident in the moral status of human being. Where was the "moral law within" when the trench warfare of 1914 I began? When the university-trained Nazis devised the concentration camps? When the annihilation of whole cities became standard strategy for victory in war from 1939 to 1945? When at the

---

[1] Mahmood Mamdani, *Good Muslim, Bad Muslim: America, the Cold War, and the Roots of Terror* (New York: Pantheon Books, 2004), p. 262.

[2] Stackhouse, p. 21.

end of this century, as a world "community," we had compiled a record for organized killing in the range of 150 million? The pre-Enlightenment French philosopher Blaise Pascal spoke of the "grandeur and misery" of human nature. We know about the grandeur in our moon walks, our computers, and our Declarations of Human Rights. But on some deep levels, we are haunted by the misery.[1]

More recent developments among some scientists and engineers do not bode well for the idea that there is anything "sacred" about humans. In "The Mystery of Consciousness" by Steven Pinker, the author speaks about scientists eventually locating consciousness somewhere within the brain. About this development, Pinker wrote, "Not only does it strangle the hope that we might survive the death of our bodies, but it also seems to undermine the notion that we are free agents responsible for our choices--not just in this lifetime but also in a life to come."[2] In June 2008, the internationally renowned IEEE's journal *Spectrum* came out with a special report on "the singularity." The conclusion that many—but not all—of the participants provided is that humans are nothing more than machines in essence. Some predicted that computers may shortly be able to reproduce "human consciousness" while others spoke about downloading one's consciousness to a computer, such that one will live on after one's physical's death—that is, if nobody deletes the person.[3]

Given that there is such a discussion and debate about what a "human" is, what does this mean for the concept of human rights? When it comes to human rights, there is no question that some definitions of "human" will be more helpful than others. However, who can force upon everyone else the one understanding of

---

[1] Carrie Gustafson and Peter Juviler, "Foreword," in Carrie Gustafson and Peter Juviler, eds., *Religion and Human Rights: Competing Claims* (Armonk, New York: M. E. Sharpe, 1999), p. ix.

[2] Steven Pinker, "The Mystery of Consciousness," *Time Magazine* (Friday, Jan. 19, 2007). Strangely, Pinker concludes that somehow such conclusions will lead to the "core of morality."

[3] Just to take one example from *Spectrum*, in the article, "I, Rodney Books, am a Robot," by Rodney Brooks, the author wrote, "Of all the hypotheses I've held during my 30-year career, this one in particular has been central to my research in robotics and artificial intelligence. I, you, our family, friends, and dogs—we all are machines... Accepting this hypothesis opens up a remarkable possibility. If we really are machines and if—this is a big *if*—we learn the rules governing our brains, then in principle there's no reason why we shouldn't be able to replicate those rules in, say, silicon and steel. I believe our creation would exhibit genuine human-level intelligence, emotions, and even consciousness."

human that human rights advocates may conclude with? How can one possibly overcome the types of differences that Donnelly describes in the following passage,

But if human nature were infinitely variable, or if all moral values were determined solely by culture (as radical cultural relativism holds), there could be no human rights (rights that one has "simply as a human being") because the concept "human being" would have no specificity or moral significance. As we saw in the case of Hindu India (§5.5), some societies have not even recognized "human being" as a descriptive category. The very names of many cultures mean simply "the people" (e.g., Hopi, Arapahoe), and their origin myths define them as separate from outsiders, who are somehow "not-human."[1]

Ignoring the fact that even the concept of "human" and what may be special about a "human" is neither truly defined or agreed upon by human rights advocates, one can now move on to some of the various justifications used to support the contemporary human rights paradigm. The concept of "natural law," which is tied into a specific view of humanity, shall be discussed first.

Natural Law

One of the arguments behind the case for human rights is the invoking of what is termed "natural law." The history of this concept of "natural law" is once again a Western phenomenon. The concept or understanding of "natural law" may be summarized as a belief that there are some laws or principles that are derived from "nature" and which must be adhered to, whether they form part of the rules of society (positive law) or not.[2]

---

[1] Donnelly, p. 91.

[2] One of the early proponents of this theory, Hugo Grotius (1583–1645), insisted on the soundness of "natural law" "even if we were to suppose…that God does not exist or is not concerned with human affairs." The heyday of the support for natural law thinking was in the 17th and 18th centuries. However, its thought does continue today with some human rights thinkers and just war advocates. See "Natural Law," *Encyclopædia Britannica Ultimate Reference Suite* (Chicago: Encyclopædia Britannica, 2009).

Resorting to natural law to justify the concept of human rights, which contemporaries like George still do[1], is questionable at best. Even if there is some moral code that is "present" via nature, that moral code certainly does not provide details to humans. Again, the human rights paradigm is about much more than general principles of being good to other humans. Secondly, it may be very difficult to determine what that "natural law" is. This could lead scholars to affirm laws that actually are in violation of "human rights" or that have very negative consequences. As Spain was moving across the new world, Francesco Victoria, one of the early scholars of "natural law," was asked whether the Christians could use military force to convert the Indians to Christianity. His reply was in the negative. However, he further stated that the Spaniards, by natural law, had the "right" to preach Christianity as well as the right to pass through Indian lands. If the Indians refused these two, which they should know by virtue of the fact that it is natural law, the Spaniards would then have the right to use military force against them. As James Turner Johnson wrote, "The rights of which Victoria spoke were conceived by him as universal, as 'natural'; yet the Indians knew nothing of them. They were in fact historically derived from the customary practices of European societies. In the name of natural law Victoria was justifying cultural imperialism."[2]

A leading proponent of the natural view, George, demonstrates how it is a very fragile justification for human rights—and in the process demonstrates how all "rational" theories are bound to be error-prone. He wrote,

As human beings, we are rational animals; but we are imperfectly rational. We are prone to making intellectual and moral mistakes and capable of behaving grossly

---

[1] For a general discourse, see the discussion with Robert George in Robert P. George, "Natural Law and Human Rights: A Conversation," in Bucar and Barnett, pp. 135-144.

[2] James Turner Johnson, "Historical Roots and Sources of the Just War Tradition in Western Culture," in John Kelsay and James Turner Johnson, *Historical and Theoretical Perspectives On War And Peace In Western And Islamic Traditions* (New York: Greenwood Press, 1991), p. 26. Also see p. 17 of the same work. Bainton also notes Victoria's reasoning and then states, "Later the great theologian Sepulveda adapted the theory of the just war to the new situation by having recourse to its most ancient formulation declared by Aristotle, who had said that a just war is one waged to enslave those who by nature are destined to be slaves and who resist their destiny." Roland H. Bainton, *Christian Attitudes Toward War & Peace: A Historical Survey and Critical Re-Evaluation* (Nashville, TN: Abingdon Press, 1990), p. 166.

unreasonably-- especially when deflected by powerful emotions that run contrary to the demands of reasonableness. Even when following our consciences, as we are morally bound to do, we can go wrong. A conscientious judgment may nevertheless be erroneous. Some of the greatest thinkers who ever lived failed to recognize the human right to religious liberty. Their failure, I believe, was rooted in a set of intellectual errors about what such a right presupposes and entails. The people who made these errors were neither fools nor knaves. The errors were not obvious, and it was only with a great deal of reflection and debate that the matter was clarified.[1]

In reality, anyone who advocates human rights from a "secular/ humanistic/ rational" perspective, turning his or her back on revelation from God, is inevitably falling prey to the same types of faults and errors that George describes in this passage. In fact, one could argue that the human kind cannot escape such shortcomings. As is well-known, the social sciences are very different from the physical sciences. Many years ago, Aristotle recognized the shortcoming in human reason but his solution was just to opt for a lesser standard of rigor for ethics and politics, saying "ethics and politics do not afford the same kind of rigorous proof standards that math and science demand."[2] One cannot study humans in a vacuum. As such, no human, simply based on human reasoning, experimentation or study, should have the audacity to claim that any right is undoubtedly and unquestionably a human right. Such a claim is, in reality, beyond the realm of human reasoning and rational conclusion. Yes, one may be very convinced that something, based on all of one's understanding and reasoning, must be considered a human right. However, as George's passage demonstrate, great minds in the past also passed judgment on many aspects of human life with the same kind of certainty and exuberance only for the humans of today to look back upon them and realize how wrong and misguided they were.

Actually, George makes the claim that most natural law theorists are deists. They seem to believe in a concept of *fitrah* (human disposition) that, it could be

---

[1] George, p. 140.

[2] Quoted in Brian Orend, *Human Rights: Concept and Context* (Ontario, Canada: Broadview Press, 2002), p. 68.

argued, is close to the Islamic concept.[1] However, Muslims would argue that the deists fail to realize that this *fitrah* is not sufficient for the complete guidance of humankind. Thus God revealed more than simply general moral precepts in the nature of humans. Instead, God has revealed a complete law to guide humankind through His Messengers. This is part of God's overall mercy and compassion to His creatures.

Touching on both Darwinian consequences and natural law, Jean Bethke Elshtain recognizes the problems of both approaches as being the basis for any human rights scheme:

There are other bases, critics responded, than the theistic one. Perhaps one might make recourse to nature and nature's laws, although here the post-Darwinian understanding of nature and the survival of the fittest does not seem the stuff out of which human rights is derived. Nature pre-Darwin could be appealed to in a strongly teleological sense. But nature post-Darwin seems a rather different sort of entity--far more likely to feed the fancies of authors of tomes arguing that pitying and trying to spare the weakest and least fit is womanish sentimentalism (though "womanish" would likely be avoided in a day and age when sensitivity about gender, not about weakness, is pervasive). There are all sorts of ways to dress the thesis of survival of the fittest up in its Sunday-best, of course, so it sounds a good bit less harsh. We are more likely, therefore, to read about "evolutionary strategies" than about a harsh neo-Darwinism, but, one way or the other, it comes down to the conclusion that, if nature structures anything, it is the quest for survival. Although the new natural law thinkers…are doing

---

[1] George stated (p. 141), "Natural law theorists do not deny that God can reveal moral truths and most believe that God has chosen to reveal many such truths. Natural law theorists also affirm, however, that many moral truths, including some that are revealed, can also be grasped by ethical reflection apart from revelation. They assert, with St. Paul, that there is a law "written on the hearts" even of the Gentiles who did not know the law of Moses. So the basic norms against murder and theft, though revealed in the Decalogue, are knowable even apart from God's special revelation. The natural law can be known by us, and we can conform our conduct to its terms, by virtue of our natural human capacities for deliberation, judgment, and choice. The absence of a divine source of the natural law would be a puzzling thing, but only in the sense that the absence of a divine source of any and every other intelligible order in human experience would be a puzzling thing."

their best to revive the older notion of natural law as it indeed survives, especially in Thomistic philosophy and theology theirs is often a lonely struggle.[1]

Human Dignity and Human Rights

The concept of human dignity is often cited as the ultimate justification for human rights. In fact, according to Louis Henkin,

Human rights discourse has rooted itself entirely in human dignity and finds its complete justification in that idea. The content of human rights is defined by what is required by human dignity—nothing less, perhaps nothing more.[2]

Others who invoke this concept include G. Vlastos, J. Maritain, and J. Finnis.[3] Orend noted, "The fact that so many in the field subscribe to this view is evidence of a kind in favour of its persuasiveness."[4]

Orend, though, is also quick to critique this view, as are many others. He argues that one is left with rather circular reasoning when invoking "human dignity" as the justification for human rights. He writes,

So the concept of human dignity refers to nothing outside of itself; here is where the chain of reasoning showing human rights justification must end. Such a chain would run like this:

1. All human beings should be treated in accord with human dignity.

2. Human rights protect human dignity.

3. Therefore, all human beings should have their human rights respected.[5]

Perhaps the greatest problems in using human dignity as a justification for human rights is that the concept of human dignity is encompasses to many aspects of

---

[1] Jean Bethke Elshtain, "Afterword," in Bucar and Barnett, p. 292. Edmund Burke, Jeremy Bentham and Karl Marx are known for presenting some of the same and the strongest arguments against the concept of "natural rights." See J. Waldron, ed., *"Nonsense Upon Stilts": Bentham, Burke and Marx on the Rights of Men* (London, England: Methuen, 1987), *passim*.

[2] Louis Henkin, "Religion, Religions, and Human Rights," in Bucar and Barnett, P. 147.

[3] Cf., Orend, p. 87.

[4] Orend, p. 87.

[5] Orend.

life. It is also too vague and too difficult to define. Always being picked last when teams are chosen in school could be an affront to one's dignity but could hardly be considered a violation of one's human rights.

Additionally, one person's view of human dignity may not be another person's view of human dignity. A few brief examples shall be sufficient to highlight this point. The Muslim woman's dress is a topic that is repeatedly attacked by human rights advocates, especially the more radical feminists among them. However, can it not be reasonably argued that to be accosted and presented with semi-nudity virtually everywhere—public parks, billboards, all forms of media—is an affront to human dignity?[1] Could one plausibly make such an argument? There is no question that many Muslims throughout the world would agree with such an argument and one would expect or hope that many Christians, Jews and members of other faiths would also agree. At the same time, though, as stated above, human rights advocates demand such freedoms and defend them. In fact, many of them demand and defend even greater affronts to human dignity, such as pornography, sometimes even bordering on child pornography.[2] How can such human rights proponents expect others to take them seriously when they claim that their entire theory is based on human dignity when they support such affronts to human dignity?

These difficulties concerning the concept of human dignity led Ignatieff to write,

I still have a difficulty about dignity. There are many forms and expressions of human dignity, and some of them strike me as profoundly inhumane. Rituals of sexual initiation, like genital cutting, for example, are linked to an idea of womanly dignity and worth. Likewise, ultra-Orthodox Judaism imposes a role on women that secular women find oppressive, but that religious women find both fulfilling and respectful of their dignity. So ideas of dignity that are supposed to unite different cultures in some shared attachment to human rights actually divide us. There is no easy way round the culturally specific and relative character of the idea of dignity.[3]

---

[1] Feminists used to complain a lot about the exploitation of women via pornography, media, prostitution and the like. However, it seems that today there is so much lesbian "exploitation" of the female body via the same means that one rarely hears such arguments any more.

[2] Such as a not too distant art display in Cincinnati, Ohio.

[3] Ignatieff, p. 164.

In sum, what truly does respect for human dignity have to do with the permissibility of pornography, homosexuality, all sorts of forms of freedom of speech (including hate literature and attacks on religion, etc.) and the like? Can one truly make such a link? Again, one must emphasize that when one is speaking about human rights today, one is speaking exactly about these types of rights. It is exactly these kinds of detailed issues that cannot be vindicated by such broad justifications as "human dignity."

Ignatieff, in the following passage, also argues that a foundation of this nature simply divides rather than unites the issue concerning justifying human rights.

It may be tempting to relate the idea of human rights to propositions like the following: that human beings have an innate or natural dignity, that they have a natural and intrinsic self-worth, that they are sacred. The problem with these propositions is that they are not clear and they are controversial. They are not clear because they confuse what we wish men and women to be with what we empirically know them to be. On occasion, men and women behave with inspiring dignity. But that is not the same thing as saying that all human beings have an innate dignity or even a capacity to display it. Because these ideas about dignity, worth, and human sacredness appear to confuse what is with what ought to be, they are controversial, and because they are controversial, they are likely to fragment commitment to the practical responsibilities entailed by human rights instead of strengthening them. Moreover, they are controversial because each version of them must make metaphysical claims about human nature that are intrinsically contestable. Some people will have no difficulty thinking human beings are sacred, because they happen to believe in the existence of a God who created Mankind in His likeness. People who do not believe in God must either reject that human beings are sacred or believe they are sacred on the basis of a secular use of religious metaphor that a religious person will find unconvincing. Foundational claims of this sort divide, and these divisions cannot be resolved in the way humans usually resolve their arguments, by means of discussion and compromise. Far better, I would argue, to forgo these kinds of foundational arguments altogether and seek to build support for human rights on the basis of what such rights actually do for human beings.[1]

---

[1] Ignatieff, p. 54.

(In typical vein, Ignatieff finds no acceptable justification for the human rights paradigm and concludes that it is simply best to sidestep this issue, emphasizing what human rights supposedly does for human beings.[1]) His passage highlights an interesting point: if a justification is contested, it will lead to division and must be rejected.[2] Since there are numerous people who believe in God and who believe that there overall beliefs about life have to be related to their belief in God, they will never be able to accept a justification for human rights that does not involve their perceptions about God and life. This means that without demanding them to give up such beliefs, it is impossible that there could ever be a unified agreement on the justification for human rights. If there is no agreement on the justification for human rights, chances are that there is not going to be agreement about many other aspects of human rights, especially detailed laws and applications. This spells doom for the human rights paradigm as a whole. Other than agreement on some general principles, maybe not much more could be reasonably expected. This is exactly the struggle that is currently taking place in the world between human rights dogmatists and those who believe in other sources of law and culture.

Henkin actually accepts the fact that the religious understanding of human dignity is going to be very different from the secular one that he proposes. He stated,

To be sure, religions also accept human dignity as a cardinal theme and motif. One finds hints of it in the principal Western religions. But the contours of the religious morality developed around this concept are not congruent with the implications of human dignity as commonly conceived in the domain of human rights.[3]

---

[1] The reality is that division is caused by human rights when there is no agreed upon justification. Thus, one will find portions of a population fighting in the streets against those who wish to follow a different way-one following the way of human rights and the other a cultural or religious view of the world. Is this the good that results that should lead one to overlook the justifications? It is only good when one starts out with the premise that "freedom" is the best of all possible worlds and submission to God is a bygone premise that has no reality. Otherwise, the suffering and sadness that results when people are forced to give up their cultures and religion in the name of human rights in itself, it can be argued, is enough to say that the "results" of human rights can also not be used as a justification for human rights.

[2] Incidentally, Orend also says that, among other things, human dignity is "contested a concept to serve as a solid starting point for justifying rights."

[3] Henkin, p. 147.

Henkin then goes on to discuss many of the differences between the secular concept of human dignity and religious understandings of it. The differences, in many cases, are very true. In fact, he states, "Some years ago, I characterized religion as an alternative ideology, indeed, as a competing ideology, and a source of resistance to the ideas of human rights."[1]

His presentation is an argument against any claim that a universal human rights scheme can be rooted in the concept of "human dignity." This demonstrates once again that a vague, undefined concept of "human dignity" cannot form the basis for human rights…

Accepting the Fact that they are part of International Law Today—or Once Again Begging the Question

An-Na'im, who calls for a complete reform of the understanding of the Shariah in the name of international human rights, can offer very little to substantiate the authority of human rights, save for the fact that they have become part of international law today.[2] He then goes on argues that international human rights are those that people deserve simply because they are human.[3] However, once again, that does not prove anything. In fact, he is arguing that there are basic rights that are found throughout the various cultures in the world while at the same time arguing that the traditional Shariah stands in the way of those human rights. But the Shariah is a culture for numerous peoples throughout the world. This means that he is contradicting himself. How can all of those cultures agree on those principles while those of the Shariah cultures, hardly a small number in the world, are violating them?

His argument is: "Applying the principle of reciprocity among all human beings rather than just among the members of a particular group, I would argue that universal human rights are those which a cultural tradition would claim for its own members and must therefore concede to members of other traditions if it is to expect reciprocal treatment from those others."[4] But this must be a question of a "lowest

---

[1] Henkin, p. 148. Incidentally, he repeats a rather fallacious claim, "The Bible—and the Qur'an, too, I think—knew not rights but duties" (p. 149).

[2] See An-Na'im, *Toward*, p. 162.

[3] An-Na'im, *Toward*, pp. 163-164.

[4] An-Na'im, *Toward*, p. 164.

common denominator." If, as he claims, Islamic culture does not give X, Y and Z rights to women and non-Muslims, he is, in essence, saying that Islamic culture does not recognize these rights for all the members of its community. Thus, any such rights which are not afforded these two groups within Islamic culture cannot be considered fundamental human rights, according to his own manner of arguing. Unless he is arguing that fundamental human rights are those that each culture offer the "privileged" members of its society. However, that is not what he is arguing and would also contradict the premise of his claims.

Actually, the argument that such laws are now part of international law and agreements may be strongest argument to compel Muslims to live by such a platform, if they choose to sign said agreements. However, a number of points need to be made here:

(1)   Although the status of international law itself is questionable, some, such as Mayer and others, argue that what has been generally accepted by international law becomes binding upon all, even if specific countries never agreed to such conventions.

(2)   Those who signed the earliest human rights accords in the 194os certainly did not expect, for example, that sexual freedom would be part of the agenda. Hence, how can they be held accountable for it?

(3)   If the agreements are binding, then the reservations put forward by Muslim countries should be accepted as binding. In other words, if they never truly agreed to the accords, how can they be held accountable for them?

(4)   There may be a great difference from the Islamic perspective and what secular Muslim states may agree to. This has been a cause of friction in Muslim lands and has led to the rise of "fundamentalism." The paradox between what governmental leaders and lawyers agree to and what the masses may desire in their lives should be a fundamental point of issue for any human rights movement. However, by taking this view—that simply because it is law it must be abided by— the rights and wants of individuals are simply overruled.

(5)   Finally, it should be noted that it seems that even "international law" can be trumped by human rights claims. Note the following critique by Bricmont of other "left-leaning liberals":

The ideas criticized in this book are often implicit, but have recently been more explicitly expressed by groups defining themselves as liberals, democrats, and progressives. A perfect illustration of these ideas is to be found in a 2005 book, entitled *A Matter of Principle: Humanitarian Arguments for War in Iraq*, a collective work by a number of writers who argue in favor of the war in Iraq on the basis of human rights. The authors consider that the United States had not only the right but the duty to use its superior military force to intervene and liberate the Iraqi people from the dictatorship of Saddam Hussein. Neither the absence of weapons of mass destruction in Iraq nor the fact that such an intervention flouts international law troubles them in the least, convinced as they are that human rights are a value far more fundamental than respect for international law.[1]

Brief Conclusion on the Foundation of Human Rights

As shall be noted in the following chapter, in the Islamic scheme of things, the foundation and ultimate source of "human rights" is the commandments from God. Obviously, different groups have very different perceptions of God. Hence, in their desire to make something "universal," the human rights theorists are forced to find some foundation other than God upon which to lay their new humanistic/secular view of the world. In all honesty, though, it seems that they have met with no success whatsoever. By removing God, they were not able to come up with any convincing upon which to base human rights for all.

The following passage from Stackhouse does a good job of demonstrating the quagmire and confusion surrounding the foundation for human rights. Stackhouse wrote,

Ironically, one of the leading international advocacy organizations for human rights, Amnesty International, has sponsored lectures by outstanding political philosophers that reveal the fragility of contemporary secular thinking about universalistic principles. In their defenses of human rights, they provide thin,

---

[1] Bricmont, p. 61.

mutually contradictory, and often precisely Hobbesian or Nietzschean, grounds for doing so.[1] For the most part, they say, human rights emerge under sociological conditions of modernity as an assertion of the will of sovereigns. They offer no explanation as to when, where, or why these social conditions arose, or when, where, or why this will was exercised. Some, to be sure, turn to the nature of human imagination, with its presumptions of linguistic construction, to see what the character of language and discourse itself tells us. And while they note that it has a grammar, it is not clear that one can get from grammar to human rights, for the opponents of human rights also have a grammar. Their arguments read thin precisely because they share a disregard of, sometimes a contempt for, theology as a possible resource in the interpretation of, or the guidance of, the common life. The dependence on sociological or linguistic analysis alone (although sometimes a blend of the two) as the bases for ethical and jurisprudential values suggests that, in substantial measure, political philosophy as practiced today is groundless and more culturally and contextually variable than theology. These philosophers tend to share the Enlightenment view that theology is the more or less rationalized articulation of otherwise quite irrational religious dogmas. This questionable view is suspect on empirical and rational grounds, and remains quite unaware of the traditions of "public theology" in relation to human rights.[2]

This author cannot emphasize enough the weight of this question of the foundation of human rights in the light of what human rights proponents are demanding of Muslims and the "changes" they are supposed to make in their religion. Secularly minded people, such as many human rights activists are, may not be able to perceive exactly what is going on when they make strong demands upon Muslims with very little or nothing to back up their premises. The reality, though, is that not everyone in the world in the world is secular minded and definitely not every Muslim is secular minded.

---

[1] Stackhouse notes that the lecturers were Steven Lukes, John Rawls, Catharine MacKinnon, Richard Rorty, Jean-Francois Lyotard, Agnes Heller, and Jon Elster.

[2] Stackhouse, p. 19.

What should be considered a human right?

Once it is realized that the foundations for human rights in the first place are not solid, the question of what can be considered a human right becomes even more so an astonishing question. If one cannot determine the foundation of something—the basis on which the thought is constructed—how can then one conclude what forms part of the locus of that thought? Upon what parameters can someone possibly claim that X or Y should be a human right when the initial parameters themselves cannot be established?

Orend stated,

The devil, though, is in the details: even if we all endorse some understanding of "human rights," it still seems to matter importantly whether we all endorse the same understanding of that to which "human rights" refers. In other words, Walzer may make a compelling argument that commitment to the ideal of human rights is universally shared, or very nearly so. But an equally important question is whether there is near-universal agreement on the practical side of the commitment, namely, to provide the same set of objects to everyone.[1]

Who can say what should be considered a human right? In other words, on what basis are human rights to be determined? On what basis are the following topical questions to be answered:

(a)   Should homosexuals have the same sexual/marriage/family rights as heterosexuals?

(b)   Should pornography be considered repugnant to human dignity or a free expression of art that is protected by the concept of human rights?

(c)   Should there be no laws distinguishing men and women in any way, as is claimed by gender feminists?

(d)   Should one have the right to blaspheme religion and God as a form of freedom of expression?

---

[1] Orend, pp. 78-79.

(e)   Should a pregnant woman or anyone else have the right to have a fetus aborted in the first, second or third trimester?

(f)   Is the death penalty considered a violation of human rights?[1]

(g)   Is male circumcision-not simply female genital mutilation-a violation of human rights[2]?

These questions actually lie at the crux of the human rights debates today—and the questions are going to become more and more complex and perplexing as biomedical sciences continue to progress.[3] Again, these all go back to the question of the foundation of human rights, which would answer questions like what is a human right and who has the right do determine what a human right is. Amazingly though, there are no satisfactory answers for these questions.

In any case, upon reading human rights theorists one quickly recognizes how subjective the list of human rights can be. Note, for example, the discussion concerning homosexuality from Donnelly. At one point he admits, "[H]omosexuality is widely considered-by significant segments of society in all countries, and by most people in most countries-to be profoundly immoral. The language of perversion and degeneracy is standard."[4] The first point that one can note is that even after admitting this fact that most of the world's population is not willing to accept this

---

[1] It is interesting to note that many human rights advocates, especially those from Europe, are completely against the death penalty, even if the criminal were a serial murderer. At the same time, though, many of the same people accept the concept of military intervention in the case of gross human rights violations. In the latter case, one guilty individual who had taken the lives (and human rights) of others is punished for his deed while in the latter numerous innocent lives are put at risk in what could certainly be a futile attempt to correct an undesirable situation.

[2] That male circumcision is a violation of human rights is exactly the argument made in George Denniston, Frederick Hodges and Marylin F. Milos, *Circumcision and Human Rights* (Springer, 2009), *passim*. This is quite a contrast to some Muslim authors who mention circumcision as one of the rights of a child. See Yaaseen, pp. 309-312 and al-Jaarid, pp. 534-536. Both of those authors also demonstrate the fact, quoting scholars from long before contemporary times, that was is commonly referred to today as female genital mutilation is prohibited in Islamic Law and has negative consequences for the woman.

[3] For example, for a discussion of genetics and artificial procreation, see the various relevant articles in Marie-Therese Meulders-Klein, Ruth Deech and Paul Vlaardingerbroek, *Biomedicine, the Family and Human Rights* (The Hague: Kluwer Law International, 2002).

[4] Donnelly, p. 233.

practice, he continues by arguing that homosexuality is still a human right that people cannot trample upon.[1] He goes on from that point to attempt to argue while no matter how repugnant their act may seem, it still must be considered a human right. This is what he had to say,

Even accepting, for the purposes of argument, that voluntary sexual relations among adults of the same sex are a profound moral outrage, discrimination against sexual minorities cannot be justified from a human rights perspective. "Perverts," "degenerates," and "deviants"-' have the same human rights as the morally pure and should have those rights guaranteed by law. Members of sexual minorities are still human beings, no matter how deeply they are loathed by the rest of society. They are therefore entitled to equal protection of the law and the equal enjoyment of all internationally recognized human rights.
Human rights rest on the idea that all human beings have certain basic rights simply because they are human. How one chooses to lead one's life, subject only to minimum requirements of law and public order, is a private matter—no matter how publicly one leads that life. Human rights do not need to be earned, and they cannot be lost because one's beliefs or way of life are repugnant to most others in a society.[2]

Interestingly, though, earlier in the same work Donnelly stated,

To require identical treatment of all individual or group differences-consider, for example, pedophiles, violent racists, those who derive pleasure from kidnapping and torturing strangers, and religious missionaries committed to killing those they cannot convert-would be perverse.[3]

There are legal lobbies pushing for the acceptance of such practices in the US. In fact, recently a Catholic Priest named Shanley was found to be advocating such an organization. Is Donnelly not willing to accept pedophiles simply because they have not yet-emphasis on yet-been accepted by Western culture? If and when their organizations are accepted by law in the United States and the majority of the

---

[1] This would imply that human rights would take precedence over democratic rule. However, as shall be noted later, when convenient, the roles seem to be reversed and human rights are subjected to the principles of democracy.

[2] Donnelly, pp. 236-237.

[3] Donnelly, p. 207.

world's population still finds that practice repugnant, will pedophilia then be a human right according to Donnelly and people like him? In any case, it is clear from Donnelly, a leading theorist on human rights, that the entire question of what is a human right is simply subjective. If Donnelly would remain firm on not accepting pedophiles, the next generation of human rights writers may well be promoting pedophilia as the frontier of human rights demands upon the world. Perhaps Donnelly does not acquiesce to pedophiles because he believes that there must be some moral limits somewhere. But, alas, the human rights paradigm certainly does not provide moral limits of that nature.

The Paradox of the Human Rights Paradigm

The human rights movement is, obviously, foremost about "rights" or "freedoms." Is it possible that some rights can be "absolute" or does every country/society recognize the fact that with respect to virtually all rights, some limits must be placed on the exercise of those rights? What about freedom of religious belief and practice? Article 18 of the Universal Declaration of Human Rights (UDHR) 18 states: "Everyone has the right to freedom of thought, conscience and religion; this right includes freedom to change his religion or belief, and freedom, either alone or in community with others and in public or private, to manifest his religion or belief in teaching, practice, worship and observance."

Ann Mayer is one who certainly gives the impression that some rights are absolute and non-negotiable. Mayer writes,

The Universal Declaration of Human Rights (UDHR) treats a number of rights as absolute or non-derogable rights, meaning that there could be no justification for curtailing them. Among these are the right to freedom and equality in dignity and rights; the right to equality before the law and to equal protection of the law; the right in fill equality to a fair and public hearing by an independent and impartial tribunal; the right to marry and the right to equal rights in marriage and divorce; freedom of thought, conscience, and religion, including the freedom to change one's religion; and the right to work and to free choice of employment." The UDHR would not accept any criteria that would deny these rights.[1]

Later, Mayer makes the following very bold statement: "International human rights law allows no constraints on a person's religious beliefs: Freedom of religion is an unqualified freedom."[2] This is a rather amazing statement from Mayer. The entire tone of her book is that "traditional Islam" is not compatible with human rights and therefore must change. In fact, could Article 18, wherein it states that anyone is free to adhere to his or her religion, "either alone or in community with others and in public or private, to manifest his religion or belief in teaching, practice, worship and observance," be true or is it simply a façade?

Suppose a religion does not believe in unrestricted interreligious marriage. Could that religious belief be absolutely protected under Article 18 of the UDHR? According to Oh, not only could that belief be contradicted by international human rights law but it could also be a grounds for military intervention. Here is what she wrote,

If governments by and large agree, even with few detractors, that interreligious marriage is a genuinely universal human right, that is, a condition necessary for human dignity that others can and should protect, then intervention-though not necessarily a military one[3]—would be justified and cannot rightly be labeled imperialist.[4]

How could it be that a system that is supposedly so pro-rights is, in essence, anti-freedom of religious belief? The reality is, as Mayer herself knows very well,

---

[1] Mayer, *Islam and Human Rights*, p. 78.

[2] Mayer, *Islam and Human Rights*, p. 168. Mayer herself notes earlier how so many rights are not "absolute". She is probably these exaggerated claims at this portion of her book in order to try to critique Islam and its stance on freedom of religion, as she made statements a part of her discussion of the law of apostasy. Otherwise, previously (on p. 77), she wrote, "International law recognizes that many rights protections are not absolute and may be suspended or qualified in exceptional circumstances such as wars or public emergencies or even in normal circumstances in the interests of certain overriding considerations."

[3] "Though not necessarily" implies that it is still a viable option if deemed necessary—all because a people did not believe in interreligious marriages.

[4] Oh, p. 32.

the freedom of religion is not absolute or an unqualified freedom.[1] Furthermore, Mayer, who critiques Islam's view on "freedom of religion," and others know very well that there is a text clearly stating that there is no such thing as absolute freedom of religion. Under Article 18(3) of the ICCPR International Covenant on Civil and Political Rights (ICCPR) , the right to freedom of religion and beliefs is not absolute. There is a restriction by the provision that:

Freedom to manifest one's religion or beliefs may be subject only to such limitations as are prescribed by law and are necessary to protect public safety, order, health, or morals or the fundamental rights and freedoms of others.

There is obviously a contradiction or paradox here. This is the fundamental paradox of human rights teaching that should be obvious to all. There are always have to be limits to freedom and rights. Most importantly, though, for the human rights paradigm, everything outside of the human rights paradigm has to be rejected—all in the name of rights and freedom.

This paradox was well delineated by Larry Alexander while speaking about "liberalism,"[2] in a discussion which is perfectly analogous to the human rights paradigm paradox. Alexander summarizes his thesis in the following:

In Chapter Eight [of his book], we saw the source of the problem: Evaluative neutrality is the hallmark of freedom of expression, but no moral theory can support evaluative neutrality without generating a paradox. Any moral theory will deem certain states of affairs to be desirable and demanding of legal promotion, and certain interests to be demanding of legal protection from acts that threaten those interests. But both the media of expression and the messages conveyed may cause undesirable states of affairs and threaten protectable interests (per the moral theory in question); and conversely, suppression of expression by reference to its content (Track One) or its media (Track Two) may cause desirable states of affairs and safeguard protectable interests (per that moral theory). Therefore, government cannot permit the harmful

---

[1] Unless, of course, one means by freedom of religion that which someone believes in his or her heart. In reality, there is no possible way to constrain what a person believes in his or her heart. However, this is not what Article 18 seems to be speaking about, as it speaks about in public, private and so on.

[2] See Larry Alexander, *Is There a Right of Freedom of Expression?* (New York: Cambridge University Press, 2005), *passim.*

expression without contravening the moral theory, which means, in turn, that the moral theory cannot demand protection of the harmful expression without generating a paradox. It must, instead, demand suppression of the harmful expression and permit only that expression that is consistent with the goals of the theory. But that evaluative *non*neutrality is the antithesis of freedom of expression.[1]

Alexander then argues that liberalism and religion are on the same epistemological level—and this is the same for the human rights advocates who are overruling religion in the name of human rights. Although the following quote from Alexander is quite lengthy, it must be quoted in full, as Alexander is one of the few to be willing to admit and state the conclusions that he has made concerning liberalism and religion. In Alexander's words,

I come to the conclusion, then, that liberalism and religion are on the same epistemological level, and that the knowledge each claims, if it be knowledge, has the same pedigree in experience and reason. There are not two ways of "knowing," religious and secular/liberal; there are not both sectarian and secular/liberal "truths." As a consequence of epistemological unity, liberalism must establish its tenets by rejecting conflicting religious ones, not by the illusion of "neutrally" banishing them to the "private" realm, where they can somehow remain "true" but impotent, but by meeting them head on and showing them to be false or unjustified. Liberalism is, as many critics claim it to be, the "religion" of secularism. That does not mean that liberalism is false or that antiliberal religious views are true. What it does mean is that both liberalism and antiliberal religious views inhabit the same realm and make conflicting claims within it. Liberalism is not at a different level, where it can remain neutral and impartial with respect to religious controversy that is truth-seeking within a restricted domain, but not within the domain of liberalism.

That liberalism and religion are epistemological rivals has two basic implications. One, obvious and banal, is that the truth of those core, defining tenets of liberalism entails the falsity of all conflicting religious tenets. That much follows from the law of noncontradiction. More importantly, and the burden of the bulk of my argument, liberalism cannot establish its core tenets and its repudiation of

---

[1] Alexander, p. 185.

illiberal religious ones (and banishment of religion from public policy making) by claiming to inhabit a different epistemological realm from that occupied by religion, a realm whose truths not only trump those of religion, but whose truths can be seen to be reasonable even by those whose religious truths they trump. No epistemological perspective exists from which one can simultaneously hold Ann's views and, barring a belief that to do so would be self-defeating, hold that the state should not impose them. Furthermore, to the extent that liberalism defines itself by the proposition that religious views can be "true" and important enough to protect, but cannot be fairly imposed through public policy, a public policy that draws its "truths" from a different epistemological well, to that extent the unity of epistemology undermines liberalism.

Liberalism can rest on agnosticism regarding some truths, but not regarding its own truth. Toleration of illiberal religions may rest on the value of autonomy (so long as those religions do not threaten autonomy), or toleration of illiberal religions may rest on a prediction that intolerance would provoke a backlash that would threaten liberalism to a greater extent than toleration. The case for toleration of illiberal religions, however, cannot rest upon their possible truth without self-contradiction.

Ultimately, then, the only reason to exclude religious views from the realm of coercive public policy – for the liberal or anyone else – is because those views are wrong. And the liberal's particular problem is that he believes it wrong to extirpate erroneous views coercively…

Liberalism's attempt to claim neutrality vis-à-vis religious views through some sort of epistemic abstinence is a failure. And from the failure issues a paradox: Liberalism can be neutral only toward those religions and religious views that are compatible with the tenets of liberalism, which is to say that if liberalism is defined in part by neutrality toward religious beliefs, liberalism is impossible.[1]

The same arguments that Alexander makes concerning liberalism can be made concerning the contemporary human rights movement. One can literally replace every instance of the word "liberalism" above with "the human rights paradigm." Once one claims that the human rights paradigm is the paradigm for all

---

[1] Alexander, pp. 163-164.

of humanity, one has essentially declared that no other paradigm is free to exist except to the extent that it is compatible with the human rights paradigm. It is freedom as long as one accepts its principles of freedom—much like Henry Ford's statement, "You can have the Model T in any color you like as long as it is black."

Nowhere, perhaps, is this paradox better highlighted than when it comes to religion. Especially given the fact that there is now a conflict with something that is very central to a human's life, perhaps much more central and important than his belief in "human rights."

One of the few to be willing to mention and discuss this topic in his discussion of human rights was Michael Freeman. He says that human rights are not "compossible," highlighting in particular the conflict with religion. He states,

Article 18 says that everyone has the right to freedom of religion. How should we define the right to freedom of religion of those whose religion denies that all human beings are equal in rights? How can we make sense of human rights if the implementation of some human rights requires tne violation of others? Here the problem of implementing human-rights ideals derives, not from lack of political will or conflicts of political interests, but from the fact that human rights are not 'compossible', that is, the implementation of one human right can require the violation of another, or the protection of a human right of one person may require the violation of the same human right of another. If a religious group, for example, forbids its members, on the basis of its religious beliefs, to change their religion, then the religious freedom of the group will conflict with that of any members who wish to change their religion. If we support human rights that are not compossible, our thinking must surely be confused.[1]

Once this is finally admitted, one will have to recognize that choices are going to have to be made and priorities are going to have to be given to some rights over others. The rights, in other words, are not absolute in any sense whatsoever. But who is going to decide what rights should take precedence and how is that decision going to be made? Should each people or nation make that decision on its own or

---

[1] Michael Freeman, *Human Rights* (Cambridge, England: Polity Press, 2002), pp. 4-5.

does the conclusion have to be universal? Can a religion which dominates a society make that decision on behalf of society?

In fact, the problem is not just with respect to religion. So many restrictions on freedom of expression that one cannot call it a human right—however, this is the same kind of reasoning that the human rights advocates put on the practice of religion. Hence, one cannot say that freedom of religion is a human right from the perspective of how the human rights advocates themselves speak about it.

The Dogmatism of Human Rights Schemes: As Fanatic as Religious Extremism?

In the most complete report to date on religious freedom, co-editors Kevin Boyle and Juliet Sheen conclude that the inclinations of religions to view themselves as the sole guardians of truth can tempt them to intolerance and "to fight against whatever [each] defines as deviant, either within [their] own faith or at [the] boundaries."[1]

Would such interreligious fighting include economic sanctions and "coalitions of the willing"? Do the human rights activists and lawyers see themselves as "the sole guardians of truth" and that is why they invoke the largest armies in the name of human rights?

The human rights movement seems to answer many of the essential questions about human's existence and yet, of course, at no time has it claimed to be a religion or even an ideology. Furthermore, it has been demonstrated that no one can claim that human rights has some kind of physical or undeniable proofs for its foundations. Instead, the belief in the human rights paradigm is no different—or even weaker—than the belief in any other religion or ideology. The propagators of the human rights paradigm are, in reality, no different from any other missionary who believes that his way of life, philosophy or religion is the best for all of humankind.

Donnelly has an interesting passage in which states in no uncertain terms—but without stating this word—that human rights activists must be dogmatic and not allow the presence of any other view on issues that they have determined to be non-negotiable. Donnelly writes,

---

[1] Bucar and Barnett, *Competing Claims*, p. 7.

Consider, for example, slavery. Most people today would agree that no matter how ancient and well established the practice may be, to turn one's back on the enslavement of human beings in the name of cultural relativity would reflect moral obtuseness, not sensitivity. Human sacrifice, trial by ordeal, extrajudicial execution, and female infanticide are other cultural practices that are (in my view rightly) condemned by almost all external observers today.

Underlying such judgments is the inherent universality of basic moral precepts, at least as we understand morality in the West. We simply do not believe that our moral precepts are for us and us alone. This is most evident in Kant's deontological universalism. But it is no less true of the principle of utility. And, of course, human rights are also inherently universal.

In any case, our moral precepts are our moral precepts. As such, they demand our obedience. To abandon them simply because others reject them is to fail to give proper weight to our own moral beliefs (at least where they involve central moral precepts such as the equality of all human beings and the protection of innocents).

Finally, no matter how firmly someone else, or even a whole culture, believes differently, at some point—slavery and untouchability come to mind— we simply must say that those contrary beliefs are wrong. Negative external judgments may be problematic. In some cases, however, they are not merely permissible but demanded.[1]

Note that although one may argue that Donnelly's examples in the passage above are acceptable, the premise of his claim against others, even in those obvious cases, is still not acceptable—and that is the important point. Donnelly, like other human rights supporters, has no basis upon which to claim the right to remove such "evils." If there are people who are still practicing such "evils," then it moves that there is not a unanimous consensus on their "evilness." One must ask the proverbial question: Who has died and made the human rights activists and lawyers the kings of the world?

Donnelly and his likes argue that they deem such acts to be so evil that even if others accept them, they must be eradicated. The next question must arise: When does this self-righteous claim to police the remainder of humanity come to an end?

---

[1] Donnelly, pp. 92-93.

Where do the human rights activists stop and say, "Now we can no longer render judgment even we, for ourselves, consider acts X, Y and Z evil"? There are a few voices writing on human rights who can understand the dilemma here. Thus, Orentlicher states,

> But however appealing, this account cannot by itself offer a complete response to the relativist challenge. Like any version of substantive accommodation, Ignatieff"'s account raises—and, if it is to persuade, must be able to answer—the question, By whose lights does one determine which rights are, in Donnelly's terms, ''prima facie universal" and what local variations in interpretation are permissible? If adherents to Islam in a particular culture believe that amputations undertaken pursuant to judicial determination do not constitute torture, does their claim fall within Donnelly's zone of permissible local variation in the interpretation of norms that are universal (in this case, the prohibition of torture)? Or do such amputations violate a norm that is not subject to local exceptions or variations in interpretation? Who decides?[1]

Who decides is the question, indeed.

Perhaps if this dogmatic attitude were put in an another perspective, the human rights proponents could understand the issue better. From an Islamic perspective, the most despicable is associating partners with God. In fact, it is this despicable act that leads people to commit so many of the other evils of the world. Thus, from an Islamic perspective, bowing down to an idol is completely unacceptable. Suppose a Muslim scholar would write a passage similar to Donnelly's passage and say, "Finally, no matter how firmly someone else, or even a whole culture, believes differently, at some point—worshipping idols come to mind— we simply must say that those contrary beliefs are wrong." Would this approach not be considered extreme and dogmatic? But this is exactly what human rights activists and lawyers do on a daily basis. And they do not do it with respect to the clear-cut cases that Donnelly chose to mention. Instead, they do it on a myriad of issues ranging from the rights of homosexuals to the right of marriage to anyone one wishes to marriage to even the rights of a child within a household—and all based on nothing but a dogmatic and blind faith in their human rights paradigm and ideology.

---

[1] Orentlicher, in Ignatiefff, p. 144.

This dogmatism, of course, has real ramifications to it. Once the human rights people determine that human rights have been violated, they then demand a response. In the words of Howland, for example, who is speaking in reference to rather specific laws related to women and marriage, "All enforcement mechanisms at the community's disposal should be used *to coerce these pariah states* to cease violating articles 55 and 56. It is time for the international community to live up to the standards of the Charter and the Universal Declaration."[1]

Oh echoes the same kind of feeling when speaking about interreligious marriage, that has somehow become a universal human right in her eyes. She states,

[G]overnments should not dismiss certain human rights because of the fear that such rights would invite scrutiny or because of the belief that interventions taken to protect that right would be interpreted as imperialistic. Given the situation where a Muslim nation denies, for example, interreligious marriage, this nation might argue that such unions do not constitute a universal human right but is simply a form of Western imperialism. Other nations may fear being labeled imperialist if they intervene to protect interreligious marriage as a human right. If governments by and large agree, even with few detractors, that interreligious marriage is a genuinely universal human right, that is, a condition necessary for human dignity that others can and should protect, then intervention—though not necessarily a military one—would be justified and cannot rightly be labeled imperialist.[2]

In the footnote to this passage, Oh interestingly writes,

This example raises the question of whether a majority agreement among nations would constitute a "universal" human right. Although majority rule has never guaranteed the unquestionable morality of a policy, it is arguably the best of our flawed options. Unfortunately, this profound philosophical problem of how humans can come to recognize the perfect form of goodness or justice lies beyond the scope of this book.[3]

---

[1] Howland, in Bucar and Barnett, p. 317 (emphasis added).

[2] Oh, p. 32.

[3] Oh, p. 123.

This is an eye-opening passage: The "best of our flawed options" are sufficient for possible military intervention and demands that Muslims change their religious beliefs about interreligious marriage. In other words, it is dogmatism based on an admittedly flawed system.[1] Of course, the "profound philosophical problem" is beyond the scope of her work on human rights because, in reality, that problem is beyond the scope of the human rights paradigm.

Rousseau was famous for speaking about forcing people to be free. This is where one group of people determine what it means to be free and then they force upon others their wonderful understanding of what it means to be free, regardless of whether others actually want this "freedom." Although Donnelly claims that he thinks Rousseau went to far when he made such a statement admits that, in essence, he is in agreement with Rousseau. Here are the words of the human rights theorist himself:

When Rousseau speaks of forcing people to be free, however, he seems to me (as a liberal) to go too far. *But he nonetheless points toward an important insight.* Some forms of behavior cannot be tolerated in a rights-protective society. Some interests must be excluded from the calculation of the public interest, no matter how deeply their proponents are attached to them.[2]

The approach of the human rights proponents, especially those who have written about Islam and demand changes in this widely accepted religion, is the same kind of dogmatism that led people to speak of the "end of history"[3] and to make statements like "There is no intellectual ground remaining for any regime other than democracy."[4] There is no other worldview left or acceptable save for the human rights paradigm. Given, though, the fundamental questions surrounding human rights and the fact that human rights theorists themselves are forced to admit

---

[1] At least when Muslims proclaim that Islam is the real guidance for all humankind they are making this statement on the belief that it is the true, complete and perfect guidance from God.

[2] Donnelly, p. 52. Emphasis added.

[3] See Francis Fukuyama, "The End of History," *National Interest*, 16 (Summer 1989).

[4] Allan Bloom's famous statement in *The Closing of the American Mind* (New York: Simon and Schuster, 1987), p, 330.

that there are no sound responses to these fundamental questions, this belligerent attitude towards all other ways smacks of nothing but arrogance and bigotry.[1]

Human Rights between Theory and Practice

The world has certainly not been devoid of human rights abuses since the signing of the UHDR or any related documents. As Donnelly noted, in a survey of a number of countries (excluding the most blatant violators) and their human rights performances,

Many states in the post-Cold War world include respect for internationally recognized human rights as part of their national self-images and as an objective in their foreign policies. Few, however, make more than occasional, modest sacrifices of other foreign policy interests in the name of human rights.[2]

In the words of Freeman, "Human-rights declarations are cheap, whereas human-rights implementation is rather expensive."[3]

The divide between theory and practice is well-known and certainly does not need to be documented in detail here. The details of violations of human rights are presented by several organizations (such as Human Rights Watch and Amnesty International) and independent authors. The recent events and plight of Abu Ghuraib, Guantanamo and "extraordinary rendition" (in which European states took an active part) demonstrate that even the most vocal supporters of human rights are willing to violate and abuse the concept when needed. The reality, though, is that

---

[1] The contemporary dogmatic liberalism (which must include the human rights paradigm) has been called the rise of the new Jacobins. This is a reference to Revolutionary France where the Jacobins "saw themselves as virtuous champions of a great moral cause and as joined by fraternity and solidarity. They were guardians of revolutionary principles. They were ushering in a new way of life, a society of equality and democracy, a glorious goal that permitted no mercy for those who stood in the way. Jacobinism inspired the French Revolution's murderous hatred of traditional elites, its reign of terror, and its messianic ambitions." Claes G. Ryn, *America the Virtuous: The Crisis of Democracy and the Quest for Empire* (New Brunswick, New Jersey: Transaction Publishers, 2004), p. 19. See that entire work for the discussion of the rise and dangers of this new Jacobinism.

[2] Jack Donnelly, "An Overview," in David P. Forsythe, ed., *Human Rights and Comparative Foreign Policy* (Tokyo, Japan: United Nations University Press, 2000) p. 310.

[3] Freeman, p. 171.

those are simply the tip of the iceberg in a long, inglorious history of human rights violations throughout the world.

Human rights has been abused in the following manners:

(1) Human rights abuses—some quite gross—are regularly overlooked when it is one's allies and partners involved in such abuses. Once again, there is no need to give numerous examples of this nature. Perhaps the Shah of Iran's relationship with the United States is enough of an example.

(2) Human rights is also used as a political tool against one's enemies. Enemies are often threatened with economic sanctions in the name of human rights violations. Indeed, war can also be declared in the name of human rights violations.[1] Such war is even justified when there is obviously other motivations for such a war. James Turner Johnson is perhaps the leading expert and theoretician of the Western concept of a "just war." Yet he completely justifies going to the war in the name of human rights violations even though other, not so legitimate, motivations are also part and parcel of the purpose behind the war. In fact, this is the gist of his argument in *The War to Oust Saddam Hussein: Just War and the New Face of Conflict* wherein he justifies the invasion of Iraq on the basis that part of its justification is actually justifiable, although other motivations are not. Previously, Bricmont was quoted wherein he critiques a work entitled *A Matter of Principle: Humanitarian Arguments for War in Iraq*, which defended the war on Iraq on the basis of human rights regardless of the fact that the war violated international law.

In general, the abuse of a principle is not necessarily evidence that the principle itself is faulty. This is true unless there is something intrinsic within the principle that leads to its abuse. In this author's view, such is the case with human rights abuses. The intrinsic failure of human rights, as shall be demonstrated in the next chapter, is that it

---

[1] The motives and ultimate goals behind such interventions can always be questioned. An interesting work challenging the claim of altruistic and "progressive" motivations is David Chandler, *From Kosovo to Kabul: Human Rights and International Intervention* (Sterling, VA: Pluto Press, 2002). Ignatiefff (p. 40) also notes that in the 1990s humanitarian interventions were only seriously considered if the area in which human rights violations were taking place were considered "strategically important" to the most powerful nations in the world. Ignatiefff (pp. 47f) further emphasizes that such humanitarian interventions have actually made matters worse rather than better.

is not based on anything "substantial." It is not surprising, then, to see a principle abused when, in reality, that principle has a very weak moral or logical foundation to support it. In such a case, it should even be *expected* that people will put other priorities above that principle and abuse it whenever necessary or needed. Sadly, such has been the history of the application of human rights in many cases.

Furthermore, theoretically speaking, the great divide between the theory and the practice of human rights is problematic as it:

(a) Demonstrates that human rights as a whole is more utopian than its proponents wants one to believe and as presented currently are neither practical nor feasible.

(b) Demonstrates that there may be other goals that are more important than human rights, such as goals of national security and so forth. Actually, this fact seems to be fairly well accepted among the international community. It was probably the American statesman George Kennan who expressed this reality the best. He is famous for his statement in a 1948 State Department classified document, "We have about 50 percent of the world's wealth, but only 6.3 percent of the world's population. Our real task in the coming period is… to maintain this position of disparity… We need not deceive ourselves that we can afford today the luxury of altruism and world-benefaction… We should cease to talk about vague and… unreal objectives such as human rights… lW]e are going to have to deal in straight power concepts."[1] If national security, economic security or other national goals can triumph human rights, one must then also question if one's submission to God (one's internal security) can also triumph human rights.

(c) Finally, the inconsistency between word and deed does—rightfully so—make one question the entire human rights project. Muslims, in particular, have the right to be particularly wary about such beautiful words coming from the "West" while the reality behind them may be something very different. Baderin quotes an Egyptian critic of the international human rights movement, Sayf al-Dawla, who rejected the UDHR exactly on this basis.[2] No less a political theorist as Samuel

---

[1] Quoted in Ishay, p. 227.

[2] See Baderin, p. 15.

Huntington recognizes this fundamental issue with the human rights agenda. He wrote,

Non-westerners… do not hesitate to point to the gaps between Western principle and Western action. Hypocrisy, double standards, and 'but nots' are the price of universalist pretensions. Democracy is promoted but not if it brings Islamic fundamentalists to power, nonproliferation is preached for Iran and Iraq but not for Israel; … human rights are an issue with China but not with Saudi Arabia;… Double standards in practice are the unavoidable price of universal standards of principle.[1]

Actually, the realization of the existence of a double standard reached Muslim states very early in the modern history of human rights. Bricmont highlights the following example,

Or consider Article 13 of the Declaration, which ensures the right to leave one's own country. During the final stages of the Cold War, the United States was unflinching in its demand that Soviet Jews be allowed to leave their country, mainly to emigrate to Israel (an emigration that ran into Soviet objections concerning the cost to the state of having educated the candidates for emigration). But the same Article 13 also guarantees the right of return to your country of origin. The day after ratification of the Declaration, the United Nations adopted Resolution 194, which gave Palestinians driven from their territories the right to return home (or else to receive compensation). Everyone knows perfectly well that this return will never take place without a profound shake-up in the world relationship of forces. On the other hand, the Israeli settlers who were obliged to leave the Gaza strip colonies they had illegally occupied received an average of a quarter of a million dollars per family in compensation.[2]

Worse than anything, this dichotomy between practice and theory concerning human rights does not stop at national governments. Unfortunately, human rights organizations themselves are very selective about what they chose to object to, with

---

[1] Quoted in Baderin, p. 15.

[2] Bricmont, p. 76.

respect to the religion of Islam in particular[1] but even more generally with respect to egregious violations of human rights. This has led Bricmont to lament,

In recent decades, there has been a proliferation of organizations, essentially based in rich countries, watching and denouncing violations of human rights in poor countries. Whenever I happen to discuss with representatives of these organizations why they do not denounce military aggressions, for example in Iraq, the answer is roughly that this is not their field and that they can't do everything. They are concerned with human rights, period. That response would be defensible if the discourse of these organizations had not become hegemonic to a point that scarcely any other viewpoint, for example the defense of national sovereignty, can get a hearing. Moreover, they push their own priority to the point of being strictly neutral concerning aggressive wars, while denouncing the violations of human rights brought about by those wars—that is, they act as if there were no necessary link between the two. After all, those organizations do not refrain from denouncing those who are responsible for violating human rights—why then not include in that denunciation those who start wars?[2]

The simple point is this: Even those countries that are the most vocal about implementing and believing in human rights have demonstrated time and again that they are willing to violate this sacred belief whenever and wherever convenient— not just whenever and wherever necessary. These countries include the United States as well as many, if not all, European countries (although the European countries are still much more covert than the US in this field). This is not to say that those countries do not have an overall decent record of respecting human rights. However, it does demonstrate that even these countries, from which the human rights beliefs and movements were born, believe in and recognize that there are other things that are more important than human rights. In their particular cases, these other things include both national security and the economic well-being of their nation.

Albeit the West has, for the most part, turned its back on religion, what could be a response from them to the following statement: "Like you envision national

---

[1] Due to a Western problem with Islamophobia, as Baderin (pp. 11f) points out.

[2] Bricmont, pp. 157-158. Bricmont then goes on to explicit critiques of both Human Rights Watch and Amnesty International.

security and economic well-being to be more important than human rights, I view my religion and submitting to God as more important than human rights. Thus, I will adhere to human rights doctrine as long as and only if it does not violate what I believe to be part of my submission to my Lord and Creator?" Granted, they may argue that one cannot compare "religion" to national security—perhaps, the same could not be said for economic well-being. However, for the Muslim or the Muslim community that believes in God, they will say that their belief and religion is more important than national security and economic well-being. Many a Muslim would prefer to be oppressed and poor rather than have to compromise or violate any of the foundations of his faith. Certainly someone coming from a human rights perspective should be willing to accept the other's "freedom" to put his religion first in his own life.

The UDHR in Practice

It is interesting to take a glance at the Universal Declaration of Human Rights signed over fifty years ago and see how many nations who are seemingly proponents of human rights today are actually fulfilling the rights that they devised, agreed to and exhort the rest of the world to adhere to—especially, it seems, the Muslim world.

Here is a sampling of some of the rights of that original convention (for the sake of brevity the later conventions that were also agreed to shall be ignored here[1]):

Article 5

No one shall be subjected to torture or to cruel, inhuman or degrading treatment or punishment.

---

[1] Other important international treaties include: the Convention on the Prevention and Punishment of the Crime of Genocide (1948), the International Convention on the Elimination of All Forms of Racial Discrimination (1965), the UN Covenant on Civil and Political Rights (1966), the Covenant on Economic, Social and Cultural Rights (1966), the Convention on the Elimination of All Forms of Discrimination Against Women (1979), the Convention against Torture and Other Cruel, Inhuman or Degrading Treatment or Punishment (1984), and the Convention on the Rights of the Child (1989). Each of these is ratified by numerous countries. Interestingly, the Convention on the Rights of the Child has been ratified by virtually every country in the world except the United States, the accepted leader of the "family of civilized nations" and Somalia, obviously a member, many of the West would imply, of the "barbaric" nations of the world.

In the history of mankind, two sets of people are well known for compiling manuals and research on the art of torture: the members of the Inquisition and the CIA. In recent times, perhaps everyone is familiar with the current debate in the United States about the use of torture on "terror" suspects.

Although it is a very general reference source, it is interesting to note what the *2004Microsoft Encarta* has to say about torture:

Until the 13th century torture was apparently not sanctioned by the canon law of the Christian church; about that time, however, the Roman treason law began to be adapted to heresy as *crimen laesae majestatis Divinae* ("crime of injury to Divine majesty"). Soon after the Inquisition was instituted, Pope Innocent IV, influenced by the revival of Roman law, issued a decree (in 1252) that called on civil magistrates to have persons accused of heresy tortured to elicit confessions against themselves and others; this was probably the earliest instance of ecclesiastical sanction of this mode of examination… In the 20th century the use of torture was revived on a major scale by the National Socialist, Fascist, and Communist regimes of Europe, usually as a weapon of political coercion. In addition, the Communist governments made use of the so-called brainwashing technique, a form of psychological torture in which mental disorientation is induced by methods such as forcing a prisoner to stay awake indefinitely. Brainwashing was practiced extensively on prisoners held by the Communists during the Korean War. Complaints about the use of physical and psychological torture have also been lodged against many other regimes in Latin America, Africa, and Asia.[1]

The nerve of those fascists and communists! The nerve of those uncivilized countries in Latin America, Africa and Asia! This is not the proper place to enter into a critique of the use of torture by the "family of civilized nations" who first and foremost uphold "human rights." The interested reader may consult, just to name a few books, Alfred McCoy's *A Question of Torture* or Jennifer Harbury's *Truth, Torture and the American Way* as well as two books more specific about the recent debate *Abu Ghraib: The Politics of Torture* and *The Torture Papers: The Road to Abu Ghraib*. The amazing aspect to mention is that during this debate in the media,

---

[1] © 1993-2003 Microsoft Corporation. All rights reserved.

there has been very little or no mention that freedom from torture is, according to what the United States' government signed, a fundamental human right.

It should be noted that for decades now Muslim activists have faced torture in prisons throughout the world with, for the most part, the West turning a blind eye to such activities. Indeed, some Western writers—even one who claims to be Sufi— defend such practices. For example, in Stephen Schwartz's *The Two Faces of Islam: The House of Sa'ud from Tradition to Terror*, he states that Nasser's regime's "brutal repression of the Muslim brotherhood…was both necessary and justified."[1] Of course, he never notes that it was this brutality and torture in Nasser's prisons that truly led to the emergence of extremism in the Muslim world.[2]

Article 7

All are equal before the law and are entitled without any discrimination to equal protection of the law. All are entitled to equal protection against any discrimination in violation of this Declaration and against any incitement to such discrimination.

Article 9

No one shall be subjected to arbitrary arrest, detention or exile.

Article 10

Everyone is entitled in full equality to a fair, and public hearing by an independent and impartial tribunal, in the determination of his rights and obligations and of any criminal charge against him.

Article 11

---

[1] Stephen Schwartz, *The Two Faces of Islam: The House of Sa'ud from Tradition to Terror* (New York: Doubleday, 2002), p. 134.

[2] Many of those extremists, it should be noted, found their way later to Afghanistan. For more on the development of this extremism under Nasser, see Abdul Rahmaan al-Luwaihiq, *Religious Extremism in the Lives of Contemporary Muslims* (Denver, CO: Al-Basheer Company for Publications and Translations, 2001), pp. 95-123.

1. Everyone charged with a penal offence has the right to be presumed innocent until proved guilty according to law in a public trial at which he has had all the guarantees necessary for his defence.

These "fundamental human rights" are very interesting in the light of the manner in which both the United States and the European Union have responded in their "war on terror." Numerous countries in Europe have been implicated in the United States' "extraordinary rendition," which would be difficult to defend from a human rights' perspective.

This point and the earlier comments seem to make it very clear that these fundamental human rights, which these very same nations speak so highly of, are by no means absolute. The "family of civilized nations" is more than ready to deny these human rights for the sake of "national security," in other words, for the purpose of state. This is very telling. It clearly demonstrates that even from these countries' points of view, the interest of the state is the most compelling factor. One simply has to understand and realize that his human rights can be suspended if necessary in the interest of the well-being of the state.

Article 19

Everyone has the right to freedom of opinion and expression; this right includes freedom to hold opinions without interference and to seek, receive and impart information and ideas through any media and regardless of frontiers.

Obviously, freedom of religion and opinion is something that the West stands for—or does it really? In March 2006, David Irving, a British historian, was sentenced to three years in prison in Austria for denying the existence of gas chambers at Auschwitz during the Nazi holocaust. The Austrian law states that it is illegal to deny or "grossly play down" the Nazi genocide.[1] This is a crime that has landed someone in prison. Yet where is the outcry from the "pro-human rights" governments of the West. Why are the Western leaders not asking in relevant forums, "When is Austria going to join the 'family of civilized nations'"? The EU,

---

[1] See *Time Magazine*, March 6, 2006, p. 15.

perhaps the most vocal supporters of human rights, does not seem to have a problem with a law of this nature from one of its own.

Article 23

1. Everyone has the right to work, to free choice of employment, to just and favourable conditions of work and to protection against unemployment.

2. Everyone, without any discrimination, has the right to equal pay for equal work.

3. Everyone who works has the right to just and favourable remuneration ensuring for himself and his family an existence worthy of human dignity, and supplemented, if necessary, by other means of social protection.

4. Everyone has the right to form and to join trade unions for the protection of his interests.

Aren't these the kinds of things that people demonstrate for outside of the World Trade Organization's meetings? If the powerful nations (along with their friends in the powerful corporations) were fully in favor of these agreed upon human rights, wouldn't they be embracing the demonstrators with open arms? Is that what occurs or are they met with the largest battalions of riot police the world has ever seen?[1] Could it possibly be the case that, according to the "family of civilized nations," if "noble" profits are involved, then one may ignore human rights?

Today, there is a movement in the United States demanding the institution of a "living wage" as opposed to a "minimum wage." The movement, so far, has not met with much success or acceptance.

Incidentally, beginning in 1923, Congress introduced the Equal Rights Amendment, to give equal rights to women, including the right to equal pay for equal work. Although the deadline to ratify that amendment was extended all the

---

[1] The Abrahamov scandal has shown that there are even forced abortions among the labor force in Saipan, a land owned by the United States and therefore what is manufactured there may have the label, "Made in the U.S." The referred to labor force includes a large number of young women brought in from other countries, such as the Philippines.

way until 1982, it was not ratified by enough states and has never become part of the US constitution.

Article 22

Everyone, as a member of society, has the right to social security and is entitled to realization, through national effort and international co-operation and in accordance with the organization and resources of each State, of the economic, social and cultural rights indispensable for his dignity and the free development of his personality.

Article 25

1. Everyone has the right to a standard of living adequate for the health and well-being of himself and of his family, including food, clothing, housing and medical care and necessary social services, and the right to security in the event of unemployment, sickness, disability, widowhood, old age or other lack of livelihood in circumstances beyond his control.

These are truly amazing articles. It can be argued that anyone who believes in or promotes free market, liberal capitalism is, in essence, stating and showing that they do not believe in this human right. Free market capitalism, due to the violation of its essential assumptions, is not geared to producing "the best of all possible worlds" and only produces what the skewed market demands. A mixture of capitalism and socialism, at best, can provide something but probably not all that is needed. But it is this very mixture of capitalism and socialism that has been the target of attack in recent years. The policies of the World Bank, the IMF and the WTO, which are nothing but tools in the hands of the "family of civilized nations" have been nothing short of an assault on any such "socialist" practices on the part of governments, especially those of lesser developed countries. The "liberalization" policies are in complete contrast to the "fundamental human rights" of the individuals of those countries.

Perhaps there is no need to go into the wide divide between human rights theory and the actual record of human rights violations, even by those countries who speak the loudest when it comes to human rights. As Freeman noted, "However, human-rights declarations are cheap, whereas human-rights implementation is rather expensive."[1] Furthermore, the works of Noam Chomsky, William Blum (*Killing Hope* and *Rogue State*), John Pilger (*Hidden Agendas*) and the like are all available for people to read. Even Ann Elizabeth Mayer has recognized this problematic issue when speaking about human rights to Muslims. She wrote,

As an American, I realize that my expressions of concern regarding the human rights violations that can result from applying Islamic criminal law in current circumstances are inevitably associated with hypocritical U.S. government stances regarding human rights and the gross double standards applied by the United States in judging human rights issues involving Muslims and Muslim countries. It is admittedly awkward to be talking about the deficiencies of the criminal justice systems of other countries at a time when under U.S. auspices so many Muslims have been casually and/or arbitrarily accused of involvement in terrorism, incarcerated in horrendous conditions in which they must endure severe indignities, and denied the basic elements of due process -- even being subjected to appalling abuses like the ones exposed at Abu Ghraib and reported by detainees held at Guantanamo.[2]

The Universality of Human Rights

The theory of universalism is that human rights are the same (or must be the same) everywhere, both in substance and application. Advocates of strict universalism assert that international human rights are exclusively universal. This theory is mostly advocated by Western States and scholars who present universalism in human rights through a strict Western liberal perspective. They reject any claims of cultural relativism and consider it as an unacceptable theory advocated to rationalize human rights violations. Scholars who argue that human rights were developed from Western culture also often argue that Western norms should always be the universal normative model for international human rights law. The theory of universalism is that human rights are the same (or must be the same) everywhere, both in substance and application. Advocates of strict universalism assert that international human rights are exclusively universal. This theory is mostly advocated by Western States and scholars

---

[1] Freeman, p. 171.

[2] Ann Elizabeth Mayer, "Reconsidering the Human Rights Framework for Applying Islamic Criminal Law," p. 3. Found at http://lgst.wharton.upenn.edu/mayera/Documents/mayerislamabad05.pdf.

who present universalism in human rights through a strict Western liberal perspective. They reject any claims of cultural relativism and consider it as an unacceptable theory advocated to rationalize human rights violations. Scholars who argue that human rights were developed from Western culture also often argue that Western norms should always be the universal normative model for international human rights law. The theory of universalism is that human rights are the same (or must be the same) everywhere, both in substance and application. Advocates of strict universalism assert that international human rights are exclusively universal. This theory is mostly advocated by Western States and scholars who present universalism in human rights through a strict Western liberal perspective. They reject any claims of cultural relativism and consider it as an unacceptable theory advocated to rationalize human rights violations. Scholars who argue that human rights were developed from Western culture also often argue that Western norms should always be the universal normative model for international human rights law.

Finally, this question is not truly relevant when it comes to the Islamic position on human rights. As shall be discussed in detail in the following chapter, the Islamic view on human rights should not be based on the question of cultural diversity or anything of that nature. The premises of the human rights movement have to be established before any question of universality or cultural relativism come into play. The purport of the this chapter has been to question the very premises of the movement. If the premises are found faulty, then the question of universal application and strict universality becomes a moot point.[1]

Some Important Conclusions

This chapter has admittedly been a fairly grim expose of human rights theory. From its very foundations to its practice, the human rights paradigm is far from perfect, to say the least.

---

[1] For those interested in the universality versus cultural relativism debate, Baderin has presented a good summary and critique of the various issues involved. See Baderin, pp. 23-32. In fact, he questions whether there is any true uniformity or universality within the "Western" approaches to human rights themselves.

Very little is offered by human rights theorists as to why anyone should believe in or accept this paradigm. Once it is recognized that that issue is not solvable, the problem of what or what is not a human right actually becomes insurmountable—as everything from homosexuality, interreligious marriage and not being circumcised are presented as "human rights." In fact, it was found that the human rights paradigm as a whole is self-contradictory. It claims to offer human rights and freedoms to others but will only do so within its own framework, meaning that human rights and freedoms are only those human rights and freedoms that the human rights paradigm allows. Thus, there are no true freedoms and to real rights. Finally, it was shown that the human rights paradigm is about a utopia that is very far from being achieved. In fact, even those who are most vocal in their support of human rights demonstrate that from their own point of view other priorities can still take precedence over human rights.

One is left with a very grim outcome. In the end, one must keep in mind that the human rights movement and paradigm is not simply about affirming some general human rights that the majority of the world's inhabitants would probably accept. The movement is about much more than that. The movement is about changing countries, societies and even religions to adhere not just to general principles but specific forms of regulation and laws.

Now comes the question: Why? Why should people give up their cultural practices and submit to this new paradigm? Why should people give up what they believe in to be ultimate truths, such as parts of their religion, to be in accordance with the demands of this movement?

If, in answering these types of questions, the human rights advocates could argue that they have a firm foundation for their beliefs, that they can prove that their movement will bring about the "best of all possible worlds,"[1] that their system is a logical and consistent system will allow all to be "free," and so on, then one could rationally argue that perhaps everyone in the world should take the demands of the

---

[1] Of course, for those who believe in a Hereafter, most human rights advocates would have to admit that they cannot guarantee anything with respect to what will happen to an individual if he forsakes a portion of his religion in the name of "human rights."

human rights movement seriously. However, the human rights paradigm cannot make such claims.

The reality is that the justifications for the human rights paradigm are weak—virtually, unidentifiable, disputed and doubtful at best. No one can say what kind of world will result if everyone is given all of the "freedoms" that many human rights advocates are calling for. Instead of leading everyone to be free, its self-contradictory framework has simply led to more and more disputes as to what constitutes a violation of human rights and what does not. Thus, as of September 18, 2008, there were 100,000 cases pending before the European Court of Human Rights, while in its entire history it had only been able to render 10,000 judgments[1]—and a case only goes to that court if all domestic remedies have failed.

Again, these realities—as well as all the points made in this chapter—actually lead to what should be a more obvious and specific question: Why should anyone who believes in Islam as the ultimate truth be willing to compromise or sacrifice any part of his religion and relationship to God on the basis of such a paradigm? This leads directly into the next chapter, which is a discussion of Islam and "human rights."

---

[1] Rudiger Wolfrum and Ulrike Deutsch, eds., *The European Court of Human Rights Overwhelmed by Applications: Problems and Possible Solutions* (Berlin, Germany: Springer, 2009), p. v.

Islam and "Human Rights"

The term "human rights" or *huqooq al-insaan* is not found in either the Quran or Hadith, although the word *haqq* or "right" can be found throughout both of them. Similarly, Islam, like other so-called "premodern" systems, faces a standard critique of emphasizing "obligations" rather than rights.[1] However, there is a well-known expression among Muslim scholars that says that "there shall be no dispute over an issue of semantics." The important point is whether there are aspects that Islam established that can be considered comparable to what many today would call "human rights." In this author's view, there is no question that there are such "rights" sanctioned by the Quran and Sunnah.

At the same time, though, not every "right" that people claim to be a human right today is sanctioned in Islam. Instead, what one will find is that there are a large number of contemporary "human rights" that Islam accepted and established over fourteen hundred years ago. At the same time, though, there are some fundamental differences between Islam's "human rights" and the contemporary human rights platform. These differences also need to be highlighted. (Incidentally, these differences may also be looked upon as the unique features of an Islamic view of "human rights" or they may be looked upon as ways in which Islam is "incompatible" with contemporary human rights theory.)

There have been a plethora of books written by Muslims that discuss, some in great detail, the rights that Islam has given humankind.[2] In fact, conferences have

---

[1] Khalid Abou El Fadhl has demonstrated that in reality both obligations and rights have been historically emphasized by the jurists of Islam. Abou El Fadhl in Bucar and Barnett, pp. 83ff.

[2] Examples include the following: Hathout, Maher with Uzma Jamil, Gasser Hathout and Nayyer Ali (Los Angeles, CA: Muslim Public Affairs Council, 2006); Mohammad Khoder, *Human Rights in Islam* (Beirut: Dar Khoder); Ibrahim al-Marzouqi, *Human Rights in Islamic Law* (Abu Dhabi, UAE: 2000); Adnaan al-Wazzaan, *Mausooah Huqooq al-Insaan fi al-Islaam* ("Encyclopedia of Human Rights in Islam") (Beirut, Lebanon: Muasassah al-Risaalah, 2005, eight volumes); Khadeejah al-Nabraawi, *Mausooah Huqooq al-Insaan fi al-Islaam* ("Encyclopedia of Human Rights in Islam") (Cairo, Egypt: Dar al-Salaam, 2006); Abdul Lateef al-Ghaamidi, *Huqooq al-Insaan fi al-Islaam* (Riyadh, Saudi Arabia: Naif Arab Academy for Security Sciences, 2000); Marwaan al-Qaisi, *Mausooah Huqooq al-Insaan fi al-Islaam* ("Encyclopedia of Human Rights in Islam"), available at http://www.scribd.com/doc/970694/1-. There are also a few books that emphasize the human rights aspects that are found in the Sunnah in particular, such as Hikmat Yaaseen, *Inaayah al-Sunnah al-Nabawiyyah bi-Huqooq al-Insaan* (Riyadh,

been held[1] and documents have been produced outlining the Islamic version of universal human rights.[2] Obviously a discussion of that nature is not the purport of this work.[3] The present work is more concerned with "fundamental" issues. Thus, this chapter will be restricted to discussing some of the fundamental issues related to "human rights" and Islam, in particular answering some of the same questions that were raised last chapter concerning the human rights paradigm, such as:

The justification for human rights

What should be considered a human right

The paradox of human rights

Human rights between theory and practice

Before discussing any of those questions, it is important to understand the general purpose of the Law (*Shareeah*) in Islam. The nature of the Law in Islam is actually directly related to the understanding of "human rights" in Islam.

A Basic Perception of the *Shareeah* (Islamic Law)

According to Muslim belief, Islamic Law or the *Shareeah*[4] has been revealed for the benefit and betterment of humankind. The *Shareeah* is not meant to be a burden upon humankind. In fact, there is no concept in Islam of making oneself suffer or undergo extreme burdens as a means of worship of God. One does sacrifice for God's sake but one does not intentionally harm oneself as a means of getting

---

Saudi Arabia: Naif Prize, 2005), Faatimah al-Jaarid, *Inaayah al-Sunnah al-Nabawiyyah bi-Huqooq al-Insaan* (Riyadh, Saudi Arabia: Naif Prize, 2005) and Sayid Thaur al-Nakhoori, *Inaayah al-Sunnah al-Nabawiyyah bi-Huqooq al-Insaan* (2007).

[1] A discussion of human rights was undertaken by the OIC's Majma al-Fiqhi and by the Muslim World League. Their papers are published, respectively, in *Majallah Majma al-Fiqh al-Islaami* (No. 13, vol. 1, 2001) and *Nadwah Huqooq al-Insaan fi al-Islaam* (Makkah, Saudi Arabia: Raabitah al-Aalim al-Islaami, 2000).

[2] Two such documents are included as appendices to this work.

[3] The author considers it sufficient to include some of the "Islamic human rights documents" as appendices.

[4] Technically speaking, the word *shareeah* refers to the clear texts of the Quran and Sunnah. Rules that are derived from those sources and which are not clear in and of themselves are known as *fiqh*. A number of writers who have touched upon Islamic Law and human rights have confused or blurred the meaning of these two terms.

closer to God. In fact, Allah has said, "[He] has not laid upon you any hardship in the religion" (*al-Hajj* 78), and "Allah does not intend to make difficulty for you, but He intends to purify you and complete His favor upon you that you may be grateful" (*Al-Maaidah* 6).

It is important for the reader to have a familiarity with the Muslim's concept of the *Shareeah*. This will shed some light on a Muslim's attitude toward this Law vis-à-vis the human rights paradigm. Unless a non-Muslim is fully aware of some of these aspects, he or she will not be able to fully comprehend the Muslim's respect for the *Shareeah* and, in turn, the Muslim's view toward abandoning it and accepting any other approach to life.

The Islamic view of the *Shareeah* can be understood in the light of numerous verses of the Quran. For example, in the Quran, Allah says about Himself, "He has prescribed for Himself mercy" (*al-Anaam* 12) and, "Your Lord has prescribed for Himself mercy" (*al-Anaam* 54). These two verses, among many others, make it clear that Allah is Merciful. In particular, His sending of the Prophet Muhammad (peace and blessings of Allah be upon him) and his message was an act of mercy on His part, as Allah says, "We have not sent you [O Prophet] except as a mercy for the worlds" (*al-Anbiyaa* 107).

It is therefore inconceivable that the *Shareeah* does not grant humans the rights that they deserve. That would not only not be mercy, that would be injustice on God's part. Thus, Allah says about the Quran that He revealed to the Prophet Muhammad (peace and blessings of Allah be upon him), "Verily this Quran guides to that which is most right" (*al-Israa* 9).

In describing the Prophet Muhammad, once again, in particular, Allah says, "Those who follow the Messenger, the unlettered prophet, whom they find written in what they have of the Torah and the Gospel, who enjoins upon them what is right and forbids them what is wrong and makes lawful for them the good things and prohibits for them the evil and relieves them of their burden and the shackles which were upon them" (*Al-Araaf* 157). Clearly, the Prophet's message is that of fulfilling what is right, allowing all good and pure things, making things easier upon the people by removing improper burdensome laws and remaining away from evil.

Once again, certainly all good "rights" must have been embodied in what the Prophet (peace and blessings of Allah be upon him) espoused while all extreme and harmful "rights" must be among those wrongs that the Prophet repelled.

Thus, one starts with this foundation: The *Shareeah* is a manifestation of God's mercy—God who is the all-Wise, all-Knowing Creator of this cosmos. Who, other than God, the Compassionate Creator, truly knows what humans need and what is best for them? Allah actually reminds all humans of this fact when He said, "Should He not know, He that created? And He is the One that understands the finest mysteries (and) is well-acquainted (with them)" (*al-Mulk* 14). In fact, no one can make a better decision for humans than Allah. Thus, He informs humankind: "Do they then seek after a judgment of (the Days of) Ignorance? But who, for a people whose faith is assured, can give better judgment than Allah?" (*al-Maaidah* 50).

Incidentally, it should be noted that Mayer lambasts the idea of holding Revelation above human reasoning. In fact, this is one of her main critiques of those who drew up the Islamic human rights declarations.[1] The entire tenor of her passage points to her considering this attitude toward revelation as a weakness in the Islamic schemes. At the same time, though, at no time did she ever demonstrate that reason should be given priority over revelation. It was as if she was simply preaching to the choir and expecting the readers to join along with her that reason must take precedence over revelation.

On the other hand, there is a very solid logical basis for giving revelation from God precedence over human reasoning. Allah reminds humans of a very important point, a point that is directly related to the question of human rights and how human rights should be determined. Allah says in the Quran, "Fighting has been enjoined upon you while it is hateful to you. But perhaps you hate a thing and it is good for you; and perhaps you love a thing and it is bad for you. And Allah Knows, while you know not" (*Al-Baqarah* 216). This verse is a stark reminder concerning the weaknesses of humans. Humankind's knowledge of the reality and secrets of this universe is admittedly limited. Furthermore, human vision is

---

[1] See Mayer, *Islam and Human Rights*, pp. 60ff. She also gives the impression that Muslim scholars are against the use of "reason." In reality, reason has its role in Islamic Legal Theory but Mayer, at least from this passage, does not seem to understand or recognize its role.

repeatedly obscured by biases and desires. Hence, it is not unlikely that humans may determine a thing to be good while in reality it is very harmful and vice-versa.

Furthermore, one of the main goals of sending messengers and revelations is the establishment of justice in this world, free of the biases and deviations of humans. Allah has clearly stated, "We have already sent Our messengers with clear evidences and sent down with them the Scripture and the balance that the people may maintain [their affairs] in justice" (*al-Hadeed* 25). But that could only be the case if said messengers and revelations were providing for humans the rights and opportunities that they truly deserve—nothing more and nothing less, as anything else would be the essence of injustice.

In fact, throughout the Quran, Allah has explicitly stated that He has ordered the establishment of justice: "Allah commands justice, the doing of good, and liberality to kith and kin, and He forbids all shameful deeds, and injustice and rebellion: He instructs you, that you may receive admonition" (*al-Nahl* 90). Repeatedly, Allah commands the believers that they must stand up for justice, even if it be against their own wishes or against the interests of those closest to them: "O you who have believed, be persistently standing firm in justice, witnesses for Allah , even if it be against yourselves or parents and relatives. Whether one is rich or poor, Allah is more worthy of both. So follow not [personal] inclination, lest you not be just" (*al-Nisaa* 135); "O you who have believed, be persistently standing firm for Allah , witnesses in justice, and do not let the hatred of a people prevent you from being just. Be just; that is nearer to righteousness. And fear Allah; indeed, Allah is Acquainted with what you do" (*al-Maaidah* 8).

Furthermore, one of the negations of justice, corruption, has been explicitly prohibited via many verses of the Quran. Note, "So fulfill the measure and weight and do not deprive people of their due and cause not corruption upon the earth after its reformation. That is better for you, if you should be believers" (*al-Araaf* 85). In fact, in numerous verses one can find the command: "Do not commit abuse on the earth, spreading corruption" (*al-Baqarah* 60; *al-Araaf* 74; *Hood* 85; *al-Shuaraa* 183; *al-Ankaboot* 36).

Thus it is clear from the texts of the Quran itself that the Islamic message has been sent as a mercy from God that seeks to establish justice and righteousness in this world and it is not simply a message concerning another world or "heavenly Kingdom," as the Christians would describe it. In sum, the Islamic argument is that there cannot be anyone better than God to lay down rights and obligations that are just and fitting for human beings.[1]

This aspect of the *Shareeah* has been well recognized by Muslims throughout their history. In fact, when asked by the Emperor of Persia what brought the Muslims to their lands, two different Companions answered in similar terms: "Allah has sent us to take whoever wishes from the servitude of mankind to the servitude of Allah and from the tightness of this world to its expanse and from the injustice of the ways of life [in this world] to the justice of Islam."[2]

The Muslim scholars thus recognized the fact that the ultimate purpose of humans was to worship God and abide by His Guidance. Yet, at the same time, this meant following a path that was best for the human in this world as well as the Hereafter. Hence, in Islamic thought, there is no dichotomy between what is good for the Hereafter or for this world—not like the struggle between the flesh and the soul found in Christianity.[3] Since the law was revealed for the betterment of humankind, it follows that the actions of humans should also be for the betterment of humans.

In fact, Muslim scholars went beyond this point and argued that every point of law in the *Shareeah* is in humankind's best interest (*maslahah*). Thus, ibn al-Qayyim, who died in 1350, stated,

---

[1] An important issue that is, however, beyond the realm of this work has to do with the preservation of that revealed message. Obviously, to make such claims about the revelation would be irrelevant if the revealed message was not preserved. The author discusses this issue in detail in his *What is Islam* (Riyadh, Saudi Arabia: Ministry of Religious Affairs, 2005), pp. 74ff.

[2] Ismaaeel ibn Katheer, *Al-Bidaayah wa al-Nihaayah* (Beirut: Dar al-Kutub al-Ilmiyya, n.d.), vol. 7, pp. 39-40.

[3] It is important to highlight this aspect of Christianity as it contributed to the rift between science and religion that eventually resulted in what could be called the first of the Western human rights movement. That rift and the resulting attitude toward religion continues to have its influence today and has undoubtedly influenced many a human rights proponent.

If you examined the laws of His religion that He has prescribed for His servants, you will find that none are other than achieving a pure *maslahah* (interest, welfare) or a predominant one whenever possible—and when there is a conflict between them, allowing for the greater or more important one, even if the lesser one is lost—or the ending of a pure *mafaasid* (evil, harm) or a predominant one whenever possible—and if there is some conflict between them, the ending of the greater evil, even if it means bearing a lesser one.

On this basis has the Most Just of Judges laid down the laws of His faith, pointing to it, witnessing by it to His perfect knowledge and wisdom and His kindness to His Servants and His goodness to them. This generality is not doubted by anyone who has had the slightest taste of the Shareeah and has been fed from its breast or has been provided to drink from its cistern. The more one becomes experienced in it, his witnessing of its goodness and *maslahah* becomes more complete…

If one reflects in the proper way upon the Shareeah with which Allah sent His Messenger, he will find that from its beginning to its end, it is witnessing to this fact and explicitly stating it. He will find wisdom, *maslahah*, justice and mercy clearly exhibited on each of its pages, calling to them and calling the intelligent and wise people to those principles…[1]

Ibn al-Qaayim points to this aspect of the *Shareeah* as being one of its greatest miracles and pointing to it coming from God alone. He wrote,

It is most amazing that a person can allow himself to reject the wisdom, causative legal reason and *maslahah* that are included in this complete Shareeah, which is part of the greatest evidence testifying to the veracity of the one who came with it and the fact that he was truly the Messenger of Allah. Had he been given no other miracle than that, it would have been sufficient and satisfying. What it contains of wisdom, *maslahah*, praiseworthy ends and sound results all witness that the One who legislated and revealed this is the Best of all Judges and the Most Merciful of the merciful. The witnessing of that in its contents and meanings is like what is witnessed of the wisdom, *maslahah* and benefits that are found in the highest and

---

[1] *Miftaah Daar al-Saadah*, vol. 2, pp. 22-23. For similar passages, see *Ilaam al-Muwaqieen*, vol. 3, p. 3 and *Majmoo Fataawaa ibn Taimiyyah*, vol. 20, p. 48; vol. 13, p. 96; vol. 11, pp. 352 and 354.

lowest forms of creation as well as what is between them of animals, vegetation, elements and remnants by which the needs of living are ordered.[1]

This attitude toward the jurists have continued to this day. In the last century, the famed Egyptian scholar Muhammad Abu Zahrah wrote, "This point [that *maslahah* is the basis of the Law] is an accepted principle agreed upon by all Muslim jurists. None of them said that the Islamic Shareeah came with an order that was not consistent with the *maslahah* of humankind. Also, none of them said that that there is something harmful in the laws and rulings that have been legislated for the Muslims."[2]

Building on the fact that the Law intends *maslahah* or public well-being and by what could be described as "juristic induction," the Islamic legal scholars determined that the Shareeah had some very specific primary goals. In essence, the main body of laws were pointing to the establishment, protection and perfection of what became known as "the necessities of life"[3]: religion, life itself, mental capacity, wealth and familial ties.[4] The scholars also concluded that these necessities and priorities of life come in the order just presented. That is, even among these necessities, some are given priorities over others.

This conclusion about Islamic Law demonstrates that what Islam envisions as the "good life" for humans, filled with proper rights and human dignity, may be very different from that envisioned by the contemporary human rights paradigm. For

---

[1] *Shifaa al-Aleel fi Masaail al-Qadha wa al-Qadar wa al-Hikmah wa al-Taleel*, p. 205. He has a similar passage in *Madaarij al-Saalikeen*, vol. 1, p. 242.

[2] Muhammad Abu Zahrah, *Maalik: Hayaatuhu wa Asruhu Araauhu wa Fiqhuhu* (Daar al-Fikr al-Arabi), pp. 293-294.

[3] It is important to note that these basic priorities of the *Shareeah* are easy to define and identify by reading the texts of the Quran and Sunnah. One set of verses that alludes to many of them is *al-Anaam* verses 151-153. Beyond the "necessities," the Law then attempts to fulfill the needs and amenities of life. However, for the purposes here, a reference to the "necessities" is sufficient. Furthermore, like all "principles" rather than specific laws, one has to be careful not to take this principle to an extreme and somehow try to give it precedence over the laws themselves. This is an approach that some "modernists" have attempted to make in contemporary times.

[4] Sherman Jackson argues that the scholars were correct in identifying these general goals but they failed to extend the idea of these goals beyond mere empiricism. See Sherman Jackson, "Concretizing the Maqaasid: Islam in the Modern World," *International Conference on Islamic Jurisprudence and the Challenges of the 21st Century: Maqasid al-Shari'ah and its Realization in Contemporary Societies* (Kuala Lumpur, Malaysia: International Islamic University Malaysia, 2006), pp. 1-9.

example, religion being given the highest priority, over that of life, demonstrates that Islam considers life without the sound religion is not a true life indeed.[1] Contemporary human rights advocates have definitely argued that their determined human rights must take precedence over any religion, as was discussed earlier.

On the other hand, the recognition of these five goals of the Shareeah should be important to human rights advocates as they demonstrate a clear recognition of rights on the part of human beings. It is the role and responsibility of the Muslim state, community and individuals to attempt to fulfill these necessities for everyone in the same way that the Law is setup to assist in the fulfillment of these necessities. Furthermore, many of these goals are similar to some of the demands of the human rights paradigm. In fact, an example shall be given later related to "the family," which can be considered one of the five necessities and which is also explicitly mentioned in the international documents on human rights.

An additional important point that human rights advocates have yet to grapple with completely is also highlighted in the concept of the goals of the Shareeah. These goals of the Shareeah are also about limitations, not just about freedoms and rights. In other words, these goals need to be protected. They cannot be truly protected unless acts that may harm them are prohibited or greatly limited. In this light, one can understand the Shareeah prohibition of alcohol and all other intoxicants. This prohibition, which one could consider a restriction on an individual's right to consume whatever he wishes, is a needed protection for human life as a whole. Thus, in one of the first revelations concerning alcohol, leading up to its eventual complete prohibition, Allah says, "They ask you about wine and gambling. Say, 'In them is great sin and [yet, some] benefit for people. But their sin is greater than their benefit'" (*al-Baqarah* 219).[2] One look at American society will allow one to understand how this prohibition—or restriction on freedom—is a must for the protection of others' human rights. One need only think about the countless

---

[1] As Allah says in the Quran, "O you who have believed, respond to Allah and to the Messenger when he calls you to that which gives you life" (*al-Anfaal* 24).

[2] In the reading of Hamzah and al-Kisaa`ee, it is, "In them is much sin." Thus, the Quran emphasizes both the quality of the harm that is resultant from alcohol as well as its quantity. See Ahmad ibn Mujaahid, *Kitaab al-Saba fi al-Qiraat* (Cairo, Egypt: Daar al-Maarif, n.d.), p. 182.

automobile accidents that are the result of drunk driving[1], the numerous cases of domestic violence that are the result of alcoholism, the early deaths and diseases accompanied with alcohol, the lost children of alcohol dependent families and so forth all demonstrate that this prohibition from the Shareeah is a great mercy for the entire society. This is the important other side of the question that human rights advocates fail to deal with adequately. One cannot simply be concerned about rights without be just as concerned with restrictions—and not simply restrictions only when they most immediately and direct violate another's rights, as is usually the case with human rights thinking.

The difference between the Islamic approach and the human rights paradigm is that Islam must be open and clear about these prohibitions while the human rights paradigm, since it is about rights, cannot. Thus one finds those bold statements about "absolute freedoms" while in reality none of them can be absolute freedoms. Islam is not about absolute freedoms. Islam has set out some very clear goals for humankind and in the line of those goals has restricted many so-called rights and freedoms, such as sexual freedoms, freedom of speech and expression and the like.

The Comprehensiveness of Islamic Law when Compared to the human rights Paradigm

Islamic Law, though, is obviously very different from the documents that form today's international human rights. Article 16 of the UDHR states the following:

Article 16

1. Men and women of full age, without any limitation due to race, nationality or religion, have the right to marry and to found a family. They are entitled to equal rights as to marriage, during marriage and at its dissolution.

2. Marriage shall be entered into only with the free and full consent of the intending spouses.

3. The family is the natural and fundamental group unit of society and is entitled to protection by society and the State.

---

[1] The crash of the Exxon Valdez demonstrates the effect that alcohol consumption can have on the environment as well.

Article 23 of the ICCPR is virtually the same.

Article 10 of the ICESCR reads as follows:

Article 10

The States Parties to the present Covenant recognize that:

1. The widest possible protection and assistance should be accorded to the family, which is the natural and fundamental group unit of society, particularly for its establishment and while it is responsible for the care and education of dependent children. Marriage must be entered into with the free consent of the intending spouses.

2. Special protection should be accorded to mothers during a reasonable period before and after childbirth. During such period working mothers should be accorded paid leave or leave with adequate social security benefits.

3. Special measures of protection and assistance should be taken on behalf of all children and young persons without any discrimination for reasons of parentage or other conditions. Children and young persons should be protected from economic and social exploitation. Their employment in work harmful to their morals or health or dangerous to life or likely to hamper their normal development should be punishable by law. States should also set age limits below which the paid employment of child labour should be prohibited and punishable by law.

Such "international laws" are meant to be vague. But then do they truly bestow rights on people? What is a family constituted of? Can it start with two men, two women or perhaps even more? The human rights documents are completely silent about these issues. They simply have some vague, general statements about equality and then they allow the courts to decide the remainder of the issues. Hence, in some places one can find two women and a child (born of one of them and a third man) making up a family. Sometimes the sperm donor is even known and involved. On occasion, one of the parties may regret what they have done and demand more rights than what the others are willing to give. When these things occur, and they do occur often, the only resort is to go to the courts. Who suffers via this entire process? It is the family itself, especially the children.

Islamic Law places a great emphasis on the role of the family and therefore provides a great deal of guidance concerning the family. It speaks about the "virtues" of marriage, what qualities to look for in a spouse, the components of a family, the rights, obligations and expectations of all of the members of the family and so on. Of course, such topics would not be expected from secular law books or international documents related to general topics like human rights. The point here is simply to demonstrate that within Islam there is support for many of the same concepts as found in the human rights documents. However, the nature of Islam being so different, Islam goes much further than those documents in giving an entire structure and support system that truly allows those "rights" to develop and prosper.

Islamic Law is a comprehensive system that takes into consideration all of the various aspects of life with enough detail to guide humans and enough flexibility to make it compatible for all times and places. The human rights advocates who attempt to eradicate the influence of Islamic Law are actually only going to leave Muslims with a great vacuum. They cannot provide Muslims with a complete and consistent system that will meet society's goals while neither going to the extreme of granting too many rights nor the extreme of prohibiting matters that do not need to be prohibited.

Islam and Human Dignity

As discussed last chapter, one of the arguments often given for the justification of the concept of human rights is the goal of attaining human dignity for all. As a justification for the human rights paradigm, as was noted, it turns out to be very weak. Furthermore, it is questionable as to simply giving people a set of determined rights does actually bring about human dignity. Without a metaphysical basis, stripping human beings to nothing but a material being, one wonders how human dignity could possibly be attained.

The religion of Islam, on the other hand, is all about human dignity. It is about releasing the potential in human beings and guiding them to a path in which they will become "the best that they can be." From the Islamic perspective, the most noble and dignified a human being can be is in being a worshipper and servant of Allah. Obviously, many human rights advocates would shutter at this very idea where the central piece moves from a glorification of the human to a deserved glorification of the One true God. However, it must be accepted that if that were what humans were meant to be, then this goal is the real fulfillment of human dignity. human rights advocates may not agree with that premise but, at the same time, they have nothing to prove it to be false or unreasonable.

Allah tells humankind about how He has honored and favored them: "We have honored the descendents of Adam; provided them with transport on land and sea; given them for sustenance things good and pure; and conferred on them special favors, above a great part of Our Creation" (al-Israa 70).[1] This means that all of humankind start out as honorable creatures of God. Allah has blessed humans with many things that He has not blessed other parts of the creation. Furthermore, according to Islamic beliefs, when Allah created the first human, He ordered the most noble of creations, the angels, to bow down to him.[2] This was indeed one of the greatest displays of showing the important place that this new creation possesses. Finally, the *rooh* or spirit that was breathed into the original human has been described by Allah as coming specifically from Him, "And when I have proportioned him and breathed into him of My soul [that I created]" (al-Hijr 29). In particular, humans have been blessed with a great intellect and will that puts them above the other creatures of this world.

Thus, from the Islamic perspective, humans are a noble creation and with a very noble purpose indeed: to become true servants and worshippers of God. The greatest of all humans according to Islamic beliefs, the Prophet Muhammad (peace and blessings of Allah be upon him) demonstrated that being a servant of God is the most honored and exalted a human being can be. Thus he said, "Do not extol me like the Christians extolled the son of Mary. I am His slave-servant, so say, 'Slave of Allah and His Messenger.'"[3] According to Islamic beliefs, being a true servant of God is the ultimate expression of humanness. In fact, there can be no other sound

---

[1] Although difficult to capture in English, the original wording of this verse in Arabic, with the Form II verb *karrama*, demonstrates the magnitude and greatness in which Allah has honored humans. Cf., Muhammad ibn Ahmad al-Qurtubi, *al-Jaami li-Ahkaam al-Quraan* (Riyadh, Saudi Arabia: Daar Aalim al-Kutub), vol. 10, p. 293.

[2] This important incident is referred to in each of the following verses of the Quran: al-Baqarah 34, al-Araaf 11, al-Israa 61, al-Kahf 50 and Taha 116.

[3] Recorded by al-Bukhari.

goal because, as Muslims believer, this is the only goal that is truly consistent with the nature and souls of humans.

However, not all humans choose to follow the path of human dignity. From the Islamic perspective, humans were created with a limited free will. Humans are free to develop their great potential or they are free to debase themselves. Allah says, for example, "Say [O Prophet], 'O humankind, the truth has come to you from your Lord, so whoever is guided is only guided for [the benefit of] his soul, and whoever goes astray only goes astray [in violation] against it. And I am not over you a manager'" (*Yoonus* 108). Allah juxtaposes the two decisions even clearer in the following verses: "We have certainly created man in the best of stature; then We return him to the lowest of the low, except for those who believe and do righteous deeds, for they will have a reward uninterrupted" (*al-Teen* 4-6).

In sum, from the Islamic perspective, true human dignity and worth comes from the human realizing his real purpose and worth, which is found in being a true and devoted servant of the Creator of the Universe. This implies submitting with true sincerity and devotion to the revelation that has come from God, without any arrogant rejection of what God has commanded. It is important for contemporary human rights activists to realize that they often demand of Muslims that they do what strikes at the very heart of the Muslim's perception of human dignity. Muslims are asked to literally disobey or "alter" clear commandments of the Quran or Sunnah—albeit very few will openly admit that such is what is being requested of Muslims. From the Muslim's perspective, this strikes at the very root of what it means to be a true and righteous human.

The Definition of "Islamic Human Rights"

Now that some general Islamic concepts have been presented, one can now move to the question of whether Islam accepts "human rights." As demonstrated in the previous chapter, the very conception or definition of "human rights" is itself disputable and not agreed upon.

There is a definitely a concept in Islam of other people having rights upon an individual, both at an individual level and at a more general level. For example, in a passage of the Quran, Allah describes characteristics of the believers. These characteristics include the fact that they recognize that those in need and the poor have a right to some of their wealth.[1]

The Prophet (peace and blessings of Allah be upon him) told one of his Companions, who used to fast everyday and pray all night, not to do that. Then he told him, "Verily, your body has a right over you, your eye has a right over you, your wife has a right over you and your visitor has a right over you."[2]

In another hadith, the Prophet (peace and blessings of Allah be upon him) emphasized that the "rights of the street/path" are to be respected. When he was asked what they were, he replied, "Lowering one's gaze, refraining from committing harm, responding to greetings, ordering good and eradicating evil."[3] This once again demonstrates the understanding that people have rights over one another. These rights are both positive and negative: One should neither bring harm to others and one must also positively work on others' behalf (which is part of the understanding of ordering good and eradicating evil).

The Messenger of Allah (peace and blessings of Allah be upon him) told some of his Companions that after his death, some rulers would give preference to others over them and would perform acts that they would disapprove of. They asked the Prophet (peace and blessings of Allah be upon him) what they should do under those circumstances. The Prophet (peace and blessings of Allah be upon him) replied, "You should fulfill their rights and ask Allah for your rights."[4] Here the Prophet (peace and blessings of Allah be upon him) was clearly speaking about the rights of rulers and the ruled. This means that in Islamic Law, by God's command and not via years of persecution and revolts, it is a must that both the rulers and the

---

[1] The Quranic passage as a whole is *al-Maarij* 19-27. Verses 24-25 state, "And those within whose wealth is a known right, for the petitioner and the deprived." In a similar vein, the Prophet (peace and blessings of Allah be upon him) was reported to have said, "In wealth, there is a right [for the poor] in addition to the [obligatory] zakat (alms)." This hadith was recorded by al-Tirmidhi, al-Baihaqi, al-Daaraqutni, al-Tabaraani and al-Daarimi; however, its chain is weak.

[2] Recorded by al-Bukhari and Muslim in their authentic collections.

[3] Recorded by al-Bukhari in his authentic collection.

[4] Recorded by al-Bukhari.

ruled have explicit and clear rights.[1] However, it is an established fact of humankind that sometimes the rulers, in particular, do not fulfill the rights of the ruled. This does not mean that one should revolt immediately as that will not produce good—nor should the ruler immediately imprison or kill his subjects when his rights are not always fulfilled. Instead, there are other means of change. The important point for the discussion here though is the recognition of the concept of rights for both.

Furthermore, by understanding Islamic Law as a whole, Islamic scholars recognized and discussed in some detail the "rights of Allah" and the "rights of humans." The "rights of humans" are individual rights with respect to people's property, honor and so forth. Since they are meant for individual interests of person, they individually have some discretion with respect to forgiveness, implementation and so on. The "rights of Allah" deal both with ritual acts of worship as well as laws that are required for the benefit of society or "public interest" (*maslahah*) as a whole. These laws cannot be overlooked or forbidden via human discretion. Instead, they are Allah's rights so they must be fulfilled.[2] (There is also a third category, which is an act that includes an aspect of it being a right of Allah as well as a right of humans.)

In the history of human rights in the West, rights-talk was originally the result of defending the individual from the oppression of the state. That historical reality is actually a very narrow sighted vision of rights. The Quran, the Prophet (peace and blessings of Allah be upon him) and Muslim jurists have used the word "right" in a much more general framework. There was no need for the conflict between the

---

[1] Beyond that, the rulers are explicitly required to behave on behalf of the ruled. An important principle states that the rulers' decisions made in regard to the ruled must be based on *maslahah* or public interest. For a detailed discussion, see Naasir al-Ghaamidi, "Qaaidah al-Tasarruf ala al-Raiyyah Manoot bi-l-Maslahah: Diraasah Taseeliyyah Tabqeeqiyyah Fiqhiyyah," *Majallah Jaamiat Umm al-Qura li-Uloom al-Shareeah wa al-Diraasaat al-Islaamiyyah* (No.46, Muharram 1430), pp. 155-218; Saeedah Bumiraaf, "Al-Taleel al-Maslahi li-Tasarrufaat al-Haakim," (Master's Thesis, University of Baatinah, Algeria, 2008).

[2] One of the differences between Islamic Law and Western thought is that the act of adultery is considered a violation of the "rights of Allah" from an Islamic perspective while it has become a matter of consent and freedom in contemporary Western thought. From the Islamic perspective, an act of that nature does not simply affect the husband, wife or family of those who commit that sin. Instead, it strikes at the very moral and actual foundation of society. Hence, it cannot be overlooked by society and the punishment for it must be great.

classes in order for Islam to recognize these specific rights. Instead, it was a command via revelation that established eternally, from an Islamic perspective, the rights of human beings.

At the same time, though, if one's conception of human rights is the "fact" that humans are somehow "sacred" in and of themselves and therefore deserving of specific general rights simply because they have been born as "humans," then one could argue that there is no such "human rights" in Islam. Actually, one could argue that such rights actually do not exist at all except in the minds of some theorists. Otherwise, rights actually have to be recognized and accepted by someone, as they cannot exist in a vacuum. (As shall be discussed later, from the Islamic perspective, humans are given rights by God.)

Similarly, if what one means by human rights is the idea that humans have a right to basically do what they please simply because they are humans, no society has ever accepted any concept of this nature. Perhaps only the most extreme of the human rights advocates would even propose or claim something of this nature. Otherwise, every society realizes that limitations must be put on the behavior of humans. Until now no society has accepted the "fact" that humans, for example, should be allowed to marry or procreate in any fashion that they wish—although there is no question that some human rights advocates are calling exactly for things of that nature.

However, if what is meant by human rights is the recognition that due to some authority, humans have rights upon each other which are inviolable, then Islam definitely supports and promotes this concept. It is this idea—that Islam gave humans numerous rights—that Islamic scholars have pointed to and can continue to point to that cannot be denied. This though does not mean that all rights are the same for every human simply because he or she is a human. That concept is foreign to Islam. Actually, that concept is foreign to most modern societies as well. Most societies, for example, distinguish between humans who are citizens and humans who are not citizens. They definitely do not give them all the same rights. Within a society, certain sectors of society are sometimes given less rights (such as those under a certain age limit) and others lose rights due to their own choices (criminals who have lost the right to vote, for example).

The conclusion is that "human rights" within an Islamic framework are rights given by Allah to humans. Since, in Islamic theology, Allah has all the authority, He is the only One who has the authority to grant humans rights, limit those rights, expand those rights or remove those rights from individuals.

Seen in this sense, and not in the extreme, secular sense of the modern human rights movement, Islam does indeed for something that could be called "human rights." However, it could be argued that all societies stood for something of this nature. It is simply a question and issue of how far one wants to go in claiming such rights for humans.

The Justification for "Human Rights" in an Islamic Framework

What is meant here by "justification for human rights" is the justification of the human rights sanctioned in Islam, as just described, and not an Islamic justification for the human rights of the contemporary human rights platform.

The question of the justification for such "human rights" in Islam is clear and uncomplicated. The source for such rights is Allah's revelation to the Prophet Muhammad (peace and blessings of Allah be upon him). Granted, non-Muslims may not find this justification convincing. However, that was the point of the earlier discussion: No one has been able to claim or declare any justification for human rights that must be or is acceptable to all. Thus, if Islam is to be faulted for supporting rights on a basis that is not acceptable to all, the human rights movement must be faulted for the same weakness. Actually, the human rights paradigm is in a much weaker position. At least among Muslims, there is a clear and definitive basis for human rights sanctioned by Islam. In the secular human rights paradigm, there is still no clear and definitive basis for human rights. The human rights movement simply has not come to terms with this reality and continues to try to enforce its will upon others, even though others simply do not believe in its rather weak foundations.

All that is being said here is that in Islam there are "human rights" and these human rights have been granted and declared by God. That should be sufficient for a Muslim to accept, respect and implement them in his or her life. These rights will be applied to any or all who are designated by Islamic Law as deserving of them. Like all systems—whether human rights utopian visionaries will admit to this or not—

some rights may be restricted to certain groups of people (like citizens) and under certain circumstances. This is simply another reality of the application of rights.

The particular justification for "human rights" in Islam, the fact that they have been revealed and sanctioned by God, has further ramifications, which are related to the unique characteristics of "human rights" within the Islamic paradigm.

Unique Features of "Human Rights" within the Islamic Paradigm

Now that it has been established that there is something within Islam that one may call "human rights,"it is also important to recognize how the "Islamic human rights" differ from the human rights proposed in the contemporary human rights paradigm.

Due to the source, foundation and basis of human rights in Islam, these "human rights" have some unique qualities that distinguish them from the human rights of the contemporary human rights paradigm. These unique aspects include the following:

(1)   "Human rights" in Islam are given by God; they are not rights that one human, a human organization or the entire body of humankind has given to any other. When humans give others anything, they may feel that they have the "right" to take it back, use it as leverage and so on. The Islamic rights have been declared by God. Humans had no role in bestowing them upon others.

(2)   Human rights, as outlined in Islam, are intrinsic and eternal rights, which cannot be cancelled, modified, abrogated or suspended; they are binding because they are ordained by the Great Creator (Allah Almighty). Therefore, no human being, whoever he may be, has the right to suspend or to transgress upon them. They do not lose their inviolability; not by willful relinquishment by the individual nor by the will of the society represented in the institutions, regardless of the nature of the institutions or of the authorities these institutions might have.

(3)   Since these rights are God-given, a Muslim believes that it is his absolute duty to believe in them and fulfill them. In other words, there should be a complete and sincere dedication to these rights on the part of the Muslim. Theoretically, these rights should not be compromised in the name of "personal interest" because a Muslim should believe that his ultimate personal interest is in

submitting to God. These are not simply political slogans put out to receive applause and praise from other countries of the world. These are the commands from Allah. Every Muslim takes them deadly seriously. They cannot be changed, tampered with, temporarily done away with—no matter how expedient that may be for the masses or the people in power. Furthermore, it is only Islam that gives these rights the moral backing and fortitude that can drive a people to truly sacrifice on behalf of these rights. The Muslim will risk his life for these rights, even if it means defending a non-Muslim of the Islamic state, for example, because he is doing that for the sake of Allah and his reward rests solely with Allah.

(4)   "Human rights" in Islam involve rights as well as prohibitions. In other words, there is more than the simple right to do something but there is also an emphasis on the obligation to do something. It is not simply a neutral system but a positive system in which people are obligated to do what is correct, noble and helpful toward others, assist in the enforcing of what is virtuous and assist in the removing of what is harmful. These societal obligations and rights rely upon one another to form the basis of a true fraternal society. Thus, when Allah speaks about the relationship between the believers, in particular, He emphasizes this mutual characteristic before mentioning any of the other characteristics of personal worship. Allah says, "The believing men and believing women are allies of one another. They enjoin what is right and forbid what is wrong and establish prayer and give zakah and obey Allah and His Messenger. Those - Allah will have mercy upon them. Indeed, Allah is Exalted in Might and Wise" (*al-Taubah* 71).

(5)   Human rights in Islam are not absolute rights. This fact is easily recognized and admitted, as opposed to some of the claims that Mayer and others make about rights in the contemporary human rights movement while in reality even in that framework, as discussed earlier, the claim to absoluteness is false. Thus, the community and individual members of society are protected by restricting even the rights that Islam has granted. Thus, there are, admittedly and for good reason, restrictions on freedom of expression in Islam, freedom of private ownership and so on. This aspect of "rights" in Islam is a distinctive feature of Islamic human rights and must be recognized from the outset.[1]

---

[1] Cf., Sulaiman al-Huqail, *Huqooq al-Insaan fi al-Islaam wa al-Radd ala al-Shubuhaat al-Mathaarah Haulahaa* (self-published, 2003), p. 53.

(6)   Human rights in Islam are fixed and not changing.[1] The Islamic view of the revelation that the Prophet Muhammad (peace and blessings of Allah be upon him) received is that it is comprehensive and flexible[2] and intended for all of humanity until the Day of Resurrection. Hence, it contains all of the basic human rights that humans shall ever need. One of the greatest disputes concerning contemporary human rights is that people are demanding "new" human rights that the nations who signed the original documents never envisioned. This is what all the commotion concerning the Cairo and Beijing Conferences was all about. From an Islamic perspective, the nature of humans has not actually changed over time. Hence, what humans need as human rights is something fixed and determinable and thus the religion of Islam came with what humans needed and there is no need for further dispute or claims for new types of human rights. Since the revelation has come from God, there is no need for groping and testing which rights may be good human rights and which may be harmful or do not make any sense. This is actually the process that is continuing to go on within the contemporary human rights movement, as they continue to debate the merits or demerits of newly proposed "rights."

---

[1] Some Islamically derived human rights will be based on texts which are definitive and there should be no debate about them. Others may be derived from conjectural (*dhanni*, non-definitive) evidences. Concerning those derived "rights," it is possible that scholars may differ over them. Such legal differences and interpretations are common among all legal systems. It should also be noted that Abou El Fadhl repeats in a number of his articles (such as the one in Runzo, et al.) a rather bogus argument in which he tries to paint all of the Shareeah as "vague" and therefore no one could say what is God's law. This is not the appropriate place to go into a lengthy refutation of his argument, but if his argument is to be taken seriously, it means that all human speech is vague and no one could say what anyone is trying to say, in contracts, law and so on. Abou El Fadhl goes into a rather bogus argument concerning knowing what is God's law. After discussing the well-known debate about whether or not every *mujtahid* is considered correct, Abou El Fadhl concludes that no one can state what is God's law and thus all laws are humans. However, he gives the impression that all the laws of Islam are a result of *ijtihaad* (juristic reasoning). But *ijtihaad* is only to be resorted to in the absence of a definitive text of the Quran and Sunnah. He never makes this point and his mostly non-Muslim audience probably does not realize the straw man argument that he is making. (Actually, if one were to take his argument seriously, then one could also not say what a human right is either because all the human rights documents have been open to discussion and debate.) Furthermore, his position is even more so weakened by the fact that many of the disputed issues related to the Islam and the human rights movement are not matters of *ijtihaad* but have to do with clear texts of the Quran and Sunnah.

[2] For more on this point, see the author's *A Guide for the New Muslim* (Islamhouse.com), pp. 18ff.

(7)   Human rights in Islam are comprehensive in nature. They include all types of rights, whether political, economic, social or cultural. They also cover rights related to the husband, wife and children, as well as rights of neighbors, travelers, elderly, and so on. In fact, even goes beyond the living to the rights of the deceased. Furthermore, it covers personal relations and ethics as well, such as rights related to one's honor and dignity, which would include positive aspects as well as prohibiting acts like envy, backbiting and so on. (Mayer, in particular, critiques these rights as frivolous, trivial and meaningless and states that they would never form part of international law[1] but this simply highlights the insufficiency of international law as every society can recognize the importance of standards of this nature.)

(8)   Human rights in Islam are practical and not simply theoretical. They have been the backbone and practice of numerous Islamic societies and communities throughout history, starting with, of course, but not ending with, the community of the Prophet and his Companions. No one claims that any society has been perfect and made up of "angels." However, for most part, these rights were there, protected and fulfilled from the top down.

(9)   Islam's view of "human rights" is also a dynamic one in the sense that it is involved with ethics, education and reformation. Once again, Islam being a complete code of life and a "closed system," brings to humans not only the rights that people deserve but also the motivation to enforce and protect those rights for others as well as for oneself. Islam inculcates within individuals the belief in Allah and Islam. It then trains the individual to become a true Muslim, thereby giving all others the rights that they deserve. For example, with respect to alcohol, Islam does not simply state that alcohol is forbidden and then expect everyone to abstain from alcohol. America's experience with prohibition demonstrated that such is a useless approach. However, when one first has a strong belief and confidence in the message, one has the internal strength and will-power to fulfill the guidance, even if it requires effort and sacrifice on one's part. Without this spiritual growth and development, humans have other forces working within them that may drive them to disrespect others' rights and not fulfill their obligations towards them. Thus, Allah

---

[1] Mayer, *Islam and Human Rights*, p. 68.

says, "Indeed, mankind was created anxious: When evil touches him, impatient, And when good touches him, withholding [of it], Except the observers of prayer - Those who are constant in their prayer…" (*al-Maarij* 19-22). This is an area in which the contemporary human rights paradigm has little direct involvement although numerous writers on human rights emphasize that the first step in truly implementing human rights is the proper education and respect for others' rights. But, once again, since the human rights paradigm has no true foundation to fall back on, this educational and developmental process will be lacking, as the content cannot be much more than an empty whole. The possible solution for the human rights paradigm is to then rely upon religion or other sources to fill this void. However, from a human rights paradigm perspective, this would probably create more problems than it would solve.

(10)   Human rights in Islam are both concerned with societal rights as well as individual rights. In the contemporary human rights movement, there has been a great deal of discussion over this question of society vis-à-vis individual. Most Western human rights proponents are somewhat adamant in their view that individual rights reign supreme. Socialist leading authors and some Muslim authors declare that the rights of society clearly take precedence over the rights of the individual.[1] The fact, as explained by al-Qaisi, is that in Islam there is a balance between the rights of the society/community and the rights of the individual.[2] Islam proposes that there is a middle ground—although it seems that proponents on both ends, such as socialists vis-à-vis writers like Mayer, cannot envision such a middle ground. There are times in which the rights of the individual will have to take precedence and then there are times in which the rights of the society will have to take precedence. Since the limitations of these are hard to define, God alone would be the only proper source to make such delineations.

---

[1] Khalid Abou El Fadhl has an illuminating discussion on this point wherein he argues that the Muslim's emphasis on societal rights is probably the remnant of socialist influences in the Third World prior to the 1980s. See Khalid Abou El Fadhl, "The Human Rights Commitment in Modern Islam," in Runzo, et al., p. 308.

[2] See al-Qaisi, p. 50. Mayer, *Islam and Human Rights*, p. 66, envisions a virtual complete dichotomy between the rights of society and the rights of individual, pointing to Islamic expressions as "trying to preserve traditional anti-individualistic, communitarian values and priorities while paradoxically trying to associate their projects with human rights."

One of the important aspects of Islam—perhaps this should actually say: one of the important aspects of those writing about Islam—is that it is honest in its treatment of issues. Instead of making such bold claims about freedom of expression and freedom of belief and then limiting freedom of expression and freedom of belief in numerous ways—which every society and nation does, no matter how much dedicated they are to the human rights platform, and one would hope that human rights advocates would have it that way—it clearly states that the rights people have are only those rights granted to them by Allah. There is no contradiction and no hypocrisy here.

Specific "Human Rights" in Islam

In this section, some important rights granted by Islam, which are often termed "human rights" today, will be discussed. Obviously, as can be seen in the documents in the Appendix, Islam grants a number of important rights that span the entire spectrum of human activity. However, here only a few examples will be given. These examples were not chosen at random. Instead, there is a particular reason for including each one of the topics discussed below. Thus, the first couple of examples highlight aspects that many seem to think are "modern inventions" and part of the entire European wave of bring rights to humans. The reality, though, is that they were established as part of the Islamic system centuries before modern European thought "discovered" them. The fourth example demonstrates how different priorities may be involved when it comes to rights. In particular, it highlights one of the greatest deficiencies of the contemporary human rights movement—the other systems that the human rights movement is tied into. Lastly, there will be a discussion of equality versus equity, wherein it will be recognized that Islam has granted many rights but those rights are not based simply on "equality" but on "equity," given the overall Islamic social framework.

Some human rights:

All Equal Before the Law: Article 7 of the UDHR states, "All are equal before the law and are entitled without any discrimination to equal protection of the law." This principle is a well-established principle in Islam. Islam starts with removing any form of racial prejudice or class distinctions.[1] Among the many texts of Islam related to this issue, the Prophet Muhammad (peace and blessings of Allah be upon him) said, "O people, truly your Lord is one and your [original] father was one. There is no superiority of an Arab over a non-Arab or of a non-Arab over an Arab or a white over a black or a black over a white except in the matter of God-consciousness."[2] With respect to the law in particular, the following hadith is relevant: One time some Muslims tried to convince a fellow Muslim who was very dear to the Prophet (peace and blessings of Allah be upon him) to intercede with the Prophet (peace and blessings of Allah be upon him) concerning a judicial case. The Prophet (peace and blessings of Allah be upon him) rejected the concept of such an intercession in the law and stated quite frankly, "The peoples before you were destroyed because if a noble committed theft among them, they would let him go while if a weak person committed theft among them, they would apply the prescribed punishment to him. I swear by God, if Fatimah, the daughter of Muhammad, were to commit theft, I would have her hand amputated."[3] This equality before the law was applied to non-Muslims, slaves and females.[4] Umar ibn al-Khattaab was the second caliph of Islam, a close Companion of the Prophet (peace and blessings of Allah be upon him) and one whose model is emulated by Muslims. He was well-known for his justice and equal treatment of all. Once, for example, he had the son of his governor in Egypt beaten by a non-Muslim citizen of Egypt, due to that son's earlier mistreatment of him.[5] When Ali[1] was the

---

[1] The interested reader may consult Muhammad al-Bahi, *al-Tafriqah al-Unsiriyyah wa al-Islaam* (Cairo: Maktabah Wahba, 1979), passim.

[2] Recorded by Ahmad and others. Authenticated by al-Albaani and Shuaib al-Arnaaoot. See, respectively, Al-Albaani, *Silsilat al-Ahaadeeth al-Saheehah*, vol. 6, p. 449; Musnad #23536

[3] Recorded by al-Bukhari and Muslim. Amputation of the hand is the prescribed punishment for theft.

[4] For numerous anecdotes demonstrating such equality, justice and removal of discrimination, see Sayed Kotb, *Social Justice in Islam* (New York, New York: Octagon Books, 1970), pp. 139-226.

[5] See Kotb, p. 161. The entire story may be found in Ali Muhammad al-Sallabi, *Umar ibn al-Khattab: His Life & Times* (Riyadh, Saudi Arabia: International Islamic Publishing House, 2007), vol. 1, pp. 191-192.

caliph, he found his stolen shield in the hands of a Christian. He brought the Christian to court and the Judge, Shuraih, asked Ali for the proof that it was his shield. When he was not able to produce any evidence, Shuraih decided the case in favor of the Christian, who later admitted his lie.[2] As for women bringing forth legal cases, a woman came directly to the highest authority in Islam, the Prophet Muhammad (peace and blessings of Allah be upon him), to register a legal complaint about her husband. This event has been preserved by Allah in the Quran, starting with the words, "Certainly has Allah heard the speech of the one who argues with you, [O Muhammad], concerning her husband and directs her complaint to Allah" (*al-Mujaadilah* 1).

Innocent Until Proven Guilty: Article 11 of the UHDR states, "Everyone charged with a penal offence has the right to be presumed innocent until proved guilty…" This is also a well-established principle in Islamic Law. In fact, Islam recognizes that individuals may or probably will make false claims against others. Thus, the burden of proof will lie upon the plaintiff and the defendant will be considered innocent unless proven otherwise. The Prophet (peace and blessings of Allah be upon him) clearly stated, "Were people to be given according to their claims, men would claim the wealth and blood of the people. But the burden of proof is upon the plaintiff and the taking of an oath is upon the one who denies [the allegation]."[3] Ibn al-Qayyim, who died in the 14th Century A.D., stated that there are three types of accused. One is an individual who has never been accused of any crime and is well-known for his righteousness. This type of person is to be released under his own recognizance until the matter is decided. The second is one who has been found guilty of crimes before or who has been clearly implicated in a crime. This person will be held until the proceedings concluded. The third is an unknown

---

[1] Ali ibn Abi Taalib was the cousin of the Prophet (peace and blessings of Allah be upon him) and the fourth caliph in Islam. Like Umar before him, he is respected and emulated by Muslims.

[2] Ismaaeel ibn Katheer, *al-Bidaayah wa al-Nihaayah* (Beirut, Lebanon: Maktabah al-Maarif, n.d.), vol. 8, p. 4; Ali ibn al-Hasan ibn Asaakeer, *Tareekh Madeenah Dimashq* (Beirut, Lebanon: Daar al-Fikr, 1995), vol. 42, p. 487. In both of these works, the chain for this report goes through Jaabir al-Jufi, which casts a great doubt on the authenticity of this story. However, a very similar story is found in a much earlier work with a different chain: Abu Nuaim al-Asbahaani, *Hilyah al-Auliyaa* (Beirut, Lebanon: Daar al-Kitaab al-Arabi, 1405 A.H.), vol. 4, p. 139.

[3] Recorded by al-Baihaqi and others.

person, who also needs to be held until the proceedings are finished.[1] It is to protect the innocent that the laws of testimony and witnessing is quite stringent in Islam.[2] Furthermore, it is also an established principle that if a case is not proven beyond doubt, the prescribed punishment is not to be meted out. Thus, Umar, the second caliph of Islam, said, "I much prefer not to implement the prescribed punishment over meting it out when there is some doubt."[3]

The rights of the poor and unfortunate—Strangely enough, in recent times, human rights has been packaged with capitalism (liberalism) and democracy. Each of these have their own great weaknesses. In the one, it is claimed by many that the rich keep getting richer and the poor keep getting poorer.[4] In the latter, it has also been claimed that it has become, instead of "one person, one vote," "one dollar, one vote." However, these structural issues, it could be argued, cause more harm to humans than any laws related to freedom or the like are rarely discussed by human

---

[1] Muhammad ibn al-Qayyim, *Al-Turuq al-Hukumiyyah* (Cairo, Egypt: Matbaah al-Madani, n.d.), p. 147.

[2] For more on this point, see Khadeejah al-Nabraawi, *Mausooah Huqooq al-Insaan fi al-Islaam* (Cairo, Egypt: Daar al-Salaam, 2006), pp. 312ff.

[3] Recorded by ibn Abi Shaibah with a broken chain. According to al-Albaani, it has been narrated in other works with authentic chains. In many books on human rights in Islam, such as al-Nabraawi (p. 312), one finds the hadith, "Put off the prescribed punishment due to any doubt." Another version of the same hadith states, "Abstain from the prescribed punishments upon the Muslims as much as possible. If the person has a way out, let him go. It is better for the ruler to make a mistake in forgiving someone than to make a mistake in meting out a punishment." However, as a hadith of the Prophet (peace and blessings of Allah be upon him) this is a weak narration. The strongest view is that it is a statement of Umar, as quoted above, and not a statement of the Prophet (peace and blessings of Allah be upon him). See Ismaaeel al-Ajalooni, *Kashf al-Khafaa* (Beirut, Lebanon: Muasassah al-Risaalah, 1405 A.H.), vol. 1, pp. 73-74; Muhammad Naasir al-Deen al-Albaani, *Irwaa al-Ghaleel fi Takhreej Ahaadeeth Manaar al-Sabeel* (Beirut, Lebanon: al-Maktab al-Islaami, 1985), vol. 7, pp. 361-362.

[4] Ishay (p. 260) notes, "Recent reports from the United Nations Development Programme show that the poorest countries are getting poorer, not just in relative terms, but also in absolute terms. Around 1.2 billion people live on less than $1 a day, and 2.8 billion on less than $2 a day. In Africa, reality shows its cruelest face: 46 percent of the population earns less than $1 a day, and foreign direct investment has fallen sharply since the mid-1990s, the $9.1 billion invested in 2000 amounting to less than 1 percent of total world investment. In Latin America and the Caribbean, the percentage of people living in poverty has increased, peaking at 40 percent during the 1990s."

rights activists. But, in the words of Freeman, "The discourse of human rights has, for example, not taken capitalism seriously."[1] Later he elaborates further,

Since the end of the cold war, Western policy-makers have presented human rights, democracy and market economies as a package. The relations between markets and human rights are, however, complex, problematic and not well understood… In many recent cases, this [deterioration of human rights] has been so because elected governments have pursued market-based economic policies that have not only worsened the protection of economic and social rights for the most vulnerable sections of society (especially women), but also provoked increases in crime that have led to restrictions on civil and political rights… Worse, the fashion for neo-liberal economic policies has reduced the protection of these rights for millions of people around the world who enjoy them least.[2]

Thus, it can be argued, when it comes to the rights of the poor, Islam takes those rights much more seriously than do the contemporary human rights movement, at least in its present form. Indeed, the focus has been so much on political rights and freedoms (and more recently on sexual rights) that alleviating poverty is not considered an aspect of "human rights." Griffin expresses a common view when he says, "This implies that welfare rights are, at most, ethical rights that one has as a citizen—civil rights, not human rights."[3] Perhaps this is not too surprising given that the contemporary human rights movement grew out of the European Enlightenment. In fact, many Western views of poverty are not kind to those who find themselves facing difficult circumstances in life.[4]

The situation in Islam is very different because Islam is not a set of laws but a complete social system that is geared to the welfare of humans. One of the institutional laws of Islam, for example, that does not receive the credit it deserves in

---

[1] Freeman, p. 173.

[2] Freeman, pp. 176-177.

[3] James Griffin, *On Human Rights* (Oxford, England: Oxford University Press, 2008), p. 177. Griffin himself concludes that "welfare" is a "human right"; however, he had to go through a long process to substantiate his claim.

[4] For a review of different worldviews on poverty, see Nasseri bin Taib, "Islam and Eradication of Poverty: An Ethical Dimension of Development with Special Reference to Malaysia's Five Year Plans" (Ph.D. Dissertation, Temple University, 1989), pp. 28-41.

fending off economic exploitation is the prohibition of interest. Although while the author is writing these words, interest-based banking and profit motive has caused a great deal of suffering to many in the United States and elsewhere, capitalist economists would probably consider it blasphemous to even speak of the removal of interest. However, the harm of interest is well-documented especially on the world's poor today.[1] Indeed, it can be argued that it has literally caused the death of many indigent persons . The debt servicing of lesser developed countries today is so great that they must sacrifice essential health and nutritional needs. It is dumbfounding to think that untold numbers of children are dying daily in lesser-developed countries due to the "tool" of modern capitalism: interest. Some African governments are forced to spend more on debt servicing than they spend on health or education.[2]

In this context, the UNDP (1998) predicted that if the external debt of the 20 poorest countries of the world was written off, it could save the lives of 20 million people before the year 2000. In other words, it means that uncancelled debt was responsible for the deaths of 130,000 children a week up until the year 2000.[3]

Ken Livingston, Mayor of London, claimed that global capitalism kills more people each year then were killed by Adolf Hitler. He blamed the IMF and World Bank for deaths of millions due to their refusal to ease the debt burden. Susan George stated that every year since 1981 between 15 and 20 million people died

---

[1] McGoldrick, p.31, notes that even some feminists are "wary of human rights approaches because they may not address structural inequalities."

[2] Cf., Noreena Hertz, *The Debt Threat* (New York: HarperBusiness, 2004), p. 3. Donnelly puts the blame for these realities on "neoliberalism," which he argues is very different from the human rights perspective that he defends. In his words (p. 48): "In fact, microeconomic, utilitarian 'neoliberalism' is fundamentally opposed to the liberal human rights perspective I defend... its logic of efficiency contrasts sharply with the logic of individual human rights. Neoliberal equality involves political indifference to competing preferences—unbiased treatment in the marketplace—rather than guaranteed access to essential goods, services, and opportunities. And neoliberal structural adjustment is very different from the welfare states of Europe and North America with which the Universal Declaration model has (rightly) been specially associated." However, those welfare states that he praises and supports have made only meager steps in solving the kinds of structural issues referred to in the text above.

[3] Ali Mohammadi and Muhammad Ahsan, *Globalisation or Reconolisation? The Muslim World in the 21st Century* (London: Ta-Ha Publishers, Ltd. 2002), p. 38.

unnecessarily due to debt burden "because Third World governments have had to cut back on clean water and health programmes to meet their repayments."[1]

Poverty can have a devastating effect on individuals and families. Worse yet, there is no question that there is today a circle of poverty wherein poverty virtually breeds poverty. The Prophet Muhammad (peace and blessings of Allah be upon him) actually instructed Muslims to seek refuge in God from poverty due to the debilitating effects in can have.[2]

At the same time, though, poverty is not considered a curse nor is it necessarily the individual's own fault. In fact, if one to honestly ponder one's own situation, one would recognize that most of an individual's money making ability is due to circumstances completely beyond his control: what parents he was born to, what society he was born in, what era he was born in, what mental and physical disabilities he was free of and so forth. Instead, being poor is a trial from God, as is being wealthy. (In fact, the trials of the wealthy are greater because they have more means and opportunities to misuse the bounties that they receive from God.) In Islam, one's value and worth is not determined by how much wealth one has. Instead, it is determined by one's piety, regardless of how poor one may be. Thus, God says, "Indeed, the most noble of you in the sight of Allah is the most righteous of you" (*al-Hujuraat* 13). Thus, the poor are full members of society, deserving of respect and good treatment. The Prophet (peace and blessings of Allah be upon him) even stated that the majority of the inhabitants of Paradise will be the poor and that they will enter Paradise forty years before the others.[3] In fact, the Prophet (peace and blessings of Allah be upon him) said about the poor and the weak in the society, "Seek your weak for me for you are given sustenance and victory due to the weak among you."

Thus, the Muslim believer realizes that it is his responsibility to aid those less fortunate than himself. Allah describes the believer as, "Those within whose wealth is a known right, for the petitioner and the deprived" *(al-Maarij* 24-25). A story in

---

[1] Mohammadi and Muhammad Ahsan, p. 43.

[2] Recorded by al-Nasaaee in *al-Kubraa*, al-Haakim and others. Authenticated by al-Albaani. Cf., *Saheeh al-Jaami al-Sagheer* #2165.

[3] Hadith of this nature may be found in *Sahih al-Bukhari.*

the Quran[1] describes how a people's attempt to prevent the poor from sharing in their wealth led to their destruction. Furthermore, the Prophet (peace and blessings of Allah be upon him) said, "One is not a believer if he goes to bed with his stomach full and his neighbor is hungry."[2] Additionally he said, "One is working on behalf of widows and the poor is equivalent to one who is striving for the sake of Allah or one who spends the entire night fasting and daytime praying."[3]

Islam therefore sets up institutional apparatus to help the poor (such as the zakat or alms-giving, which is one of the pillars of Islam, the establishment of endowments to assist the poor, other forms of wealth distributed to the poor via the public treasury, additional taxes on the rich to meet the needs of the poor and so on). In addition, voluntary assistance to the poor is greatly encouraged throughout the Quran and Hadith. According to the majority of the Muslim jurists throughout the history of Islam, the poor can be defined as, "one who has no property or no lawful and suitable earnings to meet his normal requirements such as food, clothing, accommodation and other necessities, for himself and his dependents, in a way which is neither prodigal nor niggardly."[4] It is this minimum level that would be considered one's "human right" from an Islamic perspective. Although this is very important for human dignity, it is not accomplished in a vacuum. In other words, it is not simply a matter of providing material means but providing material means in the overall Islamic society, which encourages all to better themselves spiritually, morally and financially.

The Limits of Governmental Power: When reading about the history of human rights in the West, numerous authors emphasize how it was a reaction to the extremes of governmental power. Europe had gone through a long history of both church control and the concept of the divine right of kings. In Islam, as is not uncommon when comparing Christianity with Islam, the situation was very different because the Prophet Muhammad (peace and blessings of Allah be upon him), as

---

[1] Found in *al-Qalam* 17-33.

[2] Recorded by al-Haakim, al-Tabaraani, al-Baihaqi and al-Bukhari in *al-Adab al-Mufrad*. Authenticated by al-Albaani. See *Saheeh wa Dhaeef al-Jaami al-Sagheer* #5382.

[3] Recorded by al-Bukhari.

[4] Taib, p. 68.

opposed to the Prophet Jesus (peace and blessings of Allah be upon him), was also the head of a government. Thus, from the outset, the rules of good governance were laid down by the Prophet (peace and blessings of Allah be upon him) himself and followed by his Companions afterward. From the outset, obedience to the ruler was conditional upon obedience to God. Hence, the limits of the ruler were already set and established. In fact, when a military leader during the time of the Prophet (peace and blessings of Allah be upon him) went too far in his demands on his soldiers, the Prophet (peace and blessings of Allah be upon him) clearly stated, "There is to be no obedience to a created being if it involves disobedience to Allah."[1] Thus, the ruler is not free to demand any more than what the Law has given him. Furthermore, the ruler must realize that he is bound to the citizens and must act in their best interests. The Prophet (peace and blessings of Allah be upon him) prayed to God, "O Allah, if anyone is in charge of anything for my *Ummah* and he is harsh upon them, then be harsh upon him. And if anyone is in charge of anything for my *Ummah* and he is gentle upon them, then be gentle with him."[2] The Prophet (peace and blessings of Allah be upon him) also said, "The just will be with Allah upon pulpits of light to the right of the Merciful, and both of His hands are right hands. They are the ones who are just with respect to rulings, people and what they are in charge of."[3] The Prophet (peace and blessings of Allah be upon him) also, "No one is given charge of the affairs of the Muslims except that if he does not strive on their behalf and act sincerely toward them, then he will not enter Paradise with them."[4]

The early caliphs followed the guidance of the Prophet (peace and blessings of Allah be upon him) and set the example for all who should come later, including today. Abu Bakr, the close Companion to the Prophet (peace and blessings of Allah be upon him), was the first caliph in Islam. His inaugural speech is probably well-known to all students of Islamic history. In it, he stated,

---

[1] Recorded by Ahmad, al-Tabaraani and others. Another narration is, "…if it involves disobedience to the Creator." According to al-Albaani and Shuaib al-Arnaaoot, it is authentic. See *Silsilat al-Ahaadeeth al-Saheehah*, vol. 1, p. 297; *Musnad Ahmad*, #1095.

[2] Recorded by Muslim.

[3] Recorded by Muslim.

[4] Recorded by Muslim.

O people, I have indeed been appointed over you, though I am not the best among you. If I do well, then help me; and if I act wrongly, then correct me. Truthfulness is synonymous with fulfilling the trust, and lying is tantamount to treachery. The weak among you is deemed strong by me, until I return to them that which is rightfully theirs, Allah Willing. And the strong among you is deemed weak by me, until I take from them what is rightfully (someone else's), Allah willing.… Obey me so long as I obey Allah and His Messenger. And if I disobey Allah and His Messenger, then I have no right to your obedience.[1]

The following anecdote demonstrates Umar's, the second caliph, view of the ruler:

'Umar stood up and delivered a speech in which he said: "O people, whoever among you sees any crookedness in me, let him straighten it." A man stood up and said: "By Allah, if we see any crookedness in you, we will straighten it with our swords." 'Umar said: "Praise be to Allah Who has put in this ummah people who will straighten the crookedness of 'Umar with their swords."[2]

As is said, "Power corrupts." Throughout Islamic history, rulers have exploited their power and position—although perhaps not like those who believed in the Divine Right of kings, as in Europe. However, scholars continually took it upon themselves to at least attempt to correct them and to use any leverage that they could against them. They had some solid to rest their complaints upon that gave them great legitimacy: The fundamental teachings of the religion of Islam. Obviously, Islam does not call for revolting against legitimate rulers and there is also a proper etiquette to be following when correcting them. But it does call for attempting to restrain the rulers and guiding them back to the straight path. For this reason, Islam has a rich history of scholars standing up to the rulers on behalf of the masses and demanding that the rulers give the people their rights—even though they may not have referred to them as "human rights." A classic example is that of al-Nawawi, who wrote and spoke directly to the rulers on a number of cases. His advice and

---

[1] Quoted in Ali al-Sallaabee, *The Biography of Abu Bakr As-Siddeeq* (Riyadh, Saudi Arabia: Daar al-Salaam, 2007), p. 246.

[2] Al-Sallabi, p. 213.

words have been well-documented and preserved. In reality, though, he was simply one among a large number of such scholars.[1]

Justice and Equity: The Arabic words for "justice, just, equity," such as *adl* and *qist* and their related terms, are some of the most repeated terms in the Quran.[2] Similarly, there is an equivalent emphasis given to prohibiting *dhulm* (wrongdoing, oppression, tyranny).[3] This emphasis on justice and equity—as opposed to mere equality—is related to Islam's stance on many of the contemporary human rights concerning women. In the contemporary human rights documents the emphasis is on equality and not on equity. The emphasis in Islam is on what is equitable. Hence, there is going to be great differences between the two approaches. Equity and justice demands that laws differ under different circumstances or for different members of society if the circumstances require that.

When it comes to being a full human being and being a servant of God, there is no difference between men and women. Hence, there has never been any discussion in Islam, like there was in the West and in Christianity, as to whether women even possess souls. This type of equality between men and women is well-established in Islam and probably recognized by Allah. The following Quranic

---

[1] For a history of the relationship between the scholars and the rulers, see Abdul Azeez al-Badri, *al-Islaam bain al-Ulamaa wa al-Hukkaam* (Madinah, Saudi Arabia: al-Maktabah al-Ilmiyyah, n.d.).

[2] For example, *adl* or justice occurs 13 times, *idiloo*, the command to be just, occurs twice, *tadiloo* occurs 4 times, the word *al-qist* (just, justice) occurs 15 times, *al-muqsiteen* (those who are just) occurs 3 times, and so on. See the relevant entries in Muhammad Fuad Abdul Baaqi, *al-Mujam al-Mufahras li-Alfaadh al-Quran al-Kareem* (Cairo, Egypt: Daar al-Hadeeth, 1364 A.H.). The emphasis on justice is so great in the Quran and Sunnah that it led the famed Islamic scholar ibn Taimiyyah to state, "Allah will support a just state even though it is a disbelieving state while He will not support a tyrannical state even if it were a Muslim state. See Ahmad ibn Taimiyyah, *Majmooah Fataawa ibn Taimiyyah* (Riyadh: collected by Abdul Rahmaan ibn al-Qaasim and his son Muhammad), vol. 28, p. 146.

[3] Kaamil al-Shareef notes how there is nothing explicit in the international human rights documents about actively opposing and eradicating *dhulm* or oppression, tyranny and related practices. (Interestingly, many countries remained colonies even after their home countries signed the UDHR.) Al-Shareef notes that from the first time the Prophet Muhammad (peace and blessings of Allah be upon him) formed the Islamic State in Madinah, he constructed a constitution with the Jewish communities and other non-Muslim communities in the area. This constitution is filled with the concept of mutual support and assistance to oppose any and all forms of oppression and tyranny. See Kaamil al-Shareef, "Huqooq al-Insaan fi Saheefah al-Madeenah," in *Huqooq al-Insaan bain al-Shareeah al-Islaamiyyah wa al-Qaanoon al-Widhiee* (Riyadh, Saudi Arabia: Naif Arab Academy for Security Sciences, 2001), vol. 1, p. 76.

verses, for example, touch upon this point: "And do not wish for that by which Allah has made some of you exceed others. For men is a share of what they have earned, and for women is a share of what they have earned. And ask Allah of his bounty. Indeed Allah is ever, of all things, Knowing" (*al-Nisaa* 32); "Indeed, the Muslim men and Muslim women, the believing men and believing women, the obedient men and obedient women, the truthful men and truthful women, the patient men and patient women, the humble men and humble women, the charitable men and charitable women, the fasting men and fasting women, the men who guard their private parts and the women who do so, and the men who remember Allah often and the women who do so - for them Allah has prepared forgiveness and a great reward" (*al-Ahzaab* 35); And their Lord responded to them, 'Never will I allow to be lost the work of [any] worker among you, whether male or female; you are of one another. So those who emigrated or were evicted from their homes or were harmed in My cause or fought or were killed - I will surely remove from them their misdeeds, and I will surely admit them to gardens beneath which rivers flow as reward from Allah , and Allah has with Him the best reward'" (*ali-Imraan* 195).

There is actually a strong movement under foot to remove any kinds of differences between men and women. The Convention on the Elimination of all Forms of Discrimination Against Women was one of the first steps to redress many unjust discriminatory acts against women. However, the language of strict equality as opposed to equity troubled some nations, leading many not to ratify this document. Even Tunisia, definitely one of the most liberal of the Muslim states, entered reservations to this convention. Baderin explains that this document may have gone too far even for this more liberal state:

It is noteworthy however that even Muslim countries, such as Tunisia, considered today as having adopted a most liberal approach in their interpretation of Islamic law, entered reservations to the Women's Convention. This may not be unconnected with the revolutionary approach of the Women's Convention. It aims at 'a change in the traditional role of men as well as the role of women in society and in family and at achieving full equality between men and women. Muslim States tend to be cautious in that regard because both the society and family are very important institutions in Islam. The family and societal structures of Muslim societies are based on principles prescribed by the religion, reinforced by the law, and cherished by the individuals. Some family rights and obligations are not considered as entirely private family affairs but of concern to society.[1]

However, the "strict equality" movement became much bolder in more recent years. Many of the proponents of this view are very active in the human rights movement and, for example, had a very strong influence at the Beijing Conference in 1995 and its resultant Platform for Action.[2] Kausar has given a rather strong warning about this movement, as she writes in the introduction to her work covering this movement and its relationship to the Beijing Conference in particular,

I hope that the questions and issues identified and discussed in this book would reveal the influence of extreme feminists and women activists in international documents and politics. It seems urgent and imperative to look into the sexual agenda of the extreme feminists in international law and politics and to remind the United Nations to stay away from the strategies of feminist colonization.[3]

The document from the Beijing Conference states, "responsibility for ensuring the implementation of the Platform for Action and the integration of a gender perspective into all policies and programmes of the United Nations system must rest at the highest levels."[4] It is this issue of "gender perspective" that is of interest and that is a strong departure from earlier calls to change and, it could be argued, from what most cultures throughout the world currently accept. When asked to explain this phrase, the preparatory committee responded, "Gender refers to the relationship between women and men based on socially defined roles that are assigned to one sex or the other."[5] Bella Abzug, a famed American politician further clarified the issue by proclaiming,

---

[1] Baderin, pp. 61-62.

[2] For a complete review of the radical feminist movement and its role in the Beijing Conference, see Zeenath Kausar, *Woman's Empowerment and Islam: The UN Beijing Document Platform for Action* (Selangor, Malaysia: Ilmiah Publishers, 2002).

[3] Kausar, p. x.

[4] Quoted in Kausar, p. 104. Kausar (p. 106) notes that the phrase "gender perspective" was never defined nor elaborated upon in the document.

[5] Quoted in Kausar, p. 108.

[We] will not be forced back into the 'biology is destiny', concept that seeks to define, confine and reduce women to their physical sexual characteristics. The meaning of the word 'gender' has evolved as differentiated from the word 'sex' to express the reality that women's and men's roles and status are socially constructed and subject to change.

The concept of gender is embedded in contemporary social, political and legal discourse. It has been integrated into the conceptual planning, language, documents, and programmes of the United Nations systems. The infusion of gender perspective into all aspects of United Nations activities is a major commitment approved at past conferences and it must reaffirmed and strengthened at the Fourth World Conference on Women.[1]

The implication is very clear: There is nothing about these relationships, they have been designated through a history of oppression of one sex over the other and this is exactly what needs to be changed throughout the world. Kausar also notes, "To the believers and promoters of the gender perspective, the great obstacles in their way of fulfillment of the absolute freedom for sexuality and reproduction are the institutions of 'wifehood' and 'motherhood.' Hence, they try to portray the images of those 'wives' and 'mothers' who do not work outside for various reasons, as 'gender stereotypes'."[2] Adrienne Rich, a leading radical feminist, once wrote, "The patriarchal institution of motherhood is not the 'human condition' anymore than rape, prostitution and slavery are."[3] Alison Jaggar, another radical feminist, explains this point even further, stating, "[T] he radical feminist equality means not just equality under the law nor even equality in satisfaction of basic needs: rather it means that women, like men, should not have to bear children."[4]

There is no need to discuss any further some of the new directions of feminist human rights advocates. It is one thing to demand for women the rights that they have been denied, such as equal work for equal pay, but it is quite another to claim

---

[1] Quoted in Kausar, p. 109.

[2] Kausar, p. 115.

[3] Quoted in Kausar, p. 116.

[4] Quoted in Kausar, p. 124.

that there should be no distinction between men and women.[1] This stance would be considered unjust from an Islamic perspective, as there are numerous laws in Islam that distinguish rights of women from rights of men. In fact, it should be unacceptable from a purely rational viewpoint. It is amazing to see that the evidence that men and women are different continues to pile up yet these people, who claim to be "rationalists," want to ignore all of these differences and insist on making no difference whatsoever between men and women, claiming that the differences which include everything from brain size, brain activity and muscle build to personal traits are nothing but culturally or socially created.[2]

The basic unit of the social system of Islam is the family. This unit has to be stable, with people having both rights and responsibilities—it could not possibly be stable if only rights were claimed and no one accepted responsibilities. Thus, rights and responsibilities have been distributed by Islam to the individual members of the family (father/husband, mother/wife, child, sibling and so on). These rights and responsibilities are based on the principles of justice and equity and not "equality." Allah says, "They [women] have rights similar to those against them" (*al-Baqarah* 228). Thus, for example, the financial burden of a family falls completely on the shoulders of the husband/father, to the point that even if the wife is independently wealth this does not absolve the husband of his responsibility. It is based on this concept that ties together both rights and responsibilities—the latter which the human rights paradigm completely ignores—that a number of laws are different with respect to men and women in Islam. These would include laws related to marriage, divorce, custody and inheritance. In some cases, laws may favor the woman, as such would be fairer, while in many other cases, the laws favor the man due to the greater corresponding responsibilities on his shoulders.

There is one final point that deserves to be mentioned concerning human rights law and the rights of women with respect to marriage. Islam does recognize

---

[1] Some of the other major issues that these feminists are explicitly demanding as human rights is the complete control over one's body, including a complete right to abortion, as well as complete freedom of sexual choices.

[2] A couple of interesting books highlighting the differences between men and women are Barbara Pease and Allan Pease, *Why Men Don't Listen & Women Can't Read Maps* (Broadway, 2001) and John Gray, *Men are from Mars, Women are from Venus* (New York, New York: Harpers Paperback, 2004).

the concept of prenuptial agreements (*al-shuroot fi al-nikaah*). In other words, the woman can put stipulations into the contract that would allow her, if the two parties agree, to have additional rights than those created by the contract itself. In some schools of legal thought, this includes the right of *talaaq*[1] similar to the right of *talaaq* that the husband possesses. Thus, the woman does some have legal redress if she so demands concerning some of the rights related to marriage.

In sum, the Islamic view of society and, in particular, of the family definitely seems to be different from that of the contemporary human rights paradigm. For this reason, it differs with the demands of many human rights activists today concerning a large range of issues, especially women, family and sexual practices. However, the Islamic laws have their own internal logic and purpose. They are based on justice and equity within the framework of the entire social system and are not build upon a utopian and impractical "equality" that some human rights activists call for.

Before leaving this issue of women's rights in Islam, it is important to critique Mayer's discussion of "sexual stereotyping" in Islam as the basis for Islamic laws.[2] There is no need here to enter into a detailed refutation of the claims she makes. Instead, the goal is simply to emphasize that the human rights movement, especially the leading feminists among them, are simply creating a new stereotype of what it means to be a full person and full human. Thus, the Platform for Action and Beijing Declaration speak about what women need and must be provided for in order to allow them to fulfill their potential. They state, "The lack of a family friendly environment, including a lack of appropriate and affordable child-care, and inflexible working hours further prevent women from achieving their full potential."[3] Commenting on what is behind such a statement, Kausar wrote,

It seems important to clarify here that economic independence of women as such is not objectionable rather desirable. But when economic independence becomes a condition for equality, it becomes objectionable. The document's emphasis on the economic independence of women not only makes men and women

---

[1] *Talaaq*, often times (probably improperly) translated as "divorce," is one of three means by which a marriage is dissolved in Islam. For the most part, the right of *talaaq* rests with the husband.

[2] See Mayer, *Islam and Human Rights*, pp. 143-146.

[3] Quoted in Kausar, p. 155.

inimical to each other but also makes economic factor a criterion for equality, development and peace for women. Only those women are considered equal, peaceful and developed who have their own independent economic resources. For the same reason, the roles of women as wives and mothers are perceived as secondary and insignificant. These roles are considered obstacles in women's economic empowerment, equality, development and peace.[1]

The phenomenon of believing that being a wife or a mother is simply not satisfying or sufficient for a woman has spread among Muslim women, partially as a result of strong criticisms leveled against who chose to follow such a path. Such women are treated as backwards, uneducated or uncivilized. This is a new type of stereotyping and it should be considered just a much a violation of a human's rights as any other stereotyping that restricts choices for people.

Islamic "Human Rights": Between Practice and Theory

There must be some discussion of the divide between the theory and practice of "rights" within Muslim societies. There is undoubtedly a wide divide between the "human rights" that Islam propagates and the situation throughout the Muslim world today. As shall be noted below, this reality is perhaps the saddest aspect of the current relationship between human rights proponents and Islam.

It is sad in the sense that, in reality, if the human rights activists were truly interested in relieving the plight of the masses throughout the Muslim world, there would be many steps that they could take within the culture, beliefs and religion of the people. Unfortunately, Muslim civilization has been in decline for a long time. Consequently, due to the people's ignorance of their own religion, many non-Islamic practices have crept into the Muslims' lives. Muslim scholars and activists have been working hard to encourage the Muslims to change their ways and sincerely apply Islam completely in their lives. Many such improper practices touch upon the "human rights" of women, laborers, children, the poor and others. Since many

---

[1] Kausar, p. 157.

human rights activists who critique Islam are often feminists, the plight of Muslim women shall be highlighted here.[1]

Freeman begins his book on human rights with the story of Lal Jamilla Mandokhel, a sixteen year old Pakistani girl who, in 1999, was repeatedly raped and then eventually killed by her own family for bring "dishonor" to them. He goes on to note that hundreds of women and children are killed in Pakistan yearly in this fashion and those that perpetrate the crimes are rarely prosecuted.[2] Unquestionably, this is an atrocious situation. Similarly, in her article on fundamentalist religious practices, Howland cited the following laws,

In 1990 Iraq decreed that according to its fundamentalist ideology, men were allowed to kill their womenfolk for adultery. Since the killing is based on the husband's (not a court's) assessment of the situation, it may easily occur if the adultery is merely feared or suspected rather than real. Kurdistan has recently passed a law absolving a man for murder of his wife if he can prove she was morally disobedient.[3]

Such practices are not part of Islam and are simply cultural in nature. In fact, they contradict the laws of Islam. Muslim scholars should definitely work to remove such a law and grant the Muslim woman her proper rights. The laws of evidence in Islam are very strict. In particular, if a man claims that his wife has committed adultery but he cannot provide four witnesses to that effect, he can only resort to *liaan*, which is a process whereby the husband and wife are simply separated (no

---

[1] There is no question that numerous rights of Muslim women are violated throughout the Muslim world. These are not simply "human rights" but rights that Islam has given such women. If human rights activists first concentrated on these types of issues, their credibility and impact upon women would be much greater. In fact, Muslim scholars and leaders themselves are struggling to meet these goals. For example, in some parts of India, the Muslim woman still pays the dowry. In some parts of the Indo-Pak subcontinent, the woman only gets a dower in case of divorce or death, and even then she does not get it. These are the kinds of things that are existing in our culture that we can agree with them that have to be removed. Indeed, all of us should work to remove it. However, of course, our goal and why we are removing it may be very different. These are not "women's rights" in Islam, they are rights of Islam. To a Muslim, it should not matter whether something is concerned with men or women. These are all munkar that need to be removed or maroof that needs to be implemented.

[2] Freeman, p. 1.

[3] Howland, p. 171.

other punishment occurs to the woman). Furthermore, legal punishments in Islam are to be implemented by the state not by individual citizens. Thus, one finds in a hadith in *Sahih al-Bukhari* that the Prophet (peace and blessings of Allah be upon him) was actually explicitly asked by someone, "If a man finds his wife with another man, should he then kill that other man?" The Prophet (peace and blessings of Allah be upon him) actually showed disdain for the question itself. It was after this incident and questioning that the laws of *liaan*, referred to above, were revealed, thus prohibiting the husband from vigilantism, killing either the man or his wife.

Unfortunately, the above mentioned practices are simply the tip of the iceberg. Abdullah Hakim Quick mentioned that he visited an area in which the sisters there told him that they were taught and they believed that they will not enter Paradise unless they are beaten by their husbands. During a lecture, Bilal Philips, another contemporary Muslim scholar, presented newspaper articles in which Muslim women were put to death because their families did not provide enough continuous dower—it must be emphasized these were Muslim families not Hindu families.[1] In some areas, women do not receive their dowers except in case of divorce or death, which is a great transgression against their economic rights. Referring to another area, Quick spoke about how the Muslims there refused to allow their daughters to be educated.

There is no excuse for this kind of behavior among Muslims. This behavior means that a sector of the Muslim community is being abused. That is something that no other Muslim should bear. In fact, there should never be any need for a woman's movement in Islam because if one individual woman is having her rights violated, it should not be a concern simply for the other females. Instead, it is supposed to be a concern for all Muslims. They all together should rally around in support of the wronged individual until that she receives her due rights. Allah says in the Quran, "The believing men and believing women are supporters, helpers, protectors and allies of one another. They enjoin what is right and forbid what is wrong and establish prayer and give zakah and obey Allah and His Messenger. Those - Allah will have mercy upon them. Indeed, Allah is Exalted in Might and

---

[1] In Islam, the only dower to be paid is directly from the husband to the wife and it becomes part of her private property.

Wise" (*al-Taubah* 71). The Prophet (peace and blessings of Allah be upon him) also warned, "If the people see a wrongdoer and they do not take him by his hand [to stop him], Allah will soon then inflict them with a punishment that will cover all of them due to that."[1]

All sorts of ills are spread throughout the Muslim world. Illiteracy and poverty is rampant in many Muslim countries. These are characteristics that are repugnant to Islam. Muslim scholars and activists have attempted to improve or rectify the situation in various ways but until the success, it must be admitted, has been rather limited.

The sad part though is that if the human rights movement wished to improve the lot of numerous people throughout the world, it could work hand in hand with Islamic leaders to eradicate some of these ills. There are many common platforms that Muslims and human rights advocates could work on together.[2] However, at least in a couple of instances, it seems that the priorities of some human rights advocates is very different. It is not simply relieving human suffering but instead their agenda is an entire package. Indeed, within that agenda, they may also be priorities that may give the suffering of humans lower priority than other "more important" goals.

The last paragraph was written based on anecdotal evidence. One would hope that these anecdotes are exceptions to the general rule and that human rights advocates are willing to work hand in hand with Muslims to relieve human suffering wherever and however it may occur.

The anecdotal evidence that this author was referring to is the following two incidences that were related to this author by the well-known Muslim scholar Jafar Shaikh Idris. On one occasion a European woman told a Sudanese diplomat that her country would be willing to help the impoverished children of Sudan if not but for

---

[1] Recorded by al-Tirmidhi and authenticated by al-Albaani. See al-Albaani, *Saheeh al-Jaami al-Sagheer* #3057.

[2] Overall economic improvement of a society itself has been found to lead to more respect of the women of a country. See Alison Swicker Gokal, "Human Rights and Shari'a: An Essay on the development and use of Shari'a in Islamic States and its meaning for Women in Iran, a country with a history of criticism from Human Rights groups and the United Nations," *Hertfordshire Law Journal* 5(1), pp. 86-106.

the fact that his government did not support the rights of homosexuals. On another occasion, a Bangladeshi woman complained to a diplomat that their problem was that they had no fresh water to live off of and not the right to lesbianism. The response was a cold one.

The Most Important Human Right

It was mentioned earlier that the *Shareeah* has been revealed for the benefit and betterment of humankind. It must be realized, though, that this benefit and betterment is not only for this worldly life. In other words, it is for the benefit of humankind in both this life and in the Hereafter. This brings up a rather tricky question that no pure secularist or humanist can attempt to grapple with: What are the ramifications of the human rights paradigm, the Islamic paradigm or any other paradigm in not only this world but in the Hereafter? This question leads to the greatest right of humans—a right that cannot and could not be known by simple human pondering, experimentation or investigation. If this right is a reality—and obviously Muslims believe it is so—then it means that the human rights proponents may be leading humans to lose out on the greatest right that they can attain while violating the most important right of their being.

The right that is being spoken about here is the one described in the following hadith:

Muaadh ibn Jabal narrated: The Messenger of Allah (peace and blessings of Allah be upon him) said, "O Maudh!" I responded, "At your beck and call, O Messenger of Allah." He then said, "Do you know what is the right of Allah upon His servants[1]?" I said, "Allah and His Messenger know best." He replied, "The right of Allah upon His servants is that they worship Him and do not ascribe any partner to Him." Then after a while, he said, "O Muaadh ibn Jabal!" "At your beck and call, O Messenger of Allah," I replied. He then said, "Do you know what the right of the servants upon Allah is if they perform that?" I replied, "Allah and His Messenger know best." He then said, "The right of the servants upon Allah will be that He will not punish them."[2]

---

[1] "His servants" refers to all human beings.

[2] Recorded by al-Bukhari and Muslim.

It is very fitting that the Prophet (peace and blessings of Allah be upon him) used the word "right" (*haqq*) in the above hadith. This hadith is intrinsically related to the conflict between the contemporary secular human rights paradigm and the message of Islam. Indeed, it points to the fact that a real right is being ignored. All of the other worldly rights that the people are fighting over are all fleeting. Thus, they cannot compare to the right described by the Prophet (peace and blessings of Allah be upon him) in this hadith—a right, by the way, declared by God, the only One who has the true ability to enforce and implement what He decrees to be rights.

The above hadith actually demonstrates what a losing proposition the contemporary human rights paradigm is from an Islamic perspective. Worshipping Allah alone and not ascribing any partner to Him involves, among other things, submitting purely to Him and not accepting any authority above His word. Once one submits to others, arrogates to himself the right to change and abrogate some of Allah's laws, he is no longer submitting to Him, he is no longer worshipping Him alone and, in fact, he is setting up partners with Allah, either setting himself up as a partner, an institution or whatever. By violating the clear precepts of God's guidance by ignoring His laws or distorting them out of recognition, the individual is violating this sacred pact with Allah. In so doing, he loses Allah's promise to him that He will not punish him. Additionally, he may further incur Allah's wrath in this world as well due to his arrogant disobedience to God.

When viewed in this light, one can understand the trepidation involved for a Muslim in embracing the contemporary human rights paradigm. Many human rights advocates are completely secular in their outlook and do not seem to comprehend this internal conflict that they are trying to force upon Muslims. Those human rights advocates who consider themselves "religious" obviously have a very different understanding of what it means to be religious than the traditional Islamic understanding based around the clear texts of the Quran and Sunnah. Hence, they also do not see this dilemma for what it is. (In fact, many of them may simply blame the Muslim believer for not holding their "progressive" understanding of religion.)

The Muslim believer feels that it is actually the contemporary human rights advocates who are missing out. They are groping to find the best possible life for themselves and others. They seem to think that this will be founded upon giving the proper rights to all. However, they do not realize that in the process they may be stealing the most precious right of any human: the right to worship Allah alone and have Allah pleased with him or her in return.

This is perhaps the true impasse between the two paradigms. No secular paradigm can truly speak about God and the Hereafter. Thus, a Muslim believer's perception is simply different, completely different. This fundamental difference is a reality and people are going to have to accept it for what it is and do what is best within the two frameworks instead of forcing change upon those who do not want such change—especially not in the name of "freedom," "rights" and "liberty."

Conclusions

Definitely there is something within "traditional Islam" that is equivalent to a theory of "human rights." However, being based on revelation from Allah, this theory of "human rights" is very distinct from the contemporary secular/humanist human rights paradigm. Secular human rights proponents recognize these distinctions as weaknesses in the Islamic system; some even see no relevance of the Islamic system to human rights. On the other hand, it is its distinctive features that, Muslims would argue, actually make it superior to the man-made human rights paradigm. After reviewing the rather weak basis for the contemporary human rights paradigm, this author is obviously of the view that the Islamic program is the ideal program for humans to realize their true potential as humans and to receive all the rights that they deserve.

However, as was pointed out with respect to human rights in general, in the current state of the world, there is a great divide between the rights that Islam gives humans and what people receive in the Muslim lands, especially the women and weak among them. This opens the door for a great deal of cooperation between the "Islamists" and human rights proponents—that is, if the two parties are sincere in wanting to bring about what is best for the humans involved.

The Islamic approach to human rights can be described as a "holistic" approach in the sense that it touches upon every aspect of human life and uses every realm of life towards it ultimate goals for humans. However, it also goes beyond the realm of this life and guarantees for humans, if they so choose to accept its conditions, a right in the Hereafter, that is the most important right of all rights.

Islam and Human Rights: Contemporary Controversies

For many around the world, there is a fear that Islamic Law seeks to greatly restrict freedoms and "human rights." This is one of the first objections raised whenever any country proposes the idea of implementing Islamic Law. Such reactions have occurred in Pakistan, Nigeria, Mauritania and Algerian in the past. In fact, according to Baderin, "Such apprehension is believed to have also contributed to the abortion of the democratization process in Algeria in 1992 through a military takeover, when it appeared that the Islamic Salvation Front (FIS) would emerge victorious in the overall elections."[1]

It has been the thesis of this author that Islam and the contemporary human rights paradigm are two very separate and distinct entities. In fact, one could say that they have competing claims about humans and what is best for them. The last two chapters have demonstrated the great divide between the two approaches. This chapter shall deal with some recent controversies surrounding the issue of Islam and human rights. It will seek to discuss how much Islam supposedly violates the contemporary human rights platform by discussing some very visible cases. It will seek to determine how much of the current debate has been nothing more than hype and how much are true impasses.

The discussion will first center on a controversial issue that has been decided by a number of courts in France and Europe as a whole, long considered the bastions of the human rights movement. Drawing from some of the arguments and conclusions from that experience, the same sorts of arguments will be applied to some particular controversial issues related to Islam, in particular apostasy and freedom of speech.

The author would further like to point out that this chapter is being finalized shortly after the killing of Marwa Sherbini in Germany (apparently simply because of her Muslim dress and with an astonishing lack of response on the part of the German government as she was killed within a German courtroom) and after the very negative statements of French President Nicolas Sarkozy's about the Muslim woman's dress. Perhaps, this chapter should begin with some comment on the question of the Muslim woman.

---

[1] Baderin, p. 231.

It is amazing how some feminist writers speak about the pressure on Muslim women to wear the *hijab* (Muslim women's dress) and they could consider this societal pressure as a violation of her human rights.[1] At the same time, though, none of them seem to mention the great societal pressure on Muslim women to discard the *hijab*. This pressure comes within Muslim societies, as they are told that wearing *hijab* is a sign of backwardness[2], as well as within the "free" countries of the West, where some Muslim women face ridicule or truly fear for their safety if they dress in *hijab* in public. This author can attest from personal experience that the number of Muslim women who feel that way is not small at all. In fact, M. Parris argues that "social disapproval would be enough to discourage the veils."[3] Certainly, if one argues against the first scenario as a violation of human rights then this also must be considered a violation of their human rights, but for some reason this is not commented upon. Thus, McGoldrick can make a statement like the following, "[The veil] can in certain circumstances be an instrument of oppression"[4] while never making a statement like, "Prohibiting the veil can be an instrument of oppression." Furthermore, the Muslim woman's dress has become, once again, one of those paradoxes of human rights. Human rights advocates are fighting against the "freedom" to wear the *hijab* in the name of defending human rights. Thus, the French philosopher Bernard-Henry Levy said, "The fight against the veil is for the liberty of women and therefore for human rights."[5]

It is in the light of this type of atmosphere the human rights advocates continue to speak about Islam's contradictions with human rights theory. The serious question being posed here is: Does the human rights movement seemingly look the other way when it is "human rights proponents" who take stances that would not be

---

[1] Others recognize that it can be an autonomous expression of one's identity.

[2] It was only fifty years ago, during France's "civilizing mission," that on "on 16 May 1958 a formal ceremony took place in which French women unveiled Algerian women to show to the world that Algerian women were on their way to becoming modern" (McGoldrick, p. 55).

[3] See McGoldrick, p. 15. Parris further states, "Whether she feels oppressed or not, the condition oppresses her and it should not be seen in the streets of a liberal modern country" (McGoldrick, p. 15). One wonders what the meaning of the world "liberal" is if it cannot even acquiesce to people holding different views about dress.

[4] McGoldrick, p. 14.

[5] Quoted in McGoldrick, pp. 13-14.

acceptable when done in the name of Islam or in the name of any other religion for that matter?

The Islamic Headscarf Debate in Europe

By all accounts, Europe is considered the leader in the human rights movement.[1] Their laws, courts and procedures are definitely the most advanced when it comes to dealing with the details of human rights law. Numerous commissions and courts exist to ensure that every citizen receives his due human rights.

In the light of these facts, it is interesting to study the "Islamic headscarf debate" in Europe.[2] One would think that a woman's wearing of a headscarf would be a matter of individual conscience, freedom, choice and personal right. One would imagine that in Europe in particular there could be no hint of non-acceptance of such a freedom. One definitely would imagine that the human rights courts would never uphold a ban on such a simple, personal choice that humans make for their lives.

The European human rights courts got the opportunity to demonstrate exactly how "flexible" human rights thinking can be—in other words, they had an opportunity to demonstrate what could be prohibited while not violating human rights law. This opportunity came in 2004, when President Chirac and the French National Assembly passed a law prohibiting Muslim women from wearing *hijab* while at a state school.[3] Article 1 of the law states,

In State primary and secondary schools, the wearing of signs or dress by which pupils overtly manifest a religious affiliation is prohibited. The school rules shall state that a dialogue shall precede the institution of disciplinary proceedings with the pupil.[4]

---

[1] It is unique even with respect to the United States. In fact, even though many European lawyers were influenced by American law and trained in the United States, Goldhaber, argues that Europe is setting the lead and the example for the United States, although the United States lags behind on many important issues. See Michael Goldhaber, *A People's History of the European Court of Human Rights* (New Brunswick, NJ: Rutgers University Press, 2007), pp. 181-185.

[2] In preparing this section, the author greatly benefited from Dominic McGoldrick, *Human Rights and Religion: The Islamic Headscarf Debate in Europe* (Portland, OR: Hart Publishing, 2006).

[3] France, of course, has some rather unique beliefs about itself and its special form of society, laicite. In particular, they claim not to accept the concept of "minorities," as all are supposed equally "French."

[4] Quoted in McGoldrick, p. 90.

McGoldrick starts off his study of this issue with a statement that sounds very strange given the loud claims of universality from human rights proponents, especially those like Mayer and others who write specifically about Islam. After posing the question of whether the law passed by the French National Assembly should be considered a violation of human rights, McGoldrick states,

As for the answer to the abstract question, as is often the case, *international human rights law does not give a clear response,* particularly because conflicting rights may be involved. Rather, there has to be a specific national and legal context for the international human rights law to be applied and interpreted and situations have to be considered on a case-by-case basis.[1]

One must keep in mind that the so-called freedom of religion is not "absolute," as some writers would make one believe. The ICCPR clearly states, "Freedom to manifest one's religion or beliefs may be subject only to such limitations as are prescribed by law and are necessary to protect public safety, order, health, or morals or the fundamental rights and freedoms of others."[2] Even though the General Comment of the Human Rights Committee explicitly mentions the outer dress as being a manifestation of freedom of religion, the seemingly innocent act of one's dress can be scrutinized and restricted by invoking this about clause from the ICCPR.

Thus, even before the passing of the controversial law in 1999, it was already prohibited in France for all public servants to wear *hijab* or any religious signals. They had to be seen as being "neutral." This obviously applies to teachers in state schools as well.[3] This is a clear situation where the "interests of the state" take precedence over any perceived human rights that individuals may hold.

It is not simply in France where the headscarf was an important issue. In fact, in the famous case Dahlab v Switzerland, of a teacher of young schoolchildren who was prohibited from wearing the *hijab*[4], the European Court of Human rights "found that Switzerland was entitled to place restrictions on the wearing of the Islamic

---

[1] McGoldrick, p. 2 (emphasis added).

[2] Article 9 of the European Convention on Human Rights states virtually the same.

[3] For a discussion of the details of such practice in France, see McGoldrick, pp. 73ff.

[4] For more details about this case, see McGoldrick, pp. 120ff.

headscarf-*hijab*, as it was compatible with the pursued aim of protecting primary school pupils by preserving religious harmony."[1] They feared that the wearing of the *hijab* by a teacher of children at such an impressionable age would be akin to proselytizing.[2] This goes against their desire for "neutrality." While ruling on this case, the ECHR even stated, "It therefore appears difficult to reconcile the wearing of an Islamic headscarf with the message of tolerance, respect for others and, above all, equality and non-discrimination that all teachers in a democratic society must convey to their pupils."[3] The ECHR further stated,

In the light of the above considerations and those set out by the Federal Court in its judgment of 12 November 1997, the Court is of the opinion that the impugned measure may be considered justified in principle and proportionate to the stated aim of protecting the rights and freedoms of others, public order and public safety. The Court accordingly considers that the measure prohibiting the applicant from wearing a headscarf while teaching was 'necessary in a democratic society'.[4]

Germany, which has a very different cultural history than France, is another very vocal leader in support of international human rights. Interestingly, it also starting banning the headscarf for teachers in public schools. Interestingly, they distinguished between displays of Western religions (Christianity and Judaism) as opposed to oriental religions, arguing that the latter formed an essential component

---

[1] McGoldrick, p. 113. McGoldrick (pp. 114-115) points out that in a German case, the Ludin case, the majority of judges found that "there was insufficient empirical data to indicate any harmful influence of the headscarf-*hijab* on children." The minority judges argued, though, that the headscarf "could be prohibited without evidence that it actually endangered school peace."

[2] It is interesting that some argued that the pupils may be "influenced" by the dress of the Muslim woman. Interestingly, they do not seem to think that children will be influenced by teachers not wearing any religious apparel, perhaps giving the sign that religious practice is not that important in life. The child might think that his or her family (ignorant folk) all wear *hijab* while their teachers (the educated folk) do not—of course, the children will not understand that that is only because those teachers are prohibited by law from being religious in that setting but all are free to be irreligious in that setting. Perhaps this would give them the impression that religious people are not into education or something like that—certainly such youth should not be expected to understand the concept that in these settings one is not allowed to display religious symbols, which of course adds to the dichotomy of the issue where the child sees that in some arenas one does not or must not practice his religion.

[3] Quoted in McGoldrick, p. 129.

[4] Quoted in McGoldrick, p. 129.

of German culture.[1] In fact, the laws in the state of Saarland clearly stated, "School has to teach and educate pupils on the basis of Christian educational and cultural values showing due respect for the feelings of differently minded pupils."[2] A number of other states also passed laws with a similar tenor.[3]

As part of its secularization and modernization programs, Turkey banned both the male fez and the female veil in the early 1900s. In more recent times, they have supported their ban on the headscarf in government positions and universities as a support for their secularism. The Turkish government has argued that wearing the headscarf in Turkey is "becoming the symbol of a vision that is contrary to the freedoms of women and the fundamental principles of the Republic."[4] Although Turkey is not "officially" part of Europe and certainly does not have the same reputation for supporting human rights as the remainder of Europe, two of its famous cases was taken up by the European Court of Human Rights. These were the case of Leyla Sahin v Turkey and the case of Karaduman v Turkey.

In Karaduman v Turkey, a woman who had completed her studies was refused a graduation certificate because her student ID had a picture of her wearing a headscarf. In her complaint, she noted that identity card, passport and driving license carried photographs of her wearing a headscarf. One of the comments made by the European Court of Human Rights was the following:

by choosing to pursue her higher education in a secular university a student submits to those university rules, which may make the freedom of students to manifest their religion subject to restrictions as to place and manner intended to ensure harmonious coexistence between students of different beliefs. Especially in countries where the great majority of the population owe allegiance to one particular religion, manifestation of the observances and symbols of that religion, without restriction as to place and manner, may constitute improper pressure on students who do not practice that religion or those who adhere to another religion. Where secular universities have laid down dress regulations for students, they may ensure

---

[1] McGoldrick, p. 115.

[2] McGoldrick, p. 116.

[3] See McGoldrick, pp. 114ff.

[4] McGoldrick, p. 135.

that certain fundamental religious movements do not disturb public order in higher education or impinge on the beliefs of others.[1]

This ruling is even more interesting when one keeps in mind the point that McGoldrick makes, "It is important to note that while foreign female students at Turkish universities had freedom to dress as they wished, if they were Muslim, they could not wear the Islamic headscarf-*hijab*."[2] He also noted,

In Bulut V Turkey, the European Commission on Human Rights again upheld the ban on students wearing the headscarf-*hijab* in secular universities. It considered that Turkey was entitled to impose the restriction because, in view of the great preponderance of Muslims in the country, wearing the headscarf-*hijab* could in the circumstances amount to a form of pressure both upon non-Muslims and upon those Muslims who did not practice their faith.[3]

Once again, the pressure, even from authorities, to be areligious or secular is completely supported by human rights law. In fact, there seems to be no consideration of this type of coercion at all. Indeed, that one not take one's religion too far into the public sphere seems to be a requirement of the human rights movement.

The Grand Chamber of the European Court of Human Rights heard the case of Leyla Sahin v Turkey. In this case, Sahin, a student, was prohibited from wearing the headscarf as a university student in a public university. She was not allowed to attend lectures or examinations simply because she wore a headscarf.

The Court invoked its doctrine of 'margin of appreciation' as being particularly appropriate when it comes to the regulation by the Contracting States of the wearing of religious symbols in teaching institutions in view of the diversity of approaches taken by national authorities on the issue and the impossibility of discerning throughout Europe any uniform conception of the significance of religion in society. The Court stressed what was at stake in determining the margin of

---

[1] McGoldrick, pp. 138-139. But if those other students *chose* to attend a school in a predominantly Muslim land, shouldn't it be expected of them to accept the fact that the majority of the people around them would display Muslim traits?

[2] McGoldrick, p. 140.

[3] McGoldrick, p. 140.

appreciation, viz, the need to protect the rights and freedoms of others, to preserve public order and to secure civil peace and true religious pluralism, which was vital to the survival of a democratic society.[1]

Further, McGoldrick wrote,

The European Court thus accepted Turkey's two central contentions, namely that secularism (i) was consistent with the values of the ECHR and (ii) was necessary to protect the democratic system in Turkey that was necessary to support the ECHR. The Grand Chamber saw no reason to depart from the approach taken by the Chamber.[2]

If one looks closely at the decisions of the European Court of Human Rights—perhaps the most progressive and established body of its kind in the world today—one of two things must be occurring. One possibility is that the Court is recognizing that a society may have some overall goals and beliefs about itself that override human rights law. For example, the French have some rather unique beliefs about their society and these beliefs seem to be supported in the decisions of this respected Court. If that were the case, then an Islamic State certainly would have specific overall goals that should trump human rights theory. Besides the ultimate goal of living in accord with what God has revealed, it has specific goals about the nature of society. An Islamic society is supposed to be a moral society in which it is understood that it is not a society in which "everything goes." Furthermore, it also has a very clear picture of how the basic foundation of society, the family, should be constituted. If these goals of society can trump human rights, then there is no true conflict between an Islamic State and human rights because none of the laws of Islam are intended to harm or discriminate against anyone but are simply meant to promote the overall, positive goals of Islam.

However, that interpretation of the decisions of the Court is probably far-fetched. The second possibility is much more likely and it reveals an amazing fact about the entire human rights paradigm. The so-called human rights law, in the eyes of the European Court, is not about human rights. It is about secularism. Human

---

[1] McGoldrick, p. 152.

[2] McGoldrick, p. 153.

rights law is used as a foundation for the implementation and support of secularism. If there is a conflict between the two (individual rights and secularism) secularism takes precedence. This is something that human rights activists do not necessarily explicitly mention, although it would be hard to imagine that they are oblivious to this fact. Human rights supporters will counter by saying that these seeming exceptions to freedoms and human rights are done in the name of democracy and secularism—which, the argument wishes one to believe, allows all religions and peoples to be free. This is nothing but circular reasoning. It is saying that religions must be restricted so that people shall be free to practice their religion. Amazingly, this circular, illogical argument was almost explicitly stated by the Grand Chamber of the European Court, which once argued,

In democratic societies, in which several religions coexist within one and the same population, it may be necessary to place restrictions on freedom to manifest one's religion or belief in order to reconcile the interests of the various groups and ensure that everyone's beliefs are respected.[1]

They have actually stated the same as above but in a manner that it is obvious contradictory nature is hidden from view.

Actually, as can be noted in some of the statements above, the goal is either secularism or "democracy." The UDHR is even more explicit in tying human rights directly into "democracy." In fact, it virtually subjugates human rights to "democracy." Article 29 of the Universal Declaration provides for the limitation of human rights to meet 'the just requirements of morality, public order and the general welfare in a democratic society.' The point to note here is that they are not only implying that one must be "democratic" and "secular" but they are also implying that only secular and democratic rules have the right to restrict the freedoms and implement laws that seemingly contradict what should be a person's human rights. Thus, the human rights paradigm is once again dictating to nations what kind of government and nation they are permitted to have.

Democracy and secularism are replete with their own problems and issues—especially, once again, when it comes to its relationship with religion, which,

---

[1] McGoldrick, p. 150.

obviously, is core to the question of the relationship of Islam with human rights. On the relationship between human rights and democracy, Freeman wrote,

It is commonly believed that human rights and democracy are mutually supportive or related to each other by definition. The Vienna declaration of 1993, for example, asserted that democracy and human rights were 'interdependent and mutually reinforcing'. The relations between the two are, however, quite complex. Similar values, such as respect for the dignity of the individual, may form the basis of both human rights and democracy. Democracy may also be, empirically, the best form of government for protecting human rights, although some electoral democracies fail to protect economic and social rights, while some authoritarian regimes do so quite well (Chun 2001). Nevertheless, human rights and democracy have different, and potentially competing, theoretical foundations. Democratic theory asks who ought to rule, and answers 'the people'. Human-rights theory asks how rulers ought to behave, and answers that they ought to respect the human rights of every individual. Democracy is a collective concept, and democratic governments can violate the human rights of individuals. The concept of human rights is designed to limit the power of governments, and, insofar as it subjects governments to popular control, it has a democratic character. But human rights limit the legitimate power of all governments, including democratic governments. Human rights are consequently often protected by entrenching them in constitutions. This transfers power from democratically elected political decision-makers to judges, who are usually not democratically elected.[1]

Then again, one has to wonder whether the European Commissions were truly deciding in favor of democracy. McGoldrick writes,

In a case like Leyla Sahin v Turkey the Court effectively decided that particular individuals, or even the majority of them, had to pay the price for maintaining the general principle of secularism because that principle was in their long-term interests. In one sense, it is analogous to a national constitutional rule that

---

[1] Freeman, pp. 71-72. People critique the socialist governments for being the worst violators of human rights yet they forget that socialism—in the eyes of many—is the greatest form of democracy.

allows restrictions on rights so as to defend a democratic national constitutional system from abuse.[1]

This highlights both the confusion of the human rights paradigm and one of the internal inconsistencies of the democratic ideal. The statement says: The majority may have to suffer in order to enforce secularism and ensure that democracy is not abused. That is a famous debate in democracy theory: How can the will of the majority be kept from being abused by the majority?

It seems that the European Commissions are just as confused about human rights as anyone else—sometimes sacrificing it for the sake of national goals, other times realizing that it is not the ultimate goal and that secularism or democracy are the true ultimate goals. In any case, it is important that these confusions and goals of human rights law be made clear for everyone to understand and see.

Certainly any Muslim or Islamic state could argue on the basis of their "culture," their unity, etc., that women should not be allowed to wear "provocative" clothing and that non-Muslim religious symbols should not be allowed in public. True this would be more far-reaching than any of the laws that were discussed above but at least they would make "rational." That is, the newly passed laws in Europe concerning *hijab*, for example, forbid women from wearing the *hijab* in the workplace or at school while they are free to wear it at home (where most of them time that would not be wearing it) or in the mosques.

It is interesting to note that some human rights organizations, such as Human Rights Watch, Minority Rights Group and the International Helsinki Federation for Human Rights considered that the French law banning the *hijab* was a violation of human rights.[2] However, they were definitely a minority view.

Before concluding this discussion of the headscarf debate in Europe, it is interesting to mention a number of other cases that existed in Europe. These cases highlight the inconsistencies of human rights law and make one wonder exactly what is the goal and purpose behind such laws. McGoldrick has mentioned a number of other cases in the following passage:

---

[1] McGoldrick, p. 289.

[2] McGoldrick, p. 98.

Unsurprisingly, the outcome of individual cases has varied even when the facts and issues appear similar. In one case, a Muslim woman in an underwear shop was considered by her employer to be dressing too modestly and thereby not encouraging shoppers to buy underwear. It was held that the employee could be dismissed. In 2003, the French Appeal Court authorized a young Muslim woman to wear her Islamic scarf at her place of work. The woman, Dallila Tahri, had been dismissed in July 2002 by a telemarketing firm, for insisting on wearing her scarf against the wishes of her employers who wanted her to wear a briefer veil that would not have covered her neck and ears. The Appeal Court's decision confirmed a French employment tribunal's ruling on 17 December 2002 that her dismissal by the telemarketing firm was 'manifestly illegal'. There have been examples of veiled women being banned from crèches, banks and *human rights organizations*[1] for refusing to remove their veils. In such cases the ideology of public sector principles, which already apply in a widely defined sector, are being carried over into the private sector. In addition, there are obvious difficulties if particular state functions are privatized or partly privatized but still subject to extensive governmental regulation.[2]

This European experience with laws pertaining to *hijab* brings up a rather interesting question that perhaps very few today have thought to: Are religions freer to practice under Islamic law than under secular/democratic rule? Given all of the propaganda concerning Islam and freedom of religion, this question probably sounds strange. In general, Islam respects the practice of each individual religion within a certain public framework. In the private framework, though, each religion is virtually completely free to practice its religion on its own, including choosing its own leaders, having its own legal system and abiding by its own set of personal laws. This is something that is not available, in general, to adherents of religions in secular societies. In secular societies, all must abide by the one general law with no exceptions for specific religious practices. Hence, for example, in the United States, Muslims cannot apply Islamic laws in matters of custody, divorce, maintenance, marriage and the like—unless such laws are completely consistent with the secular law, which makes it a moot point. On all of these points, the Muslim must sacrifice

---

[1] Emphasis added.

[2] McGoldrick, p. 81

his religious law in order to confirm with the secular law. Even in business matters, the laws of banking, real estate and investment are such that, in the United States for example, it is difficult for Muslims to run a completely Shareaah-compliant without running afoul of some specific secular law. From this author's experience, this reality of freedom under secularism has created much difficulties for Muslims attempting to practice their faith in secular lands. Thus, even though human rights supporters and secularists claim that it is their view that provides for religious freedom for all, it is precisely their practices that greatly restrict religious freedoms. In a sense, then, it is clear that in some ways religions are definitely much freer to practice their tenets under Islamic rule than under secular law.

Given this reality of secularism as well as the European headscarf debate, it is not surprising to find religiously-minded people, in particular Muslims among them, objecting to some of the trends that are existing. As has been implied throughout this work, "freedom" and "rights" seems to imply for everything except religion. Oh alluded to this reality when she wrote, "For people to have the freedom to believe, but not have the freedom to express that belief, nullifies the importance of such freedoms."[1] On this point, one also recalls the words of Larry Alexander,

Freedom of religion must mean freedom to practice religions that are "wrong" about religious truths. And freedom of association must mean freedom to associate with the "wrong" people for the "wrong" purposes.
Yet, here is the problem. Any philosophical account of political morality will, perforce, take a stand on what is true, right, and valuable and what is not.[2]

In the headscarf debate, the systems of Europe, its human rights apparatus include, have taken the state concerning what is right and wrong about expressing one's religion. Finally, Pope Benedict XVI has also chimed in on this issue, saying,

A tolerance that allows God as a matter of private opinion but which excludes him from public life, from the reality of our lives, is not tolerance but hypocrisy . . .

---

[1] Oh, p. 88,

[2] Alexander, p. 148.

When Man makes himself the only master of the world, and master of himself, justice cannot exist.[1]

Freedom of Speech: From a Hadith to Cartoons

Events in the past number of years, ranging from the Salman Rushdi affair to more recent events, can definitely give the impression that Islamic law violates the principles of freedom of speech and expression. In this section, this topic shall be discussed from a secular theoretical viewpoint, followed by the most spectacular recent case and concluded with a human rights legal perspective on the issue.

Is Freedom of Speech a Human Right?

Stanley Fish is an outspoken professor and author who has written a book entitled, *There's no such thing as free speech... and it's a good thing, too*. In an interview he explained his point,

Milton's recognition of a general condition: free speech is what's left over when you have determined which forms of speech cannot be permitted to flourish. The "free speech zone" emerges against the background of what has been excluded. *Everyone* begins by assuming what shouldn't be said; otherwise there would be no point to saying anything.

Another example: one of the foremost proponents of free speech in this country is Nat Hentoff, a journalist well known for his jazz criticism and who has also taken up the cause of free speech no matter how disreputable or offensive the speech in question. But about two years ago he recanted, when he drew the line at campuses allowing certain forms of anti-semitic speech to flourish. Disciples of a certain Muslim group came to campuses and began to talk about "bagel eating vermin who had escaped from caves in the middle ages and were now, as then, infecting the world". Hentoff said this has gone too far. My point is that everyone has such a trigger point, which is either acknowledged at the beginning or emerges in a moment of crisis.[2]

---

[1] Quoted in McGoldrick, p. 16.

[2] "'There is no such thing as free speech': an interview with Stanley Fish" (http://www.australianhumanitiesreview.org/archive/Issue-February-1998/fish.html).

Obviously, in an Islamic social framework, freedom of speech and expression is going to be restricted—like it is in any other society. The purpose and goal behind such restrictions are very clear. One is not free, for example, to attack religion and other's personal honor. Similarly, for the sake of the morality of society, one is not free to display pornographic materials of any kind.[1]

It is interesting at this point to compare, contrast and analyze two very separate events—one event involves the banning of a hadith of the Prophet (peace and blessings of Allah be upon him) and the other involves defaming the Prophet (peace and blessings of Allah be upon him) in newspaper cartoons. The reactions to them—or the lack thereof—demonstrate once again that "human rights" is a very slippery slope, that sometimes seems very arbitrary and other times simply seems anti-religion.

Banning a Hadith of the Prophet (peace and blessings of Allah be upon him)

In late 2008, some right-wing organizations in the United States forced the Muslim Students' Association at the University of Southern California to remove some "offensive hadith" from the organization's website, which was run under the auspices of the university. This university is a private organization and has more freedom in such issues but the entire fiasco does spread some light on the realities of "human rights" today.

The hadiths in question were those related to events that will occur before the Day of Judgment, in which there will be a battle between Muslims and Jews. One such hadith from the website reads, "Abdullah b. 'U mar reported Allah's Messenger (may peace be upon him) as saying: You and the Jews would fight against one another until a stone would say: Muslim, here is a Jew behind me; come and kill him." This is a statement from the Prophet (peace and blessings of Allah be upon him) that simply

---

[1] There is no question that one can go overboard when it comes to restricting "free speech" and the like. It is interesting to note that Mark Twain's *The Adventures of Huckleberry Finn* is among the most censored books of the 20th Century. "In the ALA's overall list of the 100 most censored books for 1990–2000, *The Adventures of Huckleberry Finn* ranked fifth." Some of the common complaints about this book that was written many years ago and whose author died in 1910 are, "in addition to complaints of racial slurs, profanity, and violence, the objector noted that traditional values were not represented and that the novel was culturally insensitive." See Jonathon Green and Nicholas J. Karolides, *Encyclopedia of Censorship* (New York, NY: Facts on File, Inc. 2005), p. 5.

describes the reality of a future event—much like the story of the Rapture believed in by some Christians that state that all others will perish and be destroyed. There is no command to kill those people today nor is there any command to bring that event about as soon as possible. However, these words of the Prophet (peace and blessings of Allah be upon him) were greatly distorted in order to bring about an attack on them and force their removal. Thus, David Horowitz referred to them as, "hadith calling for Muslims to murder Jews as a condition for redemption."[1] The David Horowitz Freedom Center worked with the Simon Wiesenthal Center to draft a letter because they were "disturbed that a call for genocide should be on the USC server."[2] The hadith wss indeed duly removed but somehow this entire incident, with its gross distortion of what the hadith stated, barely caused on a blip on the media radar. One would have expected that there would have been at least a stir and media movement from the other student organizations concerning what forms of free speech will be banned next by the university.

That hadith, it was felt, was such that it needed to be removed from an educational website in a society that believes in "free speech." What then should be the response to cartoons which maliciously depict the Prophet Muhammad (peace and blessings of Allah be upon him) and which it could have been known from the outset would lead to outrage and possibly violence? That incident is the next topic of discussion.

Defaming the Prophet (peace and blessings of Allah be upon him) in Newspaper Cartoons

As opposed to the first incident above, the publishing of cartoons in Danish newspapers defaming the Prophet (peace and blessings of Allah be upon him) and picturing him as a terrorist was well-covered in the media for a number of reasons.

---

[1] This kind of argument resonates with many Christians who somehow believe that by acts like supporting the creation of Israel they are somehow facilitating Armageddon and the return to Jesus. See Grace Halsell, *Forcing God's Hand: Why Millions Pray for a Quick Rapture ... and Destruction of Planet Earth* (Amana Publications, 2002).

[2] The details of this event and the false accusations concerning the hadith may be found at http://www.reutrcohen.com/2008/08/usc-provost-orders-usc-msa-to-remove.html. Obviously, there is no call for genocide in the hadith nor is there any hint of it being a requirement for redemption. Indeed, the entire battle could be one of self-defense on the part of the Muslims.

In September 2005, the Danish newspaper *Jyllands-Posten* published twelve cartoons about the Prophet Muhammad with the reasoning that they had been suffering under "self-censorship" when it came to the Prophet (peace and blessings of Allah be upon him). In other words, the entire goal seems to have been to demonstrate freedom of expression as a human right.[1]

This leads to the following very important question that actually is a critique of human rights theory as a whole: What is the benefit of providing such "human rights" and defending them when, in reality, it seems that they contributed nothing to human dignity and welfare except to the vague notion of someone have a "right"?

The Legal Framework

Those who engage in the practice of defaming Islam or the Prophet Muhammad (peace and blessings of Allah be upon him) have claimed that they are simply exercising their rights of freedom of speech, opinion and belief. Within the Western framework, they may have an argument. At the end of January 2006, the Blair government was defeated in attempting to pass a law that would have made ridiculing faiths and religious leaders a type of hate crime. In an interview with BBC on February 1, 2006, a Member of Parliament who opposed the bill said that the law must protect life and property but need not protect "feelings." Thus, as long as a person's "life or property" is not physically attacked, one should be free to express what one wishes. This approach reflects the currently accepted Western emphasis on individual rights as opposed to social welfare. Indeed, in the aftermath of the dispute concerning the cartoons mocking the Prophet Muhammad (peace and blessings of Allah be upon him), some in Europe are proudly—actually, arrogantly—proclaiming that they have the right to insult God if they want to.

---

[1] For a discussion of what led up to the cartoons and some of the responses, see Human Rights Watch, "Questions and Answers on the Danish Cartoons and Freedom of Expression," at http://www.hrw.org/legacy/english/docs/2006/02/15/denmar12676.htm; Rachel Saloom, "You Dropped a Bomb on Me, Denmark—A Legal Examination of the Cartoon Controversy and Response as it Relates to the Prophet Muhammad and Islamic Law," *Rutgers Journal of Law and Religion* (Volume 8, Fall 2006); Ana Belen Soage, "The Danish Caricatures Seen from the Arab World," *Totalitarian Movements and Political Regimes* (Vol. 7, No. 3, September 2006).

Whatever the man-made legal rights may be and ignoring the gravity of the manner in which such insults have been done, what if such statements do eventually lead to harm and attacks on life and property? What is the logic behind permitting "causes" that lead to "harm" while prohibiting the act of harm in itself? For example, is there anything reprehensible about drunk driving in itself or is it prohibited by law only due to the harm that it can result in, the loss of life and property?

In any case, of course, simply because something is legal by law does not necessarily imply that it is moral or even wise. In the current environment, this is the more important issue. One should never invoke one's "rights" in defense of harmful and hateful actions that could eventually even lead to bloodshed. Thus, it is not a matter of passing new laws, as was attempted in England. Instead, it is a matter of recognizing the morally correct path to follow and the prudent path to follow.

At the same time, though, according to European Human Rights law prohibiting such cartoons should not have been considered a violation of human rights, at least not if some other cases may be taken as precedence. In the case of Hertzberg and Others v. Finland, the State Party was being sued because it had censured television programs dealing with homosexuality. Their defense was that the action was done in order to protect public morals. The Human Rights Commission found that the State Party had not violated Article 19 of the ICCPR and further stated,

It has to be noted, first, that public morals differ widely. There is no universally applicable common standard. Consequently, in this respect, a certain margin of discretion ought to be accorded to the responsible national authorities.[1]

Furthermore, in Murphy v Ireland, the European Court of Human Rights upheld a decision banning a commercial religious broadcast in Ireland on the basis that it would be too divisive, given Ireland's tumultuous history of religious conflict.[2]

---

[1] Quoted in Baderin, p. 231.
[2] See McGoldrick, pp. 167-168.

The Dangers of Defamation and Ridicule in the Media: Why Freedom of Speech Must be Restricted

No one can doubt that images and stereotypes presented in the media are very powerful. In many cases, they form a person's perception of reality. In particular, many of the West, more so in the US than in Europe, do not have first hand experiences with Muslims and therefore they must rely on the media to develop their perception of Islam and Muslims. Nacos and Torres-Reyna write, "Some 55 years ago, before the advent of television, Walter Lippmann observed that what people know about the world around them is mostly the result of second-hand knowledge received through the press and that the 'pictures in our heads' are the result of a pseudo-reality reflected in the news."[1]

Thus, the press bears a great responsibility. What and how the press presents something can ultimately lead to decisions of life and death or war and peace. Indeed, political cartoons and yellow journalism can be sufficient to drive a country into a war frenzy—as they appeal to the emotions of the masses. Anyone familiar with the Spanish-American War is well aware of this fact. There were powerful forces in the United States who were determined to go to war against Spain, fearing the "Spanish threat" on the Americas. *The New York Morning Journal* (headed by William Randolph Hearst) and *The New York World* used yellow journalism to depict Spanish oppression in Cuba. Even though President McKinley wanted to follow a hands-off policy, the effect of the media was such that it led to great popular support to come to the aid of the Cubans. This put great pressure upon President McKinley, leading him to send the Battleship Maine to Havana in 1898. The Battleship Maine exploded. The Navy at that time was unable to determine the cause of the explosion—although more recently many have concluded that it was due to mechanical problems. At that time, the Spanish offered to turn the issue of responsibility over to an arbitrator. However, even without being able to identify the exact cause of the explosion, the media pounced on the opportunity, spread the slogan "Remember the Maine, to hell with Spain" and continued to depict the evil

---

[1] Brigitte L. Nacos and Oscar Torres-Reyna, "Framing Muslim-Americans Before and After 9/11," in Pippa Norris, Montague Kern and Marion Just, eds. *Framing Terrorism: The News Media, the Government and the Public* (New York: Routledge, 2003), p. 135.

Spaniards in their cartoons. The United States was now definitely going to war. The lessons of those events should not be lost on the world today.

Another example of the influence of the press is discussed in the following passage: "The racism that led to the internment of Japanese-Americans during World War II was created partly by the motion picture industry, which for years typecast Orientals as villains, and partly by the press, especially the newspapers of William Randolph Hearst."[1] Today, of course, the internment of the Japanese is something that Americans remember with shame—while at the same time, the media continues to play its role, as can be seen by the fact that even years after the Invasion of Iraq, many people still believed that Saddam Hussein was directly involved in the 9/11 attacks..

The result—if not the goal—of blatant defamation and ridicule is the dehumanization of the enemy. When the enemy is dehumanized, one no longer cares how much they suffer. One can then do things to them that humans would, under normal circumstances, completely shun—such as all forms of horrendous torture and humiliation.

Defamation versus Critique

Most of the inhabitants of the West are non-Muslims. Many of them are not Muslim because they feel that there is something unacceptable in Islam. Hence, it is to be expected that they would have thoughts about the Prophet Muhammad (peace and blessings of Allah be upon him) that Muslims would not share. The Prophet (peace and blessings of Allah be upon him) himself debated with Jews, Christians and polytheists who did not believe in him and even after discussions with the Prophet (peace and blessings of Allah be upon him) himself they remained true to their own faiths. Thus, no one, Muslim or otherwise, should be surprised if a non-Muslim has a lesser opinion of the Prophet (peace and blessings of Allah be upon him) than a Muslim has.

The Quran welcomes discussion and dialogue with the non-Muslims: "Invite (mankind, O Muhammad) to the Way of your Lord with wisdom and fair preaching,

---

[1] Nacos and Torres-Reyna, p. 152.

and debate with them in a way that is better. Truly, your Lord knows best who has gone astray from His Path, and He is the Best Aware of those who are guided" (*al-Nahl* 125). In fact, more than once, the Quran even asks the non-Muslim to, "Produce your proof if you are truthful" (*al-Baqarah* 111; *al-Naml* 64; *al-Qasas* 75).

Thus, the objection is not to non-Muslims—especially in their own lands—expressing their view about the Prophet Muhammad (peace and blessings of Allah be upon him). If what they state is sincere and rational, then they can be spoken to on a rational level with sincerity. Indeed, Muslims welcome such discussions and, in reality, such discussions are best for Islam, because, to this day, most of the people in the West have distorted views of Islam. If they wish to express their views honestly and discuss them honestly, they can be presented with the truth of Islam. This act in itself may reduce the tension and discord that exists between non-Muslims and Muslims. In fact, after the events of 9/11, many Americans took the effort to find out more about Islam and there was much more exposure of Islam and Muslims. Thus, in comparing surveys before 9/11 and after 9/11, Nacos and Torres-Reyna found that "the American public in general viewed Muslim-Americans more favorable after September 11, 2001."[1]

One can respond to rational arguments with an honest and straightforward rational discussion. However, there is no real response to something that is meant only to ridicule, insult or harm.

In sum, if non-Muslims want to debate and discuss the real issues of religion and belief, Muslims are more than ready to do that. If they resort to defamation and ridicule, then they should not be surprised if they are in turn responded to with hatred and disrespect. There is no need for them to then ask, "Why do they hate us?" The answer should be clear.

Actually, there is one author who makes the point that those in the past who attacked the Prophet Muhammad (peace and blessings of Allah be upon him) did so in an attempt to avoid discussing the real issues. Minou Reeves writes in a work entitled *Muhammad in Europe: A Thousand Years of Western Myth-Making,*

---

[1] Nacos and Torres-Reyna, p. 152.

The trouble started with early medieval Christian polemicists. They chose not to attack Islamic theology, which was too seductive in its simplicity and clarity, and which raised too many awkward questions about Christian dogma. Nor could they cast doubt on the pious practice of ordinary Muslims. Instead, anticipating the worst excesses of tabloid journalism, they personalized the issue and attacked the Prophet of Islam, dispensing with all but the barest knowledge of any facts and inventing falsehoods. Muslims could not reply in kind, since they are told by the Qur'an to revere Jesus as a holy prophet.[1]

It seems that not much has truly changed over the centuries.

Summary

Islam restricts manners to be consistent with the public morals and welfare of the people. From an Islamic perspective, any publication that would be offensive to religion must be considered the most threatening and dangerous. The question of restricting such "freedoms" is well-known and established in every society. While restricting such "freedoms" one can still have respect for the freedom itself. Donnelly explained this issue well while discussing another aspect of freedom of speech, pornography. He stated,

This is particularly important because most of the "hot button" issues in recent discussions have occurred at the level of implementation. For example, debates about pornography are about the limits—interpretation or implementation— of freedom of expression. Most Western countries permit the graphic depiction of virtually any sex act (so long as it does not involve and is not shown to children). Many others countries punish those who produce, distribute, or consume such material. This dispute, however, does not suggest a rejection of human rights, the idea of personal autonomy, or even the right to freedom of speech. We should also note that controversy over pornography rages internally in many countries. Every country criminalizes some forms of pornography, and most countries—Taliban Afghanistan being the exception that proves the rule— permit some depictions of sexual behavior or the display of erotic images that another

---

[1] Minou Reeves, *Muhammad in Europe: A Thousand Years of Western Myth-Making* (Washington Square, New York: New York University Press, 2000), p. x.

country has within living memory banned as pornographic. *Wherever one draws the line, it leaves intact both the basic internationally recognized human right to freedom of speech and the underlying value of personal autonomy.*[1]

Freedom of Religion: The Controversy over Apostasy

Much has been said in recent years concerning the law of apostasy in Islam. Again, Article 18 of the Universal Declaration of Human Rights, signed by the vast majority of today's countries, reads: "Everyone has the right to freedom of thought, conscience and religion; this right includes freedom to change his religion or belief, and freedom, either alone or in community with others and in public or private, to manifest his religion or belief in teaching, practice, worship and observance."

On the other hand, Muslims believe that the Prophet Muhammad (peace and blessings of Allah be upon him) said, "It is not legal [to spill] the blood of a Muslim except in one of three cases: the fornicator who has previously experienced legal sexual intercourse, a life for a life and one who forsakes his religion and separates from the community." (Recorded by al-Bukhari and Muslim.) The Prophet (peace and blessings of Allah be upon him) is also reported to have said, "Whoever changes his religion is to be killed."[2] (Recorded by al-Bukhari and others.)

---

[1] Donnelly, pp. 97-98, emphasis added.

[2] It should be noted that this hadith does not give the "wisdom" behind this law. Thus, the complete reasoning why an apostate should be killed is not explained in the text (other than the specific case in the other hadith of abandoning the community). Hence, any discussion of the reason behind the act can be considered no more than speculation and conjecture. This is a very important point because some people try to "defend" this law by deriving reasons behind it, such as the commonly heard argument that apostasy is a threat to the state and is therefore tantamount to treason; thus the state has the right to kill said individual. This rational argument is sometimes answered simply by saying, "I do not think that an individual's apostasy is a threat to the state." The fact is that the complete wisdom behind this ruling is not explained to humans in the texts of the Quran or Sunnah. For example, it could possibly be the case that if someone has grown up and is living in an Islamic state, there is no rational excuse for him to give up the religion of Islam and become an apostate. Perhaps such an act by such a person is so grave that God, his Creator, deems that he is no longer deserving of life. This would definitely be God's prerogative from an Islamic perspective. Again, this author is not stating that this is the wisdom behind the law of apostasy but is only saying that the real wisdom behind this law is not explained in the text and one must be cautious about stating what the reasoning is.

These texts from the Prophet (peace and blessings of Allah be upon him) have led the vast majority of Muslim scholars to conclude that the punishment for apostasy from Islam in Islamic Law is death. It is true that there are some, especially contemporary writers, who opt for very different conclusions and argue that such a death penalty is a misunderstanding of Islamic Law. This is not the proper place to enter into such a debate. Instead, this author shall presume that the opinion that has been held by the vast majority of the scholars is the correct opinion. This entire discussion, therefore, shall be in the light of that conclusion. If the harsher punishment can be "defended" from the current onslaught, any lesser punishments will, obviously, be even more so defensible.

Could God Legislate Death for Apostasy?

Many Christians, in particular, seem abhorred by the fact that Muslims could believe that God has legislated death for apostasy. This author has personally heard Christians claim, once again, that Islam must be some barbaric religion to believe in such a penalty. This attitude is very perplexing to this author. It is one thing to say, "We no longer believe in such a law" and quite another to say, "We do not believe in a God that would legislate such a penalty." In the former case, the individual is simply turning his back on what may have been part of his religion. Such an approach is common for modernist Jews, Christians and Muslims. However, the latter approach clearly denies what is stated in their holy books. (Unfortunately, this is also not uncommon for modernists. However, many less-extreme Jews, Christians and Muslims do not allow themselves to go that far.)

An in-depth study of all of the relevant Biblical texts is well beyond what is needed here. Hence, only one or two verses shall be commented upon.[1]

Exodus 22:20 reads, "He that sacrificeth unto *any* god, save unto the LORD only, he shall be utterly destroyed." Famed and widely respected Biblical commentator Matthew Henry had the following to say about this verse:

IV. Idolatry is also made capital, _v. 20_. God having declared himself jealous in this matter, the civil powers must be jealous in it too, and utterly destroy those

---

[1] The author would like to thank Br. Hadi Hashmi for his research paper, "Verses dealing with the Death Penalty for the Apostate."

persons, families, and places of Israel, that worshipped any god, save the Lord: this law might have prevented the woeful apostasies of the Jewish nation in after times, if those that should have executed it had not been ringleaders in the breach of it.[1]

Numbers 25:1-5 reads:

1 And Israel abode in Shittim, and the people began to commit whoredom with the daughters of Moab. 2 And they called the people unto the sacrifices of their gods: and the people did eat, and bowed down to their gods. 3 And Israel joined himself unto Baal-peor: and the anger of the **L**ORD was kindled against Israel. 4 And the **L**ORD said unto Moses, Take all the heads of the people, and hang them up before the **L**ORD against the sun, that the fierce anger of the **L**ORD may be turned away from Israel. 5 **And Moses said unto the judges of Israel, Slay ye every one his men that were joined unto Baal-peor.**

Another passage, Deuteronomy 13:6-11 is also quite telling:

6 If thy brother, the son of thy mother, or thy son, or thy daughter, or the wife of thy bosom, or thy friend, which *is* as thine own soul, entice thee secretly, saying, Let us go and serve other gods, which thou hast not known, thou, nor thy fathers; 7 *Namely,* of the gods of the people which *are* round about you, nigh unto thee, or far off from thee, from the *one* end of the earth even unto the *other* end of the earth; 8 Thou shalt not consent unto him, nor hearken unto him; neither shall thine eye pity him, neither shalt thou spare, neither shalt thou conceal him: 9 But thou shalt surely kill him; thine hand shall be first upon him to put him to death, and afterwards the hand of all the people. 10 And thou shalt stone him with stones, that he die; because he hath sought to thrust thee away from the **L**ORD thy God, which brought thee out of the land of Egypt, from the house of bondage. 11 And all Israel shall hear, and fear, and shall do no more any such wickedness as this is among you.

2 Chronicles 15:8-19 has the law being applied even to the young among the apostates. The relevant verses in that passage are verses 12-13 which read, "12 And they entered into a covenant to seek the LORD God of their fathers with all their

---

[1] Taken from *The Bible Suite Collection* (ValuSoft, 2006).

heart and with all their soul;   13 That whosoever would not seek the LORD God of Israel should be put to death, whether small or great, whether man or woman."

From the New Testament, one finds in Romans 1:20-32 that Paul approves of the death of idolaters, homosexuals and other sinners. This passage reads,

19 Because that which may be known of God is manifest in them; for God hath showed *it* unto them. 20 For the invisible things of him from the creation of the world are clearly seen, being understood by the things that are made, *even* his eternal power and Godhead; so that they are without excuse: 21 Because that, when they knew God, they glorified *him* not as God, neither were thankful; but became vain in their imaginations, and their foolish heart was darkened.   22 Professing themselves to be wise, they became fools,   23 And changed the glory of the uncorruptible God into an image made like to corruptible man, and to birds, and four footed beasts, and creeping things.   24 Wherefore God also gave them up to uncleanness through the lusts of their own hearts, to dishonour their own bodies between themselves:25 Who changed the truth of God into a lie, and worshipped and served the creature more than the Creator, who is blessed for ever. Amen. 26 For this cause God gave them up unto vile affections: for even their women did change the natural use into that which is against nature: 27 And likewise also the men, leaving the natural use of the woman, burned in their lust one toward another; men with men working that which is unseemly, and receiving in themselves that recompence of their error which was meet. 28 And even as they did not like to retain God in *their* knowledge, God gave them over to a reprobate mind, to do those things which are not convenient;29 Being filled with all unrighteousness,fornication, wickedness, covetousness, maliciousness; full of envy, murder, debate, deceit, malignity; whisperers, 30 Backbiters, haters of God, despiteful, proud, boasters, inventors of evil things, disobedient to parents, 31 Without understanding, covenant-breakers, without natural affection, implacable, unmerciful:32 **Who knowing the judgment of God, that they which commit such things are worthy of death, not only do the same, but have pleasure in them that do them.**

The above examples should be sufficient. The interested reader may further consult Deuteronomy 13:12-18 and Deuteronomy 17: 1-7.

Actually, as is well-known, the history of the official Christian church and many of its leaders on issues of this nature is very dark indeed. One did not need to be an apostate to be killed in the history of Christianity. Apostasy is to be distinguished from heresy, as is clear in the following passage from the *Encyclopedia Britannica*,

[Apostasy is] the total rejection of Christianity by a baptized person who, having at one time professed the faith, publicly rejects it. It is distinguished from heresy, which is limited to the rejection of one or more Christian doctrines by one who maintains an overall adherence to Jesus Christ.

Two examples from the history of Christianity dealing simply with heretics—not apostates—should suffice here. The Cathars, a pacifist heretical group of southern France, were crushed. Pope Innocent III declared a crusade against them. Here is how two Christian authors described part of that crusade:

In 1209, Arnold Amaury, abbot of Citeaux, called for the collective slaughter of all Cathars in the town of Beziers. His motto, which has carried forth into modern expression, stated, "Kill them all, the Lord knows those who are his." Only a small minority of the town, perhaps five hundred, was made up of Cathars, but all the city paid the price for guilt by association. Twenty thousand were killed. Thus began the wholesale slaughter of thousands of Cathars in the thirteenth century.[1]

Non-Catholics, of course, may respond to the above by putting the blood of those deeds on the hands of the evil Catholics. However, one should not forget Martin Luther's ruling concerning the Anabaptists, another pacifist heretical group who had the audacity to have themselves re-baptized when adults.[2] Martin Luther stated that such heretics are not to be tolerated and the only fitting punishment for them was hanging.[3]

This approach is in compelling contrast to the legacy of Islam. Not long after the death of the Prophet (peace and blessings of Allah be upon him), the caliph Ali

---

[1] Ergun Mehmet Caner and Emir Fethi Caner, *Christian Jihad* (Grand Rapids, MI: Kregel Publications, 2004), p. 183.

[2] One can only wonder what Martin Luther would have to say about today's "born again" Christians.

[3] See Caner and Caner, p. 162.

had to face the crisis of the heretical group known as the Khawarij. Although he sent people to preach to them to correct their misunderstandings, his approach was that they were not to be physically attacked by the state as long as they did not commit any acts of violence against the Muslims. The Khawarij did become violent and it became necessary for Ali to fight and defeat them. Afterwards, he was asked about them. He was asked if they were polytheists and Ali replied that they were fleeing from polytheism. When he was asked if they were hypocrites, he replied that hypocrites rarely remember and mention Allah. Finally, they asked him, "What are they?" He replied, "They are our brethren who revolted against us and we fought them only due to their revolting against us."[1]

In fact, one of the interesting aspects of the Sunnis compared to the different heretical groups is that the majority of the heretical groups believed in *takfeer* (declaring non-members to be disbelievers) and "the sword" (forcing others to accept their teachings and revolting against the rulers). Groups of this nature included the Mutazilah and the Khawarij, both of whom, as described earlier, Mayer praises—perhaps being unaware of this facet of Islamic history. The Sunnis would rarely resort to *takfeer* and virtually never revolted against rulers. Indeed, numerous writings were declared blasphemous and yet their writers continued to live in the Muslim community and their writings have been passed on until today, such as the writings of the majority of the "Islamic philosophers" so praised in the West.

Killing For God or For Country?

The history just referred to is actually very relevant for the contemporary discussion. It was this history that led to revulsion among Western thinkers to the idea of killing for the sake of God. There was so much killing of Christians by Christians in Europe that the great thinkers of Europe finally concluded that it makes no sense to kill "in the name of God."

It did not take long for what occurred in the particular circumstances of Europe to be accepted by Western thinkers as "universal principles." Nothing highlights this fact more than a short treatise prepared by the Institute for American

---

[1] Abu al-Fidaa Ismaaeel ibn Katheer, *Al-Bidaayah wa al-Nihaayah* (Beirut: Maktabah al-Maarif, n.d.), vol. 7, p. 290.

Values shortly after 9/11. This paper was entitled, "What We're Fighting For." It was signed by many of the leading intellectuals in the United States, including Francis Fukuyama, Samuel Huntington, Daniel Patrick Moynihan and many others—including some of the leading just war theorists of today, such as James Turner Johnson, John Kelsay and Jean Bethke Elshtain.

In the opening passages of that paper, they state the following:

We affirm five fundamental truths that pertain to all people without distinction:

1. All <u>human beings are born free</u> and equal in dignity and rights.

2. The <u>basic subject of society</u> is the human person, and the legitimate role of government is to protect and help to foster the conditions for human flourishing..

3. <u>Human beings naturally desire to seek the truth</u> about life's purpose and ultimate ends.

4. Freedom of conscience and <u>religious freedom</u> are inviolable rights of the human person.

5. <u>Killing in the name of God</u> is contrary to faith in God and is the greatest betrayal of the universality of religious faith.
We fight to defend ourselves and to defend these universal principles.

Points numbers four and five are of most interest here. This author has to admit that the logic of this preamble escapes him. For example, how did Point 5 become a universal principle?[1] It definitely goes against what the West believed in for centuries. In reality, to this day, it is not a "universal principle" within the West—as can be seen by Christians who have been fighting each other in Northern Ireland

---

[1] Note that the treatise never defines what is meant by "killing in the name of God." If they are referring to something like the Crusades or the Inquisition, such events have never been characteristic of Islamic practices and one would hope that to reject practices of that nature would be a universal principle. However, if they are referring to the concept that one believes that his belief in God requires that he may even have to kill another human for specific reasons, then it is definitely highly presumptuous of them to claim such as a universal principle. In fact, based on the texts of the Bible itself and the history of Western civilization, one could argue that the burden of proof is upon those who claim that God never condones any killing in His name as opposed to those who say that such is a possibility.

and those who have committed murder at abortion clinics in the name of God. It is astonishing to see that after mentioning the basic principles, they then say that they fight "to defend these universal principles."

At the very least, they should have said that they believe that these principles are good for all of humankind and deserving of the greatest amount of support. They way they have stated their case—and as signed by numerous dignitaries—has a fundamental logical flaw in it. How can they "fight" to defend the "universal principle" of "killing in the name of God is contrary to faith" while also fighting to defend the principle of "religious freedom" as one of the "inviolable rights of the human person"? From what they stated, one could argue that it is acceptable to fight for the sake of God against those people who kill in the name of God because killing in the name of God is contrary to faith in God, as they have stated!

But what have they done in reality? All they have done is replaced religion— for which one is not allowed to fight—with some principles that they have concluded—for which one is allowed to fight! Why should more weight be given to their devised principles rather than the principles that one believes has been revealed from God? Isn't fighting for man-made principles nothing more than a "secular holy war"? In one of his numerous writings, James Turner Johnson made a valuable comment that highlights the self-contradiction of the stance that these signatories have taken. He wrote,

However, when the state itself develops a state ideology, something very much like holy war reasoning reasserts itself in secular guise. Examples include the ideologies of nationalism, nazism, communism, ethnicity, and even democracy. The West, then, has not completely rejected war for religion, for something very like it lives on in the form of wars for various justifying ideologies.[1]

Now comes a very perplexing question for anyone who believes in God, which, it seems, is still the majority of humankind today: How is it that one is not allowed to fight for the sake of God's religion—God who created and nourished all of humankind—yet it is considered acceptable today to fight in the name of man-

---

[1] James Turner Johnson, *The Holy War Idea in Western and Islamic Traditions* (University Park, PA: The Pennsylvania State University Press, 1997), p. 60

made ideologies, such as "democracy" or "freedom"? Indeed, it is considered completely acceptable today to fight in the name of man-made "nations." People get together and form a nation, sometimes a result of most arbitrary historical events, and yet it becomes considered acceptable and logical for the people of that nation to kill others in wars carried out in the name of that nation. The same people who defend those types of wars, including many of the signatories to the above mentioned treatise, will condemn killing or fighting in the name of religion or for the sake of God. Which one should make more sense to the one who believes in God, regardless of whether he be a Jew, Christian, Muslim or whatever?

The issue becomes even more perplexing for those who believe in God: An individual can be jailed for life and even put to death for treason, all in the name of the state, yet at the same time, in the name of freedom of expression, anyone is allowed to say anything they wish about God, religion or virtually any other subject. The man-made entity called the state—which may not even exist tomorrow, such as Yugoslavia, or may even give up its overriding ideology, such as the USSR—has the right to put someone to death but God has no right to call for the death of any individual.

The result is a rather hypocritical situation. If such rights for states are accepted then they must also be accepted for God, especially when one's view of God embodies state, society and personal devotion, as in the case of Islam.

Treason and Apostasy

In sum, there is no question that the Islamic law of apostasy is a stringent one. Its most probable contemporary analogous case is that of treason. The penalty for treason ranges anywhere from life imprisonment (in many European states that have abolished the death penalty) to the death penalty (such as currently in the United States). The two cases are analogous because the type of apostasy for which a person may face the death penalty is akin to openly revolting against the Islamic state and all that the state stands for. This point is explained by Sheha as follows,

Sheha, pp. 153-154:

The killing of an apostate from the Islamic faith implies that such a person has violated the basis of Islam and attacked Islam openly and publicly with treachery and blasphemy. As such, he threatens the very basis of the moral and social order. This treachery may precipitate the beginning of internal revolution and dangerous rebellion within the Islamic society. This kind of crime is the most serious in any society, and therefore is called 'High Treason'… Execution of such an apostate is, in reality, a salvation for the rest of the society members from the maliciousness and violence he would spread if left to propagate his disbelief and blasphemy among the other members of the society. If such a person confines his disbelief and apostasy to himself, and does not proclaim and propagate it, he is left to Allah and the punishments of the hereafter. Allah knows best who believes and who rejects faith, who is sincere and who is a hypocrite. Muslim authorities only base their judgments and sentences upon open external matters and leave the internal realties to Allah.[1]

Additionally, Bilal Philips notes the following about the laws of apostasy in Islam,

One who personally abandons the faith and leaves the country would not be hunted down and assassinated. Now would one who apostates privately and remains in the Muslim state conforming to the outward rules of the state be tracked down and executed. The practice of setting up inquisition courts to examine people's faith is not a part of Islamic legal tradition.[2]

Historically speaking, the "traditional Sunnite" scholars were very reluctant to ever declare an individual a disbeliever or apostate. Naasir al-Aql noted that many famous scholars were known never to utter such a conclusion, although actions which comprise "apostasy" were present around them.[3] In fact, historically speaking, it was the, as Mayer calls them, "pro-human rights" schisms of the Kharijites and Mutazilah who were known for declaring Muslims outside of their sects as non-Muslims. In fact, those heretical groups were distinguished by two beliefs: *al-takfeer* (declaring those outside of their fold as non-Muslims) and *al-saif* (the sword,

---

[1] Abdul Rahman al-Sheha, *Misconceptions on Human Rights in Islam* (Riyadh, Saudi Arabia: Islamic Propagation Office, 2001), pp. 153-154.

[2] Bilal Philips, "Contemporary Issues, (www.bilalphilips.com), p. 23.

[3] Naasir al-Aql, *Sharh al-Aqeedah al-Tahaawiyyah* (Riyadh, Saudi Arabia: Markaz al-Najaashi), lecture 37. The Sunni scholars distinguish between acts of apostasy (*kufr*) and apostates (*kaafir*). An act of apostasy does not necessarily make one an apostate.

referring to their belief in the legitimacy of revolting against the rulers). Of course, the one belief leads to the other. The easier it is for people to be considered apostates, such as rulers, the easier it is to accept the concept that they must be revolted against.

It is beyond the scope of this work to touch upon all of the relevant points related to the question of the law of apostasy in Islam[1] in the light of contemporary thought and attitudes. It is sufficient to note here in the end that if the currently existing laws of treason and laws of war do not constitute violations of human rights, then the Islamic law of apostasy also cannot be considered a violation. Just because one punishment is on behalf of a "state" or "national interest" while the other is on behalf of God or a "religion," there can be no substantial logical (or possibly legal) difference between the two cases.

Finally, regardless of how many times Mayer may wish to claim tha freedom of religion is "absolute," as was described earlier, it must be admitted that virtually all societies have to deal internally with its own question of religious freedom. True, the resulting penalty for certain religious practices may not be death but they certainly can be imprisonment, which is still a restriction of freedom. Donnelly openly discusses this element of "freedom of religion" when he states,

Given the continuing repression of Iranian Bahais—although, for the moment at least, the apparent end to executions—this was quite a sensitive issue. Even here, though, the challenge was not to the principle, or even the right, of freedom of religion (which almost all Muslims support) but to competing "Western" and "Muslim" conceptions of its limits. And we must remember that every society places some limits on religious liberty. In the United States, for example, recent court cases have dealt with forced medical treatment for the children of Christian Scientists, live

---

[1] For example, one important issue not discussed here is the question of the conditions for applying a *hadd* (prescribed penal punishment) in Islam. In particular, given all of the conditions that must exist before *hadd* punishments are implemented, can a country like today's Afghanistan truly have the right to implement the *hadd* punishment for apostasy? It is very possible that the government itself is committing *kufr* (disbelief), not to speak of opening the door for all sorts of anti-Islamic organizations and peoples to work freely in the land. This very important issue is one that contemporary Muslim scholars must discuss in detail as the harm of misapplying the *hadd* could possibly be very great for Muslims and Islam as a whole.

animal sacrifice by practitioners of santaria, and the rights of Jehovah's Witnesses to evangelize at private residences.[1]

Freedom of Religion: Are Muslims Free to Practice their Religion under a Contemporary human rights Platform

Before leaving this topic, it is important to highlight once again that Muslims are not truly free to practice their religion under the contemporary human rights platform according to human rights activists like Mayer and Howland, as they believe that many of the tenets and practices violate human rights law and as such cannot be tolerated. It is further true that if Muslims insist upon "violating" such human rights, they will be exposed to sanctions and possibly military intervention. The results of military intervention are, most likely, death and destruction. In other words, Muslims who seek to implement their understanding of "traditional Islam" may be killed simply because they refuse to adhere to the human rights platform. In other words, they are nothing better than "apostates" or "infidels" from the point of view of these human rights proponents. Due to their "apostasy" or "infidelity," it becomes permissible to spill their blood in the name of human rights. Yet at the same time these same human rights proponents seemed to appalled by the Islamic Law of apostasy. Thus, the glaring contradictions of the contemporary human rights platform continue to grow.

Conclusions

It is amazing to see how Islam is critiqued on so many fronts when it comes to human rights. Upon closer inspection, though, one finds that it is actually human rights law that is inconsistent. The attacks on Islam and its view of human rights seem to be more based on a bias against religion in general and Islam in particular.

Islam is criticized by many by putting too many restrictions on women and not granting them the same rights as men. At the same time, European nations repeatedly have banned Muslim women from wearing the Islamic dress known as *hijab*. This is a clear restriction of their freedom in the same way that Islam telling women that they cannot go about dress provocatively is a restriction of their

---

[1] Donnelly, p. 95.

freedom. Yet the former human rights courts have no problem approving. They do so in the name of secularism, protecting public morals, equality and national unity.

However, these same European countries have no problem with publishing disparaging cartoons about the Prophet Muhammad (peace and blessings of Allah be upon him). Apparently, the same issues of protecting public morals and national unity are of no importance here. It was known beforehand that such cartoons would be divisive and may even lead to violence within the European nations. In some perverse way, all of a sudden, it is the freedom to act that reigns supreme in this situation. Human rights activists throughout the world supported the newspapers right to publish those cartoons about the Prophet Muhammad (peace and blessings of Allah be upon him).

Finally, when it comes to laws of apostasy and the like, human rights activists seem to be clear that none should be killed in the name of God or for the sake of religion. At the same time, people may be killed for numerous other reasons related to reasons of state.

Beyond the inconsistencies described above, this chapter exposed some other very important facts about the human rights paradigm.

In this chapter, a number of controversial topics related to Islam and human rights have been touched upon. Europe is considered the most progressive in the world when it comes to human rights. Hence, this chapter began with a study of how the European human rights courts have dealt with the issue of human rights. Those courts and decisions clearly exhibited the fact that human rights can be manipulated or overruled in favor of two other vague concepts, secularism and democracy. In essence, this means that there is no true human rights paradigm or movement today. If, according to the leaders of the human rights paradigm in progressive Europe, human rights can be trumped by secularism or democracy, this means that the movement is not about human rights. Human rights is simply a secondary goal or a tool that is used to promote secularism and democracy.

If the ideology or system of secularism/democracy is able to trump human rights, should the ideology or system of Islam also be allowed to trump human rights? Certainly for believers in an Islamic state, adhering to Islam is more precious and important than individual human rights. Just as it the laicite or secularism of France is given preference over individual rights in France, as endorsed by the European Court of Human Rights, certainly Islamic Law should be given the same priority in Islamic states. Of course, the standard reply is: "But secularism and democracy allows for freedom for all…" However, that is a bogus argument and it was debunked earlier in this chapter and in the previous chapter.

The reality is that states and systems of law do have the right and imperative to restrict freedoms. As Baderin noted,

By their nature, both law and political authority constitute some limitation upon the freedom and liberties of individuals. Perhaps, the correct perception is as stated by Locke that '…Liberty is to be free from restraint and violence from others, which cannot be, where there is no law:… Freedom is not, as we are told, A Liberty for every Man to do what he lists'. Under what has been described as the ' fundamental liberal principle' there only exists a kind of presumption in favour of liberty, which places the burden of proof on anyone who contends for any restriction on it. Thus the power of the State to interfere in the actions of individuals is not completely ousted under liberal theory or within human rights but only curtailed to its legitimate necessity. The necessity of control by the political authority through law is recognized, but any limitations they impose upon individual liberties and freedoms must be justifiable in accordance with the law and not be arbitrary. The justificatory principle thus establishes that restrictions upon the rights of individuals must be clearly determinable and justifiable under the law in order not to violate their freedom, liberties and fundamental human rights.[1]

This passage from Baderin would imply that the Islamic State could justify many restrictions on liberty in light of its overall goals for society. However, in the above passage Baderin has failed the important caveat that forms part of the human rights paradigm. It is recognized that rights cannot be free. They must be subjected to some greater authority. In the writings of contemporary human rights proponents and in contemporary human rights law, that greater authority can be or must be a

---

[1] Baderin, p. 45.

secular democracy and cannot be a religious authority—although they fail to explicitly prove why one should be accepted and the one rejected.

Clapham, for example, writes that rights and freedoms may be interfered with but only on the bases of the following three questions:

• is there a legitimate aim to the interference?

• is the interference prescribed by a clear and accessible law?

• is the interference proportionate to the identified legitimate aim and necessary in a democratic society?[1]

Mayer even admits that "absolute freedoms" may be restricted but never on the basis of religion. Mayer writes,

But even Mayer recognizes limits:

International law recognizes that many rights protections are not absolute and may be suspended or qualified in exceptional circumstances such as wars or public emergencies or even in normal circumstances in the interests of certain overriding considerations. In international law, one expects these overriding considerations to fall within one of several established categories. Qualifications may be placed on human rights in the aggregate common interest and to serve particular, specified policies. The latter might include the preservation of national security, public safety, public order, morals, the rights and freedom of others, the interests of justice, and the public interest in a democratic society. To ensure that accommodations and derogations are made within structures of authority and to prevent arbitrariness in decisions, the measures imposing these limitations must be taken in accordance with the law… International law does not accept that fundamental human rights may be restricted—much less permanently curtailed—by reference to the requirements of any particular religion. International law provides no warrant for depriving Muslims of human rights by according primacy to Islamic criteria. Thus, to limit or dilute human rights in deference to the requirements of the shari'a is to qualify human

---

[1] Andrew Clapham, *Human Rights: A Very Short Introduction* (Oxford, England: Oxford University Press, 2007), p. 100.

rights established under international law by standards that are not recognized as legitimate bases for curtailing rights.[1]

Similarly, Howland states that rights may be restricted based on morality and public order but,

"The terms 'morality' and 'public order' are thus limited to meaning public order and morality in the context of democratic principles… Thus, national law or religious law may not be the source for either of these standards. Furthermore, article 29 requires the same treatment for all rights, and thus corresponding situations must be treated symmetrically. For example, if a state enacts a law protecting religion to the detriment of women, a determination must be made as to whether such limitations on the rights of women are necessary for the due recognition of the religion and the just requirements of a democratic society. This must be symmetric to the case of a state that enacts a law protecting women against religious pressures and a determination must be made as to whether the limitation on religion is necessary for the due recognition of the rights of women and the just requirements of a democratic society.[2]

(According to Howland, apparently, "morality" cannot even be based on a nation's religion.)

Thus, once again, the issue is not the question of curtailing human rights. The issue is based on what are such human rights to be curtailed.

---

[1] Mayer, *Islam and Human Rights*, pp. 77-80.

[2] Howland in Bucar and Barnett, p. 184.

Final Thoughts

In this work, the different strands of writings on Islam and human rights have been covered and critiqued. After that, some fundamental questions concerning the contemporary human rights movement were discussed. This led directly into the question of where Islam stands with respect to human rights. Finally, there was a discussion of some recent controversial topics related to Islam and human rights. There are definitely some loose ends that still need to be discussed before a few final general conclusions can be made.

Protecting Humans

"At the core of *our* concept of human rights is the idea of protecting individuals (and perhaps groups) from *the abuse of power*."[1]

Today the question is: Who is going to save individuals from the abuse of power performed by the human rights lawyers, politicians and activists? These people have a great deal of power today and they have no qualms in wielding it in various different ways. They use their economic and military strength to threaten nations, communities and peoples throughout the world. They demand that people change their culture, society and even religion to conform to the demands of this new movement.

"Human rights" has come a long way from some basic fundamental principles that nations throughout the world could agree to within the contexts of their own cultures. Now human rights law has permeated into the most private of individual's affairs, be it the relationship between husband and wife or one's own attitude toward others' chosen sexual preferences. Undoubtedly, this has been an abuse of power.

Actually, the abuse of power goes well beyond that. It touches upon the most sacred aspect of a person's life: An individual's relationship with his or her Creator. Even that relationship is overruled—in fact, dominated—by the laws laid down by professional bureaucrats, politicians and lawyers. One is not even allowed to submit to God in a fashion that these supposed super guardians of morality object to.

Even well-intended individuals can easily slip and abuse their newly received powers. Perhaps one need only look at the aftermath of the French Revolution to see

---

[1] Freeman, p. 167 (emphasis is part of the original).

how power can be greatly abused, even by those who claim that they are bringing freedom to the people. Perhaps human rights advocates need to reassess exactly where they have come from and where they are now. Although everything is stated in terms of "human rights," one can definitely get a feel of "totalitarianism" in the writings of human rights advocates, especially when it comes to the place and role of religion in human society.

The Moral Choice

"[R]ights ought to be balanced with other values, and it would be dogmatic to assume that rights are always more fundamental than other values... I should identify and evaluate the moral weight of the other values at issue. Rights are important, but they are not the whole of morality."[1]

There are a number of tricky questions that are related to the issue of human rights and morality. Human rights activists could argue that morality is for states and individuals to give everyone the rights that they deserve and to fully respect those rights. That sounds excellent and very convincing. However, it leads to an obvious follow up questions: What are those rights that everyone deserves? As discussed earlier, this is actually an unanswerable question in the human rights paradigm. One could answer that it is those rights that have been agreed upon as rights. That does not answer the question, especially given that "agreed upon" simply means by the human rights lawyers and state representatives for whom morality need not have been a guiding principle. Again, the answer could be those rights that are consistent with a secular, democratic or free society. Once again, morality "has left the building." Those sources for rights are supposed to be, in a sense, "morality neutral." There is no true secular or democratic morality. Hence, one is truly left with a system that is void of "morality." It was actually meant to be that way because subjective questions of morality means that one is forced to "judge" certain ways of life and behavior. This is what the human rights paradigm theoretically seeks to avoid. But taking morality out of the equation simply opens the door for immorality. One would hope that it would be one's "human right" to be concerned about

---

[1] Freeman, pp. 62-63.

morality. One definitely should not have to sacrifice one's concern for morality in the name of some vague concept of "human rights."

If one does allow the question of moral choice to enter into the equation again, then, with respect to the contemporary human rights paradigm, the Muslim is facing a moral choice of momentous proportion. What can be a greater moral question or a greater moral dilemma for a Muslim than disobeying God or believing in a system that he knows violates his fundamental beliefs about God? The Prophet Muhammad (peace and blessings of Allah be upon him) explicitly touched upon this question when he stated, "There is to be no obedience to a created being if it involves disobedience to Allah."[1] If it is *allowed* to put forth the notion that something may take precedence over human rights, certainly, in an internal discussion among Muslims, obedience to God must be given the ability to *trump* human rights.

Secularism and Human Rights: Is There More to Life?

Human rights are not, and cannot be, grounded in religious conviction. Such a contention is factually and historically mistaken, and it is conceptually imperialistic. The human rights ideology is a fully secular and rational ideology whose very promise of success as a universal ideology depends on its secularity and rationality. No one can expect merger or full comfortable cooperation between religious and human rights organizations.[2]

Here, Henkin is representing a secular approach. If the secularists are willing to make such clear and unequivocal statements, it is high time that the Muslims also recognize that such is truly the case. One can argue that two distinct *religions or ideologies* are being spoken about when comparing the contemporary human rights doctrine with Islam. It will not work if one tries to bend Islam such that it fits the contemporary human rights schemes, in particular the more extreme versions of it, nor will it work if one tries to bend and manipulate the human rights platform to fit

---

[1] Recorded by Ahmad, al-Tabaraani and others. Another narration is, "…if it involves disobedience to the Creator." According to al-Albaani and Shuaib al-Arnaaoot, it is authentic. See *Silsilat al-Ahaadeeth al-Saheehah*, vol. 1, p. 297; *Musnad Ahmad*, #1095.

[2] Henkin, p. 154.

with Islam. In both cases, the contradictions and illogical arguments will be such that it will weaken the resolve of all concerned.

Later, actually, Henkin completely contradicts himself probably because his conception of religion or ideology is very restricted. At the same time, he points out a very important reality: the contemporary human rights schemes cannot offer humankind all of what it needs. He writes,

In fact, however, the idea of rights is not, and does not claim to be, a complete, all-embracing ideology. It is not, in fact, in competition with other ideologies. Religion explains and comforts; tradition supports; development builds. The human rights idea does none of these. In today's world—and tomorrow's—there may be no less need for what religions and traditions have always promised and provided. Representatives of religion have been right to reject any claims for human rights as a total ideology. Human rights—cold rights—do not provide warmth, belonging, fitting, significance, do not exclude the need for love, friendship, family, charity, sympathy, devotion, sanctity, or for expiation, atonement, forgiveness. But if human rights may not be sufficient, they are at least necessary. If they do not bring kindness to the familiar, they bring—as religions have often failed to do—respect for the stranger. Human rights are not a complete, alternative ideology, but are a floor, necessary to allow other values—including religions—to flourish. Human rights not only protect religions but have come to serve religious ethics in respects and contexts where religion itself has sometimes proved insufficient. Human rights are, at least, a supplemental "theology" for pluralistic, urban, secular societies. There, religions can accept if not adopt the human rights idea as an affirmation of their own values, and can devote themselves to the larger, deeper areas beyond the common denominator of human rights. Religions can provide, as the human rights idea does not adequately provide, for the tensions between rights and responsibilities, between individual and community, between the material and the spirit. [1]

Henkin is recognizing the vacuum of the human rights paradigm but, at the same time, he is failing to recognize that once the authority of religion is undermined, then the religion can actually no longer fulfill the other roles that he is

---

[1] Henkin, pp. 154-155.

describing in the passage. By accepting the human rights doctrines as paramount over the religious doctrine, what does it then mean to be worshipping and submitting to God? An individual cannot have two gods or two ultimate authorities in his heart. As An-Na'im once said, "The most serious objection to secularism as the foundation of the universality of human rights is its inability to inspire or motivate believers, who are the vast majority of the world."[1] Similarly, those believers will not be willing to relegate their belief system to a secondary role, second to the demands of the human rights paradigm.

Unless, of course, as a secularist, Henkin is thinking of religion from a secularist perspective. "Religion" simply provides those other aspects, like "comfort" but it does not provide a complete way of life. In this way, the human rights advocate is once again, ironically, forcing his view of religion upon others in the name of universal human rights. This simply cannot work and is illogical in its premise.

Eventually, one must reign supreme: the secular theology of the human rights movement or the theology of one's religion. There is a definitely a "theology" behind the human rights movement:

Max Horkheimer, an early exponent of the critical theory of the Frankfurt Institute for Social Research, and an existentialist and atheist, suggested that "behind every genuine human endeavour stands a theology." He argues that a political and ethical paradigm that "does not preserve a theological moment in itself, no matter how skilful, in the last analysis is mere business."[2]

This "theology" behind the human rights movement cannot take a back seat to any other type of theology. In the words of Donnelly,

If human rights are the rights one has simply because one is a human being, as they usually are thought to be, then they are held "universally," by all human beings. They also hold "universally" against all other persons and institutions. As the highest moral rights, they regulate the fundamental structures and practices of political life, and in ordinary circumstances they take priority over other moral,

---

[1] An-Na'im, quoted in Bucar and Barnett, p. 227.

[2] Bucar and Barnett, pp. 227-228

legal, and political claims. These dimensions encompass what I call the moral universality of human rights.[1]

One can find these admissions throughout the theoretical literature on human rights but one has to be a devoted researcher to find them. They are not part of the message that the human rights proponents are stating to the masses when they speak of their glorious human rights platform.

This "secular religion" of human rights has become the religion of contemporary times. In the words of Ignatieff,

Fifty years after its proclamation, the Universal Declaration of Human Rights has become the sacred text of what Elie Wiesel has called a "Worldwide secular religion.' UN Secretary-General Kofi Annan has called the Declaration the "yardstick by which we measure human progress." Nobel Laureate Nadine Gordimer has described it as "the essential document, the touchstone, the creed of humanity that surely sums up all other creeds directing human behavior." Human rights has become the major article of faith of a secular culture that fears it believes in nothing else. It has become the lingua franca of global moral thought, as English has become the lingua franca of the global economy.[2]

In recent decades, the world has seen a resurgence of religion, "fundamentalist" and even "extremist." One cannot doubt that part of this resurgence has been in response to this secular religion of human rights that has become so dominant yet strikes at the very core of what so many humans belief about themselves, this world and God. Unfortunately, as human rights proponents become bolder and bolder in their demands, this clash between the secular religionists, especially the extreme among them, and the traditional religionists, especially the extreme among them, will become more and more bitter and, sadly, even violent. Part of the blame for that must fall upon the human rights advocates who are not willing to say openly that they are replacing the people's religions with a secular religion of their own. Many people realize this fact only when it is too late and the human rights paradigm has been entrenched. Once the human rights

---

[1] Donnelly, p. 1.

[2] Ignatieff, p. 53.

paradigm is entrenched, its view of "freedom" does not actually allow any true voice for any competing paradigm. Hence, the friction begins.

Freedom Lost

It was on these Western traditions of individualism, humanism, and rationalism and on legal principles protecting individual rights that twentieth-century international law on civil and political rights ultimately rested. *Rejecting individualism, humanism, and rationalism is tantamount to rejecting the premises of modern human rights.*[1]

Individualism, humanism and rationalism is what the human rights movement is truly all about according to Mayer. Humanism, of course, replaces God as the center of one's life and replaces it with the human. Rationalism—such as it is called although one could argue that it is not truly rational—implies giving preference to human thought over what has been revealed from the Creator.

This passage from Mayer is one of the most explicit and honest passages from a human rights proponent. This author can speak from his own personal experience as a convert to Islam and from the experience of others that he has known that there are many even from the "West" who reject the concepts of individualism, humanism and rationalism as the basis for life. In this one passage, Mayer has aptly described why "modern human rights" morally should not be forced upon any human in this world, not to speak of those who believe in a religion like that of Islam.

Beyond Dogmatism and Blind Faith

Islam, in its essence, is not about blind faith and dogmatism. Muslims should believe in Islam because it is the truth and they can recognize the truth of Islam. This is what true faith (*imaan*) is about in Islam. One of its founding principles of *ilm* or knowledge.

The Quran teaches Muslims that if people make claims, especially great claims about life or belief, then they should be asked to present the proof for their claims, if they are truthful in what they are claiming.[2] In fact, if they can bring a

---

[1] Mayer, *Islam and Human Rights*, pp. 47-48, emphasis added.
[2] See *al-Baqarah* 111, *al-Anbiyaa* 24 and *al-Naml* 64.

teaching better than the Quran, the Muslim should follow it: "Say: Then bring you a Book from Allah, which is a better Guide than either of them, that I may follow it! (Do so), if you are truthful! But if they hearken not to you, know that they only follow their own lusts: and who is more astray than one who follows his own lusts, devoid of guidance from Allah? For Allah guides not people given to wrong-doing" (*al-Qasas* 49-50).

The reality, as an earlier chapter demonstrated, is that the human rights theorists do not present any earth shaking new theory that dispels the beliefs of a Muslim and that should convince the Muslim to put the human rights paradigm above the Islamic paradigm, even if he keeps the Islamic paradigm as a secondary source. The proofs are simply not there. It may be a very sincere attempt to establish something that seems very noble and praiseworthy but, like all the other man-made systems that came before it and which these same human rights theorists now scoff at, it falls short. It is admittedly foundationless. In the long-run, it will produce much more harm than good, as it contradicts the truths that have been revealed from God. Contradicting those truths means going against the very nature by which this cosmos was created. As Allah says in the Quran, "If the Truth had been in accord with their desires, truly the heavens and the earth, and all beings therein would have been in confusion and corruption! Nay, We have sent them their admonition, but they turn away from their admonition" (*al-Muminoon* 71).

In this work an attempt has been made to show that the contemporary human rights schemes, especially the more extreme but widespread and very vocal branch of it, has offered nothing that should convince a Muslim that he should give up tenets of his faith to bend them to meet their demands. Indeed, the opposite is the case. When one realizes how baseless their claims are, the Muslim should be more convinced in the truth of Islam. They have a very noble goal—bringing people the rights that they deserve. But they are lost and confused. They have no way of knowing what rights should be promoted. They do not even know what they should base their claims on. After studying the human rights paradigm in detail, a Muslim should flee quickly and return to Allah, realizing that without Allah's guidance there is no hope for humanity.

Furthermore, the ultimate question is not whether Islam is compatible with human rights, the question is what is the ultimate truth and way of life that a human should live. Obviously, human rights are calling to a path that is definitely deeply "religious" in its essence—meaning deeply philosophical touching on some core issues of what it means to be human. However, for the most part, one only finds them taking their assumptions as true without argument (very dogmatic, irrational, argument to authority) and enforceable by law. However, truth does not even seem to enter into the picture.

In fact, one can even go a step further than that. If one is truly interested in giving humans the rights that they deserve and need for life, then, according to Islamic beliefs, it is Islam that gives them all of those rights and prepares an entire society around allowing them to take advantage of those rights in the most beneficial manner. Islam does not give humans rights that will eventually be harmful for themselves but it does provide for them all that they need for a sound life, as shall be touched upon in the next section.

The Good Life

The enforcement of human rights in the international arena does not guarantee that anyone whose rights are effectively protected will live a wonderful life. Or even a (morally or nonmorally) good life.[1]

"Whoever does righteousness, whether male or female, while he is a believer - We will surely cause him to live a good life, and We will surely give them their reward [in the Hereafter] according to the best of what they used to do" (*al-Nahl* 97).

"O you who have believed, respond to Allah and to the Messenger when he calls you to that which gives you [true] life" (*al-Anfaal* 24).

The human rights paradigm—probably admitted even by its most staunchest supporters—is an empty hole. It does not offer anyone anything except, at the most, to say, "Here do as you please, just don't trample on the rights of others."

---

[1] Amy Gutmann, "Introduction," in Michael Ignatieff, *Human Rights as Politics and Religion* (with commentary by K. Anthony Appiah, David A. Hollinger, Thomas W. Laqueur, Diane F. Orentlicher) (Princeton, NJ: Princeton University Press, 2001), p. x.

Obviously, Islam, on the other hand, makes a much bolder claim. It claims to give human beings a "good life" in both this world and the next. Regardless of whether the reader believes in that claim or not, the reader must realize what Islam claims for itself and what the Muslim believes about Islam. Islam promises the good life, the life that is consistent with a person's nature and which leads to God being pleased with the individual and the individual being content.

However, the promise of this good life is conditional. It is conditional upon one's sincere acceptance of its principles and one's honest effort in living by those principles. It does not come by being halfheartedly committed to the faith. It does not come by sacrificing the tenets of Islam. It does not come by submitting to Islam in X percentage of one's life and then submitting to some other god/ideology/paradigm in Y percentage of one's life. These compromises are recipes for disaster as the strike at the very foundation of what it means to be a worshipper of God. Allah says in the Quran, "O you who have believed, enter into Islam completely [and perfectly] and do not follow the footsteps of Satan. Indeed, he is to you a clear enemy" (*al-Baqarah* 208). Allah also says, "And whoever desires a way other than Islam (submission to Allah) as religion - never will it be accepted from him, and he, in the Hereafter, will be among the losers" (*ali-Imraan* 85).

This ultimate choice of life has been left to the discretion of the human being. God has granted humans limited free will. But when the choices are laid out in front of an individual between the empty vacuum of the man-made human rights paradigm and the divine way of the religion of Islam that brings about real contentment in both this life and the Hereafter, it is difficult to see how any Muslim would choose the former over the latter. The saddest plight for humans, though, is if they are not given this choice and the man-made human rights paradigm is simply forced upon them—in the name of freedom.

Engaging the Muslims on Human Rights: The Concept of *Maroof*

There is no reason to end this work on a negative note. Human rights advocates and theorists seem to be sincere people who wish to bring good to their fellow humans. For that they are to be commended, even if a Muslim completely disagrees with their theory and ways.

It is an obligation upon the Muslim to stand for truth and righteousness, order good and eradicate evil wherever it may be. Allah says, "Help one another in righteousness and piety, but help not one another in sin and rancor: fear Allah for Allah is strict in punishment" (*al-Maaidah* 2). It is narrated in many of the books of *seerah* that the Prophet (peace and blessings of Allah be upon him), before being a prophet, had joined a pact known as *hilf al-fadhool*, which was dedicated to redressing the wrongs done to individuals in Makkah. After receiving his message, the Prophet said, "If they were to call me to respond to it today, I would respond to it."[1]

It must be made very clear here at the end that the conflict between Islam and the contemporary human rights movement has nothing to do with the support of numerous and various human rights. Many, if not most, of the human rights called for by the human rights paradigm are sanctioned by Islam. This means it is the obligation of Muslims to support them, as part of the overall ordering good and eradicating evil. As was noted earlier, even within the practice of Islam itself, there are many avenues by which mutual support could be given to ensure that women, children and the poor receive some of their due rights.

In the end, it must be recognized that the ideologies and the belief systems of the human rights paradigm and Islam are actually at odds with each other. That impasse cannot successfully be broken without one of the two sides suffering irreparable damage. However, if Islamicists and human rights advocates are sincerely interested in bringing good to people, there are many avenues in which they could cooperate to make this world a better place for its inhabitants.

---

[1] See Ahmad ibn Hajar, *Fath al-Baari fi Sharh Sahih al-Bukhari* (Beirut, Lebanon: Daar al-Marifah, n.d.), vol. 4, p. 473.

Appendix 1:

The Universal Declaration of Human Rights

[1948] Preamble

Whereas recognition of the inherent dignity and of the equal and inalienable rights of all members of the human family is the foundation of freedom, justice and peace in the world,

Whereas disregard and contempt for human rights have resulted in barbarous acts which have outraged the conscience of mankind, and the advent of a world in which human beings shall enjoy freedom of speech and belief and freedom from fear and want has been proclaimed as the highest aspiration of the common people,

Whereas it is essential, if man is not to be compelled to have recourse, as a last resort, to rebellion against tyranny and oppression, that human rights should be protected by the rule of law,

Whereas it is essential to promote the development of friendly relations between nations,

Whereas the peoples of the United Nations have in the Charter reaffirmed their faith in fundamental human rights, in the dignity and worth of the human person and in the equal rights of men and women and have determined to promote social progress and better standards of life in larger freedom,

Whereas Member States have pledged themselves to achieve, in co-operation with the United Nations, the promotion of universal respect for and observance of human rights and fundamental freedoms,

Whereas a common understanding of these rights and freedoms is of the greatest importance for the full realization of this pledge,

Now, therefore,

The General Assembly

Proclaims this Universal Declaration of Human Rights as a common standard of achievement for all peoples and all nations, to the end that every individual and every organ of society, keeping this Declaration constantly in mind, shall strive by teaching and education to promote respect for these rights and freedoms and by progressive measures, national and international, to secure their universal and effective recognition and observance, both among the peoples of Member States themselves and among the peoples of territories under their jurisdiction.

Article 1

All human beings are born free and equal in dignity and rights. They are endowed with reason and conscience and should act towards one another in a spirit of brotherhood.

Article 2

Everyone is entitled to all the rights and freedoms set forth in this Declaration, without distinction of any kind, such as race, colour, sex, language, religion, political or other opinion, national or social origin, property, birth or other status.

Furthermore, no distinction shall be made on the basis of the political, jurisdictional or international status of the country or territory to which a person belongs, whether it be independent, trust, non-self-governing or under any other limitation of sovereignty.

Article 3

Everyone has the right to life, liberty and the security of person.

Article 4

No one shall be held in slavery or servitude; slavery and the slave trade shall be prohibited in all their forms.

Article 5

No one shall be subjected to torture or to cruel, inhuman or degrading treatment or punishment.

Article 6

Everyone has the right to recognition everywhere as a person before the law.

Article 7

All are equal before the law and are entitled without any discrimination to equal protection of the law. All are entitled to equal protection against any discrimination in violation of this Declaration and against any incitement to such discrimination.

Article 8

Everyone has the right to an effective remedy by the competent national tribunals for acts violating the fundamental rights granted him by the constitution or by law.

Article 9

No one shall be subjected to arbitrary arrest, detention or exile.

Article 10

Everyone is entitled in full equality to a fair, and public hearing by an independent and impartial tribunal, in the determination of his rights and obligations and of any criminal charge against him.

Article 11

1. Everyone charged with a penal offence has the right to be presumed innocent until proved guilty according to law in a public trial at which he has had all the guarantees necessary for his defence.

2. No one shall be held guilty of any penal offence on account of any act or omission which did not constitute a penal offence, under national or international law, at the time when it was committed. Nor shall a heavier penalty be imposed than the one that was applicable at the time the penal offence was committed.

Article 12

No one shall be subjected to arbitrary interference with his privacy, family, home or correspondence, nor to attacks upon his honour and reputation. Everyone has the right to the protection of the law against such interference or attacks.

Article 13

1. Everyone has the right to freedom of movement and residence within the borders of each State.

2. Everyone has the right to leave any country, including his own, and to return to his country.

Article 14

1. Everyone has the right to seek and to enjoy in other countries asylum from persecution.

2. This right may not be invoked in the case of prosecutions genuinely arising from non-political crimes or from acts contrary to the purposes and principles of the United Nations.

Article 15

1. Everyone has the right to a nationality.

2. No one shall be arbitrarily deprived of his nationality nor denied the right to change his nationality.

Article 16

1. Men and women of full age, without any limitation due to race, nationality or religion, have the right to marry and to found a family. They are entitled to equal rights as to marriage, during marriage and at its dissolution.

2. Marriage shall be entered into only with the free and full consent of the intending spouses.

3. The family is the natural and fundamental group unit of society and is entitled to protection by society and the State.

Article 17

1. Everyone has the right to own property alone as well as in association with others.

2. No one shall be arbitrarily deprived of his property.

Article 18

Everyone has the right to freedom of thought, conscience and religion; this right includes freedom to change his religion or belief, and freedom, either alone or in community with others and in public or private, to manifest his religion or belief in teaching, practice, worship and observance.

Article 19

Everyone has the right to freedom of opinion and expression; this right includes freedom to hold opinions without interference and to seek, receive and impart information and ideas through any media and regardless of frontiers.

Article 20

1. Everyone has the right to freedom of peaceful assembly and association.

2. No one may be compelled to belong to an association.

Article 21

1. Everyone has the right to take part in the government of his country, directly or through freely chosen representatives.

2. Everyone has the right of equal access to public service in his country.

3. The will of the people shall be the basis of the authority of government; this will shall be expressed in periodic and genuine elections which shall be by universal and equal suffrage and shall be held by secret vote or by equivalent free voting procedures.

Article 22

Everyone, as a member of society, has the right to social security and is entitled to realization, through national effort and international co-operation and in accordance with the organization and resources of each State, of the economic, social and cultural rights indispensable for his dignity and the free development of his personality.

Article 23

1. Everyone has the right to work, to free choice of employment, to just and favourable conditions of work and to protection against unemployment.

2. Everyone, without any discrimination, has the right to equal pay for equal work.

3. Everyone who works has the right to just and favourable remuneration ensuring for himself and his family an existence worthy of human dignity, and supplemented, if necessary, by other means of social protection.

4. Everyone has the right to form and to join trade unions for the protection of his interests.

Article 24

Everyone has the right to rest and leisure, including reasonable limitation of working hours and periodic holidays with pay.

Article 25

1. Everyone has the right to a standard of living adequate for the health and well-being of himself and of his family, including food, clothing, housing and medical care and necessary social services, and the right to security in the event of unemployment, sickness, disability, widowhood, old age or other lack of livelihood in circumstances beyond his control.

2. Motherhood and childhood are entitled to special care and assistance. All children, whether born in or out of wedlock, shall enjoy the same social protection.

Article 26

1. Everyone has the right to education. Education shall be free, at least in the elementary and fundamental stages. Elementary education shall be compulsory. Technical and professional education shall be made generally available and higher education shall be equally accessible to all on the basis of merit.

2. Education shall be directed to the full development of the human personality and to the strengthening of respect for human rights and fundamental

freedoms. It shall promote understanding, tolerance and friendship among all nations, racial or religious groups, and shall further the activities of the United Nations for the maintenance of peace.

3. Parents have a prior right to choose the kind of education that shall be given to their children.

Article 27

1. Everyone has the right freely to participate in the cultural life of the community, to enjoy the arts and to share in scientific advancement and its benefits.

2. Everyone has the right to the protection of the moral and material interests resulting from any scientific, literary or artistic production of which he is the author.

Article 28

Everyone is entitled to a social and international order in which the rights and freedoms set forth in this Declaration can be fully realized.

Article 29

1. Everyone has duties to the community in which alone the free and full development of his personality is possible.

2. In the exercise of his rights and freedoms, everyone shall be subject only to such limitations as are determined by law solely for the purpose of securing due recognition and respect for the rights and freedoms of others and of meeting the just requirements of morality, public order and the general welfare in a democratic society.

3. These rights and freedoms may in no case be exercised contrary to the purposes and principles of the United Nations.

Article 30

Nothing in this Declaration may be interpreted as implying for any State, group or person any right to engage in any activity or to perform any act aimed at the destruction of any of the rights and freedoms set forth herein.

Appendix 2:

International Covenant on Economic, Social and Cultural Rights

Adopted and opened for signature, ratification and accession by General Assembly resolution 2200A (XXI) of 16 December 1966 entry into force 3 January 1976, in accordance with article 27

Preamble

The States Parties to the present Covenant,

Considering that, in accordance with the principles proclaimed in the Charter of the United Nations, recognition of the inherent dignity and of the equal and inalienable rights of all members of the human family is the foundation of freedom, justice and peace in the world,

Recognizing that these rights derive from the inherent dignity of the human person,

Recognizing that, in accordance with the Universal Declaration of Human Rights, the ideal of free human beings enjoying freedom from fear and want can only be achieved if conditions are created whereby everyone may enjoy his economic, social and cultural rights, as well as his civil and political rights,

Considering the obligation of States under the Charter of the United Nations to promote universal respect for, and observance of, human rights and freedoms,

Realizing that the individual, having duties to other individuals and to the community to which he belongs, is under a responsibility to strive for the promotion and observance of the rights recognized in the present Covenant,

Agree upon the following articles:

PART I

Article 1

1.   All peoples have the right of self-determination. By virtue of that right they freely determine their political status and freely pursue their economic, social and cultural development.

2.	All peoples may, for their own ends, freely dispose of their natural wealth and resources without prejudice to any obligations arising out of international economic co-operation, based upon the principle of mutual benefit, and international law. In no case may a people be deprived of its own means of subsistence.

3.	The States Parties to the present Covenant, including those having responsibility for the administration of Non-Self-Governing and Trust Territories, shall promote the realization of the right of self-determination, and shall respect that right, in conformity with the provisions of the Charter of the United Nations.

PART II

Article 2

1.	Each State Party to the present Covenant undertakes to take steps, individually and through international assistance and co-operation, especially economic and technical, to the maximum of its available resources, with a view to achieving progressively the full realization of the rights recognized in the present Covenant by all appropriate means, including particularly the adoption of legislative measures.

2.	The States Parties to the present Covenant undertake to guarantee that the rights enunciated in the present Covenant will be exercised without discrimination of any kind as to race, colour, sex, language, religion, political or other opinion, national or social origin, property, birth or other status.

3.	Developing countries, with due regard to human rights and their national economy, may determine to what extent they would guarantee the economic rights recognized in the present Covenant to non-nationals.

Article 3

The States Parties to the present Covenant undertake to ensure the equal right of men and women to the enjoyment of all economic, social and cultural rights set forth in the present Covenant.

Article 4

The States Parties to the present Covenant recognize that, in the enjoyment of those rights provided by the State in conformity with the present Covenant, the State may subject such rights only to such limitations as are determined by law only in so far as this may be compatible with the nature of these rights and solely for the purpose of promoting the general welfare in a democratic society.

Article 5

1.   Nothing in the present Covenant may be interpreted as implying for any State, group or person any right to engage in any activity or to perform any act aimed at the destruction of any of the rights or freedoms recognized herein, or at their limitation to a greater extent than is provided for in the present Covenant.

2.   No restriction upon or derogation from any of the fundamental human rights recognized or existing in any country in virtue of law, conventions, regulations or custom shall be admitted on the pretext that the present Covenant does not recognize such rights or that it recognizes them to a lesser extent.

PART III

Article 6

1.   The States Parties to the present Covenant recognize the right to work, which includes the right of everyone to the opportunity to gain his living by work which he freely chooses or accepts, and will take appropriate steps to safeguard this right.

2.   The steps to be taken by a State Party to the present Covenant to achieve the full realization of this right shall include technical and vocational guidance and training programmes, policies and techniques to achieve steady economic, social and cultural development and full and productive employment under conditions safeguarding fundamental political and economic freedoms to the individual.

Article 7

The States Parties to the present Covenant recognize the right of everyone to the enjoyment of just and favourable conditions of work which ensure, in particular:

(a) Remuneration which provides all workers, as a minimum, with:

(i) Fair wages and equal remuneration for work of equal value without distinction of any kind, in particular women being guaranteed conditions of work not inferior to those enjoyed by men, with equal pay for equal work;

(ii) A decent living for themselves and their families in accordance with the provisions of the present Covenant;

(b) Safe and healthy working conditions;

(c) Equal opportunity for everyone to be promoted in his employment to an appropriate higher level, subject to no considerations other than those of seniority and competence;

(d) Rest, leisure and reasonable limitation of working hours and periodic holidays with pay, as well as remuneration for public holidays

Article 8

1. The States Parties to the present Covenant undertake to ensure:

(a) The right of everyone to form trade unions and join the trade union of his choice, subject only to the rules of the organization concerned, for the promotion and protection of his economic and social interests. No restrictions may be placed on the exercise of this right other than those prescribed by law and which are necessary in a democratic society in the interests of national security or public order or for the protection of the rights and freedoms of others;

(b) The right of trade unions to establish national federations or confederations and the right of the latter to form or join international trade-union organizations;

(c) The right of trade unions to function freely subject to no limitations other than those prescribed by law and which are necessary in a democratic society in the interests of national security or public order or for the protection of the rights and freedoms of others;

(d) The right to strike, provided that it is exercised in conformity with the laws of the particular country.

2. This article shall not prevent the imposition of lawful restrictions on the exercise of these rights by members of the armed forces or of the police or of the administration of the State. 3. Nothing in this article shall authorize States Parties to

the International Labour Organisation Convention of 1948 concerning Freedom of Association and Protection of the Right to Organize to take legislative measures which would prejudice, or apply the law in such a manner as would prejudice, the guarantees provided for in that Convention.

Article 9

The States Parties to the present Covenant recognize the right of everyone to social security, including social insurance.

Article 10

The States Parties to the present Covenant recognize that:

1.	The widest possible protection and assistance should be accorded to the family, which is the natural and fundamental group unit of society, particularly for its establishment and while it is responsible for the care and education of dependent children. Marriage must be entered into with the free consent of the intending spouses.

2.	Special protection should be accorded to mothers during a reasonable period before and after childbirth. During such period working mothers should be accorded paid leave or leave with adequate social security benefits.

3.	Special measures of protection and assistance should be taken on behalf of all children and young persons without any discrimination for reasons of parentage or other conditions. Children and young persons should be protected from economic and social exploitation. Their employment in work harmful to their morals or health or dangerous to life or likely to hamper their normal development should be punishable by law. States should also set age limits below which the paid employment of child labour should be prohibited and punishable by law.

Article 11

1.	The States Parties to the present Covenant recognize the right of everyone to an adequate standard of living for himself and his family, including adequate food, clothing and housing, and to the continuous improvement of living conditions. The States Parties will take appropriate steps to ensure the realization of this right, recognizing to this effect the essential importance of international co-operation based on free consent.

2.   The States Parties to the present Covenant, recognizing the fundamental right of everyone to be free from hunger, shall take, individually and through international co-operation, the measures, including specific programmes, which are needed:

(a) To improve methods of production, conservation and distribution of food by making full use of technical and scientific knowledge, by disseminating knowledge of the principles of nutrition and by developing or reforming agrarian systems in such a way as to achieve the most efficient development and utilization of natural resources;

(b) Taking into account the problems of both food-importing and food-exporting countries, to ensure an equitable distribution of world food supplies in relation to need.

Article 12

1.   The States Parties to the present Covenant recognize the right of everyone to the enjoyment of the highest attainable standard of physical and mental health.

2.   The steps to be taken by the States Parties to the present Covenant to achieve the full realization of this right shall include those necessary for:

(a) The provision for the reduction of the stillbirth-rate and of infant mortality and for the healthy development of the child;

(b) The improvement of all aspects of environmental and industrial hygiene;

(c) The prevention, treatment and control of epidemic, endemic, occupational and other diseases;

(d) The creation of conditions which would assure to all medical service and medical attention in the event of sickness.

Article 13

1.   The States Parties to the present Covenant recognize the right of everyone to education. They agree that education shall be directed to the full development of the human personality and the sense of its dignity, and shall strengthen the respect for human rights and fundamental freedoms. They further agree that education shall enable all persons to participate effectively in a free society, promote understanding, tolerance and friendship among all nations and all racial, ethnic or religious groups, and further the activities of the United Nations for the maintenance of peace.

2.   The States Parties to the present Covenant recognize that, with a view to achieving the full realization of this right:

(a) Primary education shall be compulsory and available free to all;

(b) Secondary education in its different forms, including technical and vocational secondary education, shall be made generally available and accessible to all by every appropriate means, and in particular by the progressive introduction of free education;

(c) Higher education shall be made equally accessible to all, on the basis of capacity, by every appropriate means, and in particular by the progressive introduction of free education;

(d) Fundamental education shall be encouraged or intensified as far as possible for those persons who have not received or completed the whole period of their primary education;

(e) The development of a system of schools at all levels shall be actively pursued, an adequate fellowship system shall be established, and the material conditions of teaching staff shall be continuously improved.

1.   The States Parties to the present Covenant undertake to have respect for the liberty of parents and, when applicable, legal guardians to choose for their children schools, other than those established by the public authorities, which conform to such minimum educational standards as may be laid down or approved by the State and to ensure the religious and moral education of their children in

conformity with their own convictions.

2.   No part of this article shall be construed so as to interfere with the liberty of individuals and bodies to establish and direct educational institutions, subject always to the observance of the principles set forth in paragraph I of this article and to the requirement that the education given in such institutions shall conform to such minimum standards as may be laid down by the State.

Article 14

Each State Party to the present Covenant which, at the time of becoming a Party, has not been able to secure in its metropolitan territory or other territories under its jurisdiction compulsory primary education, free of charge, undertakes, within two years, to work out and adopt a detailed plan of action for the progressive implementation, within a reasonable number of years, to be fixed in the plan, of the principle of compulsory education free of charge for all.

Article 15

1. The States Parties to the present Covenant recognize the right of everyone:

(a) To take part in cultural life;

(b) To enjoy the benefits of scientific progress and its applications;

(c) To benefit from the protection of the moral and material interests resulting from any scientific, literary or artistic production of which he is the author.

2. The steps to be taken by the States Parties to the present Covenant to achieve the full realization of this right shall include those necessary for the conservation, the development and the diffusion of science and culture. 3. The States Parties to the present Covenant undertake to respect the freedom indispensable for scientific research and creative activity.

4. The States Parties to the present Covenant recognize the benefits to be derived from the encouragement and development of international contacts and co-operation in the scientific and cultural fields.

PART IV

Article 16

1. The States Parties to the present Covenant undertake to submit in conformity with this part of the Covenant reports on the measures which they have adopted and the progress made in achieving the observance of the rights recognized herein.

2.

(a) All reports shall be submitted to the Secretary-General of the United Nations, who shall transmit copies to the Economic and Social Council for consideration in accordance with the provisions of the present Covenant;

(b) The Secretary-General of the United Nations shall also transmit to the specialized agencies copies of the reports, or any relevant parts therefrom, from States Parties to the present Covenant which are also members of these specialized agencies in so far as these reports, or parts therefrom, relate to any matters which fall within the responsibilities of the said agencies in accordance with their constitutional instruments.

Article 17

1. The States Parties to the present Covenant shall furnish their reports in stages, in accordance with a programme to be established by the Economic and Social Council within one year of the entry into force of the present Covenant after consultation with the States Parties and the specialized agencies concerned.

2. Reports may indicate factors and difficulties affecting the degree of fulfilment of obligations under the present Covenant.

3. Where relevant information has previously been furnished to the United Nations or to any specialized agency by any State Party to the present Covenant, it will not be necessary to reproduce that information, but a precise reference to the information so furnished will suffice.

Article 18

Pursuant to its responsibilities under the Charter of the United Nations in the field of human rights and fundamental freedoms, the Economic and Social Council may make arrangements with the specialized agencies in respect of their reporting to it on the progress made in achieving the observance of the provisions of the present Covenant falling within the scope of their activities. These reports may include particulars of decisions and recommendations on such implementation adopted by their competent organs.

Article 19

The Economic and Social Council may transmit to the Commission on Human Rights for study and general recommendation or, as appropriate, for information the reports concerning human rights submitted by States in accordance with articles 16 and 17, and those concerning human rights submitted by the specialized agencies in accordance with article 18.

Article 20

The States Parties to the present Covenant and the specialized agencies concerned may submit comments to the Economic and Social Council on any general recommendation under article 19 or reference to such general recommendation in any report of the Commission on Human Rights or any documentation referred to therein.

Article 21

The Economic and Social Council may submit from time to time to the General Assembly reports with recommendations of a general nature and a summary of the information received from the States Parties to the present Covenant and the specialized agencies on the measures taken and the progress made in achieving general observance of the rights recognized in the present Covenant.

Article 22

The Economic and Social Council may bring to the attention of other organs of the United Nations, their subsidiary organs and specialized agencies concerned with furnishing technical assistance any matters arising out of the reports referred to in this part of the present Covenant which may assist such bodies in deciding, each within its field of competence, on the advisability of international measures likely to contribute to the effective progressive implementation of the present Covenant.

Article 23

The States Parties to the present Covenant agree that international action for the achievement of the rights recognized in the present Covenant includes such methods as the conclusion of conventions, the adoption of recommendations, the furnishing of technical assistance and the holding of regional meetings and technical meetings for the purpose of consultation and study organized in conjunction with the Governments concerned.

Article 24

Nothing in the present Covenant shall be interpreted as impairing the provisions of the Charter of the United Nations and of the constitutions of the specialized agencies which define the respective responsibilities of the various organs of the United Nations and of the specialized agencies in regard to the matters dealt with in the present Covenant.

Article 25

Nothing in the present Covenant shall be interpreted as impairing the inherent right of all peoples to enjoy and utilize fully and freely their natural wealth and resources.

PART V

Article 26

1.   The present Covenant is open for signature by any State Member of the United Nations or member of any of its specialized agencies, by any State Party to the Statute of the International Court of Justice, and by any other State which has been invited by the General Assembly of the United Nations to become a party to the present Covenant.

2.   The present Covenant is subject to ratification. Instruments of

ratification shall be deposited with the Secretary-General of the United Nations.

3.   The present Covenant shall be open to accession by any State referred to in paragraph 1 of this article.

4.   Accession shall be effected by the deposit of an instrument of accession with the Secretary-General of the United Nations.

5.   The Secretary-General of the United Nations shall inform all States which have signed the present Covenant or acceded to it of the deposit of each instrument of ratification or accession.

Article 27

1.   The present Covenant shall enter into force three months after the date of the deposit with the Secretary-General of the United Nations of the thirty-fifth instrument of ratification or instrument of accession.

2.   For each State ratifying the present Covenant or acceding to it after the deposit of the thirty-fifth instrument of ratification or instrument of accession, the present Covenant shall enter into force three months after the date of the deposit of its own instrument of ratification or instrument of accession.

Article 28

The provisions of the present Covenant shall extend to all parts of federal States without any limitations or exceptions.

Article 29

1.   Any State Party to the present Covenant may propose an amendment and file it with the Secretary-General of the United Nations. The Secretary-General shall thereupon communicate any proposed amendments to the States Parties to the present Covenant with a request that they notify him whether they favour a conference of States Parties for the purpose of considering and voting upon the proposals. In the event that at least one third of the States Parties favours such a conference, the Secretary-General shall convene the conference under the auspices of the United Nations. Any amendment adopted by a majority of the States Parties present and voting at the conference shall be submitted to the General Assembly of

the United Nations for approval.

2.   Amendments shall come into force when they have been approved by the General Assembly of the United Nations and accepted by a two-thirds majority of the States Parties to the present Covenant in accordance with their respective constitutional processes.

3.   When amendments come into force they shall be binding on those States Parties which have accepted them, other States Parties still being bound by the provisions of the present Covenant and any earlier amendment which they have accepted.

Article 30

Irrespective of the notifications made under article 26, paragraph 5, the Secretary-General of the United Nations shall inform all States referred to in paragraph I of the same article of the following particulars:

(a) Signatures, ratifications and accessions under article 26;

(b) The date of the entry into force of the present Covenant under article 27 and the date of the entry into force of any amendments under article 29.

Article 31

1.   The present Covenant, of which the Chinese, English, French, Russian and Spanish texts are equally authentic, shall be deposited in the archives of the United Nations.

2.   The Secretary-General of the United Nations shall transmit certified copie of the present Covenant to all States referred to in article 26.

Appendix 3:

Preamble

The States Parties to the present Covenant,

Considering that, in accordance with the principles proclaimed in the Charter of the United Nations, recognition of the inherent dignity and of the equal and inalienable rights of all members of the human family is the foundation of freedom, justice and peace in the world,

Recognizing that these rights derive from the inherent dignity of the human person,

Recognizing that, in accordance with the Universal Declaration of Human Rights, the ideal of free human beings enjoying civil and political freedom and freedom from fear and want can only be achieved if conditions are created whereby everyone may enjoy his civil and political rights, as well as his economic, social and cultural rights,

Considering the obligation of States under the Charter of the United Nations to promote universal respect for, and observance of, human rights and freedoms,

Realizing that the individual, having duties to other individuals and to the community to which he belongs, is under a responsibility to strive for the promotion and observance of the rights recognized in the present Covenant,

Agree upon the following articles:

PART I

Article 1

1.   All peoples have the right of self-determination. By virtue of that right they freely determine their political status and freely pursue their economic, social and cultural development.

2.   All peoples may, for their own ends, freely dispose of their natural wealth and resources without prejudice to any obligations arising out of international economic co-operation, based upon the principle of mutual benefit, and international

law. In no case may a people be deprived of its own means of subsistence.

3.   The States Parties to the present Covenant, including those having responsibility for the administration of Non-Self-Governing and Trust Territories, shall promote the realization of the right of self-determination, and shall respect that right, in conformity with the provisions of the Charter of the United Nations.

PART II

Article 2

1.   Each State Party to the present Covenant undertakes to respect and to ensure to all individuals within its territory and subject to its jurisdiction the rights recognized in the present Covenant, without distinction of any kind, such as race, colour, sex, language, religion, political or other opinion, national or social origin, property, birth or other status.

2.   Where not already provided for by existing legislative or other measures, each State Party to the present Covenant undertakes to take the necessary steps, in accordance with its constitutional processes and with the provisions of the present Covenant, to adopt such laws or other measures as may be necessary to give effect to the rights recognized in the present Covenant.

3.   Each State Party to the present Covenant undertakes:

(a) To ensure that any person whose rights or freedoms as herein recognized are violated shall have an effective remedy, notwithstanding that the violation has been committed by persons acting in an official capacity;

(b) To ensure that any person claiming such a remedy shall have his right thereto determined by competent judicial, administrative or legislative authorities, or by any other competent authority provided for by the legal system of the State, and to develop the possibilities of judicial remedy;

(c) To ensure that the competent authorities shall enforce such remedies when granted.

Article 3

The States Parties to the present Covenant undertake to ensure the equal right of men and women to the enjoyment of all civil and political rights set forth in the present Covenant.

Article 4

1 . In time of public emergency which threatens the life of the nation and the existence of which is officially proclaimed, the States Parties to the present Covenant may take measures derogating from their obligations under the present Covenant to the extent strictly required by the exigencies of the situation, provided that such measures are not inconsistent with their other obligations under international law and do not involve discrimination solely on the ground of race, colour, sex, language, religion or social origin.

1. No derogation from articles 6, 7, 8 (paragraphs I and 2), 11, 15, 16 and 18 may be made under this provision.

2. Any State Party to the present Covenant availing itself of the right of derogation shall immediately inform the other States Parties to the present Covenant, through the intermediary of the Secretary-General of the United Nations, of the provisions from which it has derogated and of the reasons by which it was actuated. A further communication shall be made, through the same intermediary, on the date on which it terminates such derogation.

Article 5

1. Nothing in the present Covenant may be interpreted as implying for any State, group or person any right to engage in any activity or perform any act aimed at the destruction of any of the rights and freedoms recognized herein or at their limitation to a greater extent than is provided for in the present Covenant.

2. There shall be no restriction upon or derogation from any of the fundamental human rights recognized or existing in any State Party to the present Covenant pursuant to law, conventions, regulations or custom on the pretext that the present Covenant does not recognize such rights or that it recognizes them to a lesser extent.

PART III

Article 6

1.   Every human being has the inherent right to life. This right shall be protected by law. No one shall be arbitrarily deprived of his life.

2.   In countries which have not abolished the death penalty, sentence of death may be imposed only for the most serious crimes in accordance with the law in force at the time of the commission of the crime and not contrary to the provisions of the present Covenant and to the Convention on the Prevention and Punishment of the Crime of Genocide. This penalty can only be carried out pursuant to a final judgement rendered by a competent court.

3.   When deprivation of life constitutes the crime of genocide, it is understood that nothing in this article shall authorize any State Party to the present Covenant to derogate in any way from any obligation assumed under the provisions of the Convention on the Prevention and Punishment of the Crime of Genocide.

4.   Anyone sentenced to death shall have the right to seek pardon or commutation of the sentence. Amnesty, pardon or commutation of the sentence of death may be granted in all cases.

5.   Sentence of death shall not be imposed for crimes committed by persons below eighteen years of age and shall not be carried out on pregnant women.

6.   Nothing in this article shall be invoked to delay or to prevent the abolition of capital punishment by any State Party to the present Covenant.

Article 7

No one shall be subjected to torture or to cruel, inhuman or degrading treatment or punishment. In particular, no one shall be subjected without his free consent to medical or scientific experimentation.

Article 8

1.   No one shall be held in slavery; slavery and the slave-trade in all their forms shall be prohibited.

2.   No one shall be held in servitude.

3.

(a) No one shall be required to perform forced or compulsory labour;

(b) Paragraph 3 (a) shall not be held to preclude, in countries where imprisonment with hard labour may be imposed as a punishment for a crime, the performance of hard labour in pursuance of a sentence to such punishment by a competent court;

(c) For the purpose of this paragraph the term "forced or compulsory labour" shall not include:

(i) Any work or service, not referred to in subparagraph (b), normally required of a person who is under detention in consequence of a lawful order of a court, or of a person during conditional release from such detention;

(ii) Any service of a military character and, in countries where conscientious objection is recognized, any national service required by law of conscientious objectors;

(iii) Any service exacted in cases of emergency or calamity threatening the life or well-being of the community;

(iv) Any work or service which forms part of normal civil obligations.

Article 9

1.   Everyone has the right to liberty and security of person. No one shall be subjected to arbitrary arrest or detention. No one shall be deprived of his liberty except on such grounds and in accordance with such procedure as are established by law.

2.   Anyone who is arrested shall be informed, at the time of arrest, of the reasons for his arrest and shall be promptly informed of any charges against him.

3.   Anyone arrested or detained on a criminal charge shall be brought promptly before a judge or other officer authorized by law to exercise judicial power and shall be entitled to trial within a reasonable time or to release. It shall not be the general rule that persons awaiting trial shall be detained in custody, but release may

be subject to guarantees to appear for trial, at any other stage of the judicial proceedings, and, should occasion arise, for execution of the judgement.

4.   Anyone who is deprived of his liberty by arrest or detention shall be entitled to take proceedings before a court, in order that that court may decide without delay on the lawfulness of his detention and order his release if the detention is not lawful.

5.   Anyone who has been the victim of unlawful arrest or detention shall have an enforceable right to compensation.

Article 10

1.   All persons deprived of their liberty shall be treated with humanity and with respect for the inherent dignity of the human person.

2.

(a) Accused persons shall, save in exceptional circumstances, be segregated from convicted persons and shall be subject to separate treatment appropriate to their status as unconvicted persons;

(b) Accused juvenile persons shall be separated from adults and brought as speedily as possible for adjudication.

3. The penitentiary system shall comprise treatment of prisoners the essential aim of which shall be their reformation and social rehabilitation. Juvenile offenders shall be segregated from adults and be accorded treatment appropriate to their age and legal status.

Article 11

No one shall be imprisoned merely on the ground of inability to fulfil a contractual obligation.

Article 12

1.   Everyone lawfully within the territory of a State shall, within that territory, have the right to liberty of movement and freedom to choose his residence.

2.   Everyone shall be free to leave any country, including his own.

3.   The above-mentioned rights shall not be subject to any restrictions except those which are provided by law, are necessary to protect national security, public order (ordre public), public health or morals or the rights and freedoms of others, and are consistent with the other rights recognized in the present Covenant.

4.   No one shall be arbitrarily deprived of the right to enter his own country.

Article 13

An alien lawfully in the territory of a State Party to the present Covenant may be expelled therefrom only in pursuance of a decision reached in accordance with law and shall, except where compelling reasons of national security otherwise require, be allowed to submit the reasons against his expulsion and to have his case reviewed by, and be represented for the purpose before, the competent authority or a person or persons especially designated by the competent authority.

Article 14

1.   All persons shall be equal before the courts and tribunals. In the determination of any criminal charge against him, or of his rights and obligations in a suit at law, everyone shall be entitled to a fair and public hearing by a competent, independent and impartial tribunal established by law. The press and the public may be excluded from all or part of a trial for reasons of morals, public order (ordre public) or national security in a democratic society, or when the interest of the private lives of the parties so requires, or to the extent strictly necessary in the opinion of the court in special circumstances where publicity would prejudice the interests of justice; but any judgement rendered in a criminal case or in a suit at law shall be made public except where the interest of juvenile persons otherwise requires or the proceedings concern matrimonial disputes or the guardianship of children.

2.   Everyone charged with a criminal offence shall have the right to be presumed innocent until proved guilty according to law.

3.   In the determination of any criminal charge against him, everyone shall be entitled to the following minimum guarantees, in full equality: (a) To be informed promptly and in detail in a language which he understands of the nature

and cause of the charge against him;

(b) To have adequate time and facilities for the preparation of his defence and to communicate with counsel of his own choosing;

(c) To be tried without undue delay;

(d) To be tried in his presence, and to defend himself in person or through legal assistance of his own choosing; to be informed, if he does not have legal assistance, of this right; and to have legal assistance assigned to him, in any case where the interests of justice so require, and without payment by him in any such case if he does not have sufficient means to pay for it;

(e) To examine, or have examined, the witnesses against him and to obtain the attendance and examination of witnesses on his behalf under the same conditions as witnesses against him;

(f) To have the free assistance of an interpreter if he cannot understand or speak the language used in court;

(g) Not to be compelled to testify against himself or to confess guilt.

1.   In the case of juvenile persons, the procedure shall be such as will take account of their age and the desirability of promoting their rehabilitation.

2.   Everyone convicted of a crime shall have the right to his conviction and sentence being reviewed by a higher tribunal according to law.

3.   When a person has by a final decision been convicted of a criminal offence and when subsequently his conviction has been reversed or he has been pardoned on the ground that a new or newly discovered fact shows conclusively that there has been a miscarriage of justice, the person who has suffered punishment as a result of such conviction shall be compensated according to law, unless it is proved that the non-disclosure of the unknown fact in time is wholly or partly attributable to him.

4.   No one shall be liable to be tried or punished again for an offence for which he has already been finally convicted or acquitted in accordance with the law and penal procedure of each country.

Article 15

1.   No one shall be held guilty of any criminal offence on account of any act or omission which did not constitute a criminal offence, under national or international law, at the time when it was committed. Nor shall a heavier penalty be imposed than the one that was applicable at the time when the criminal offence was committed. If, subsequent to the commission of the offence, provision is made by law for the imposition of the lighter penalty, the offender shall benefit thereby.

2. Nothing in this article shall prejudice the trial and punishment of any person for any act or omission which, at the time when it was committed, was criminal according to the general principles of law recognized by the community of nations.

Article 16

Everyone shall have the right to recognition everywhere as a person before the law.

Article 17

1.   No one shall be subjected to arbitrary or unlawful interference with his privacy, family, or correspondence, nor to unlawful attacks on his honour and reputation.

2.   Everyone has the right to the protection of the law against such interference or attacks.

Article 18

1.   Everyone shall have the right to freedom of thought, conscience and religion. This right shall include freedom to have or to adopt a religion or belief of his choice, and freedom, either individually or in community with others and in public or private, to manifest his religion or belief in worship, observance, practice and teaching.

2.   No one shall be subject to coercion which would impair his freedom to have or to adopt a religion or belief of his choice.

3.   Freedom to manifest one's religion or beliefs may be subject only to

such limitations as are prescribed by law and are necessary to protect public safety, order, health, or morals or the fundamental rights and freedoms of others.

4.   The States Parties to the present Covenant undertake to have respect for the liberty of parents and, when applicable, legal guardians to ensure the religious and moral education of their children in conformity with their own convictions.

Article 19

1.   Everyone shall have the right to hold opinions without interference.

2.   Everyone shall have the right to freedom of expression; this right shall include freedom to seek, receive and impart information and ideas of all kinds, regardless of frontiers, either orally, in writing or in print, in the form of art, or through any other media of his choice.

3.   The exercise of the rights provided for in paragraph 2 of this article carries with it special duties and responsibilities. It may therefore be subject to certain restrictions, but these shall only be such as are provided by law and are necessary:

(a) For respect of the rights or reputations of others;

(b) For the protection of national security or of public order (ordre public), or of public health or morals.

Article 20

1.   Any propaganda for war shall be prohibited by law.

2.   Any advocacy of national, racial or religious hatred that constitutes incitement to discrimination, hostility or violence shall be prohibited by law.

Article 21

The right of peaceful assembly shall be recognized. No restrictions may be placed on the exercise of this right other than those imposed in conformity with the law and which are necessary in a democratic society in the interests of national security or public safety, public order (ordre public), the protection of public health or morals or the protection of the rights and freedoms of others.

Article 22

1.   Everyone shall have the right to freedom of association with others, including the right to form and join trade unions for the protection of his interests.

2.   No restrictions may be placed on the exercise of this right other than those which are prescribed by law and which are necessary in a democratic society in the interests of national security or public safety, public order (ordre public), the protection of public health or morals or the protection of the rights and freedoms of others. This article shall not prevent the imposition of lawful restrictions on members of the armed forces and of the police in their exercise of this right.

3.   Nothing in this article shall authorize States Parties to the International Labour Organisation Convention of 1948 concerning Freedom of Association and Protection of the Right to Organize to take legislative measures which would prejudice, or to apply the law in such a manner as to prejudice, the guarantees provided for in that Convention.

Article 23

1.   The family is the natural and fundamental group unit of society and is entitled to protection by society and the State.

2.   The right of men and women of marriageable age to marry and to found a family shall be recognized.

3.   No marriage shall be entered into without the free and full consent of the intending spouses.

4.   States Parties to the present Covenant shall take appropriate steps to ensure equality of rights and responsibilities of spouses as to marriage, during marriage and at its dissolution. In the case of dissolution, provision shall be made for the necessary protection of any children.

Article 24

1.   Every child shall have, without any discrimination as to race, colour, sex, language, religion, national or social origin, property or birth, the right to such

measures of protection as are required by his status as a minor, on the part of his family, society and the State.

2.   Every child shall be registered immediately after birth and shall have a name.

3.   Every child has the right to acquire a nationality.

Article 25

Every citizen shall have the right and the opportunity, without any of the distinctions mentioned in article 2 and without unreasonable restrictions:

(a) To take part in the conduct of public affairs, directly or through freely chosen representatives;

(b) To vote and to be elected at genuine periodic elections which shall be by universal and equal suffrage and shall be held by secret ballot, guaranteeing the free expression of the will of the electors;

(c) To have access, on general terms of equality, to public service in his country.

Article 26

All persons are equal before the law and are entitled without any discrimination to the equal protection of the law. In this respect, the law shall prohibit any discrimination and guarantee to all persons equal and effective protection against discrimination on any ground such as race, colour, sex, language, religion, political or other opinion, national or social origin, property, birth or other status.

Article 27

In those States in which ethnic, religious or linguistic minorities exist, persons belonging to such minorities shall not be denied the right, in community with the other members of their group, to enjoy their own culture, to profess and practise their own religion, or to use their own language.

PART IV

Article 28

1.   There shall be established a Human Rights Committee (hereafter referred to in the present Covenant as the Committee). It shall consist of eighteen members and shall carry out the functions hereinafter provided.

2.   The Committee shall be composed of nationals of the States Parties to the present Covenant who shall be persons of high moral character and recognized competence in the field of human rights, consideration being given to the usefulness of the participation of some persons having legal experience.

3.   The members of the Committee shall be elected and shall serve in their personal capacity.

Article 29

1.   The members of the Committee shall be elected by secret ballot from a list of persons possessing the qualifications prescribed in article 28 and nominated for the purpose by the States Parties to the present Covenant.

2.   Each State Party to the present Covenant may nominate not more than two persons. These persons shall be nationals of the nominating State.

3.   A person shall be eligible for renomination.

Article 30

1.   The initial election shall be held no later than six months after the date of the entry into force of the present Covenant.

2.   At least four months before the date of each election to the Committee, other than an election to fill a vacancy declared in accordance with article 34, the Secretary-General of the United Nations shall address a written invitation to the States Parties to the present Covenant to submit their nominations for membership of the Committee within three months.

3.   The Secretary-General of the United Nations shall prepare a list in alphabetical order of all the persons thus nominated, with an indication of the States

Parties which have nominated them, and shall submit it to the States Parties to the present Covenant no later than one month before the date of each election.

4.   Elections of the members of the Committee shall be held at a meeting of the States Parties to the present Covenant convened by the Secretary General of the United Nations at the Headquarters of the United Nations. At that meeting, for which two thirds of the States Parties to the present Covenant shall constitute a quorum, the persons elected to the Committee shall be those nominees who obtain the largest number of votes and an absolute majority of the votes of the representatives of States Parties present and voting.

Article 31

1.   The Committee may not include more than one national of the same State.

2.   In the election of the Committee, consideration shall be given to equitable geographical distribution of membership and to the representation of the different forms of civilization and of the principal legal systems.

Article 32

1.   The members of the Committee shall be elected for a term of four years. They shall be eligible for re-election if renominated. However, the terms of nine of the members elected at the first election shall expire at the end of two years; immediately after the first election, the names of these nine members shall be chosen by lot by the Chairman of the meeting referred to in article 30, paragraph 4.

2.   Elections at the expiry of office shall be held in accordance with the preceding articles of this part of the present Covenant.

Article 33

1.   If, in the unanimous opinion of the other members, a member of the Committee has ceased to carry out his functions for any cause other than absence of a temporary character, the Chairman of the Committee shall notify the Secretary-General of the United Nations, who shall then declare the seat of that member to be vacant.

2.   In the event of the death or the resignation of a member of the Committee, the Chairman shall immediately notify the Secretary-General of the United Nations, who shall declare the seat vacant from the date of death or the date on which the resignation takes effect.

Article 34

1.   When a vacancy is declared in accordance with article 33 and if the term of office of the member to be replaced does not expire within six months of the declaration of the vacancy, the Secretary-General of the United Nations shall notify each of the States Parties to the present Covenant, which may within two months submit nominations in accordance with article 29 for the purpose of filling the vacancy.

2.   The Secretary-General of the United Nations shall prepare a list in alphabetical order of the persons thus nominated and shall submit it to the States Parties to the present Covenant. The election to fill the vacancy shall then take place in accordance with the relevant provisions of this part of the present Covenant.

3.   A member of the Committee elected to fill a vacancy declared in accordance with article 33 shall hold office for the remainder of the term of the member who vacated the seat on the Committee under the provisions of that article.

Article 35

The members of the Committee shall, with the approval of the General Assembly of the United Nations, receive emoluments from United Nations resources on such terms and conditions as the General Assembly may decide, having regard to the importance of the Committee's responsibilities.

Article 36

The Secretary-General of the United Nations shall provide the necessary staff and facilities for the effective performance of the functions of the Committee under the present Covenant.

Article 37

1.   The Secretary-General of the United Nations shall convene the initial

meeting of the Committee at the Headquarters of the United Nations.

2.   After its initial meeting, the Committee shall meet at such times as shall be provided in its rules of procedure.

3.   The Committee shall normally meet at the Headquarters of the United Nations or at the United Nations Office at Geneva.

Article 38

Every member of the Committee shall, before taking up his duties, make a solemn declaration in open committee that he will perform his functions impartially and conscientiously.

Article 39

1.   The Committee shall elect its officers for a term of two years. They may be re-elected.

2.   The Committee shall establish its own rules of procedure, but these rules shall provide, inter alia, that:

(a) Twelve members shall constitute a quorum;

(b) Decisions of the Committee shall be made by a majority vote of the members present.

Article 40

1. The States Parties to the present Covenant undertake to submit reports on the measures they have adopted which give effect to the rights recognized herein and on the progress made in the enjoyment of those rights: (a) Within one year of the entry into force of the present Covenant for the States Parties concerned;

(b) Thereafter whenever the Committee so requests.

1.   All reports shall be submitted to the Secretary-General of the United Nations, who shall transmit them to the Committee for consideration. Reports shall indicate the factors and difficulties, if any, affecting the implementation of the present Covenant.

2.   The Secretary-General of the United Nations may, after consultation with the Committee, transmit to the specialized agencies concerned copies of such parts of the reports as may fall within their field of competence.

3.   The Committee shall study the reports submitted by the States Parties to the present Covenant. It shall transmit its reports, and such general comments as it may consider appropriate, to the States Parties. The Committee may also transmit to the Economic and Social Council these comments along with the copies of the reports it has received from States Parties to the present Covenant.

4.   The States Parties to the present Covenant may submit to the Committee observations on any comments that may be made in accordance with paragraph 4 of this article.

Article 41

1. A State Party to the present Covenant may at any time declare under this article that it recognizes the competence of the Committee to receive and consider communications to the effect that a State Party claims that another State Party is not fulfilling its obligations under the present Covenant. Communications under this article may be received and considered only if submitted by a State Party which has made a declaration recognizing in regard to itself the competence of the Committee. No communication shall be received by the Committee if it concerns a State Party which has not made such a declaration. Communications received under this article shall be dealt with in accordance with the following procedure:

(a) If a State Party to the present Covenant considers that another State Party is not giving effect to the provisions of the present Covenant, it may, by written communication, bring the matter to the attention of that State Party. Within three months after the receipt of the communication the receiving State shall afford the State which sent the communication an explanation, or any other statement in writing clarifying the matter which should include, to the extent possible and pertinent, reference to domestic procedures and remedies taken, pending, or available in the matter;

(b) If the matter is not adjusted to the satisfaction of both States Parties concerned within six months after the receipt by the receiving State of the initial communication, either State shall have the right to refer the matter to the Committee, by notice given to the Committee and to the other State;

(c) The Committee shall deal with a matter referred to it only after it has ascertained that all available domestic remedies have been invoked and exhausted in the matter, in conformity with the generally recognized principles of international law. This shall not be the rule where the application of the remedies is unreasonably prolonged;

(d) The Committee shall hold closed meetings when examining communications under this article;

(e) Subject to the provisions of subparagraph (c), the Committee shall make available its good offices to the States Parties concerned with a view to a friendly solution of the matter on the basis of respect for human rights and fundamental freedoms as recognized in the present Covenant;

(f) In any matter referred to it, the Committee may call upon the States Parties concerned, referred to in subparagraph (b), to supply any relevant information;

(g) The States Parties concerned, referred to in subparagraph (b), shall have the right to be represented when the matter is being considered in the Committee and to make submissions orally and/or in writing;

(h) The Committee shall, within twelve months after the date of receipt of notice under subparagraph (b), submit a report:

(i) If a solution within the terms of subparagraph (e) is reached, the Committee shall confine its report to a brief statement of the facts and of the solution reached;

(ii) If a solution within the terms of subparagraph (e) is not reached, the Committee shall confine its report to a brief statement of the facts; the written submissions and record of the oral submissions made by the States Parties concerned shall be attached to the report. In every matter, the report shall be communicated to the States Parties concerned.

2. The provisions of this article shall come into force when ten States Parties to the present Covenant have made declarations under paragraph I of this article. Such declarations shall be deposited by the States Parties with the Secretary-General of the United Nations, who shall transmit copies thereof to the other States Parties. A declaration may be withdrawn at any time by notification to the Secretary-General. Such a withdrawal shall not prejudice the consideration of any matter which is the subject of a communication already transmitted under this article; no further communication by any State Party shall be received after the notification of withdrawal of the declaration has been received by the Secretary-General, unless the State Party concerned has made a new declaration.

Article 42

1.

(a) If a matter referred to the Committee in accordance with article 41 is not resolved to the satisfaction of the States Parties concerned, the Committee may, with the prior consent of the States Parties concerned, appoint an ad hoc Conciliation Commission (hereinafter referred to as the Commission). The good offices of the Commission shall be made available to the States Parties concerned with a view to an amicable solution of the matter on the basis of respect for the present Covenant;

(b) The Commission shall consist of five persons acceptable to the States Parties concerned. If the States Parties concerned fail to reach agreement within three months on all or part of the composition of the Commission, the members of the Commission concerning whom no agreement has been reached shall be elected by secret ballot by a two-thirds majority vote of the Committee from among its members.

1.   The members of the Commission shall serve in their personal capacity. They shall not be nationals of the States Parties concerned, or of a State not Party to the present Covenant, or of a State Party which has not made a declaration under article 41.

2.   The Commission shall elect its own Chairman and adopt its own rules of procedure.

3.   The meetings of the Commission shall normally be held at the

Headquarters of the United Nations or at the United Nations Office at Geneva. However, they may be held at such other convenient places as the Commission may determine in consultation with the Secretary-General of the United Nations and the States Parties concerned.

4.   The secretariat provided in accordance with article 36 shall also service the commissions appointed under this article.

5.   The information received and collated by the Committee shall be made available to the Commission and the Commission may call upon the States Parties concerned to supply any other relevant information.

6.   When the Commission has fully considered the matter, but in any event not later than twelve months after having been seized of the matter, it shall submit to the Chairman of the Committee a report for communication to the States Parties concerned:

(a) If the Commission is unable to complete its consideration of the matter within twelve months, it shall confine its report to a brief statement of the status of its consideration of the matter;

(b) If an amicable solution to the matter on tie basis of respect for human rights as recognized in the present Covenant is reached, the Commission shall confine its report to a brief statement of the facts and of the solution reached;

(c) If a solution within the terms of subparagraph (b) is not reached, the Commission's report shall embody its findings on all questions of fact relevant to the issues between the States Parties concerned, and its views on the possibilities of an amicable solution of the matter. This report shall also contain the written submissions and a record of the oral submissions made by the States Parties concerned;

(d) If the Commission's report is submitted under subparagraph (c), the States Parties concerned shall, within three months of the receipt of the report, notify the Chairman of the Committee whether or not they accept the contents of the report of the Commission.

1.   The provisions of this article are without prejudice to the responsibilities of the Committee under article 41.

2.   The States Parties concerned shall share equally all the expenses of the members of the Commission in accordance with estimates to be provided by the Secretary-General of the United Nations.

3.   The Secretary-General of the United Nations shall be empowered to pay the expenses of the members of the Commission, if necessary, before reimbursement by the States Parties concerned, in accordance with paragraph 9 of this article.

Article 43

The members of the Committee, and of the ad hoc conciliation commissions which may be appointed under article 42, shall be entitled to the facilities, privileges and immunities of experts on mission for the United Nations as laid down in the relevant sections of the Convention on the Privileges and Immunities of the United Nations.

Article 44

The provisions for the implementation of the present Covenant shall apply without prejudice to the procedures prescribed in the field of human rights by or under the constituent instruments and the conventions of the United Nations and of the specialized agencies and shall not prevent the States Parties to the present Covenant from having recourse to other procedures for settling a dispute in accordance with general or special international agreements in force between them.

Article 45

The Committee shall submit to the General Assembly of the United Nations, through the Economic and Social Council, an annual report on its activities.

PART V

Article 46

Nothing in the present Covenant shall be interpreted as impairing the provisions of the Charter of the United Nations and of the constitutions of the specialized agencies which define the respective responsibilities of the various organs of the United Nations and of the specialized agencies in regard to the matters dealt with in the present Covenant.

Article 47

Nothing in the present Covenant shall be interpreted as impairing the inherent right of all peoples to enjoy and utilize fully and freely their natural wealth and resources.

PART VI

Article 48

1.   The present Covenant is open for signature by any State Member of the United Nations or member of any of its specialized agencies, by any State Party to the Statute of the International Court of Justice, and by any other State which has been invited by the General Assembly of the United Nations to become a Party to the present Covenant.

2.   The present Covenant is subject to ratification. Instruments of ratification shall be deposited with the Secretary-General of the United Nations.

3.   The present Covenant shall be open to accession by any State referred to in paragraph 1 of this article.

4.   Accession shall be effected by the deposit of an instrument of accession with the Secretary-General of the United Nations.

5.   The Secretary-General of the United Nations shall inform all States which have signed this Covenant or acceded to it of the deposit of each instrument of ratification or accession.

Article 49

1.   The present Covenant shall enter into force three months after the date of the deposit with the Secretary-General of the United Nations of the thirty-fifth instrument of ratification or instrument of accession.

2.   For each State ratifying the present Covenant or acceding to it after the deposit of the thirty-fifth instrument of ratification or instrument of accession, the present Covenant shall enter into force three months after the date of the deposit of its own instrument of ratification or instrument of accession.

Article 50

The provisions of the present Covenant shall extend to all parts of federal States without any limitations or exceptions.

Article 51

1.   Any State Party to the present Covenant may propose an amendment and file it with the Secretary-General of the United Nations. The Secretary-General of the United Nations shall thereupon communicate any proposed amendments to the States Parties to the present Covenant with a request that they notify him whether they favour a conference of States Parties for the purpose of considering and voting upon the proposals. In the event that at least one third of the States Parties favours such a conference, the Secretary-General shall convene the conference under the auspices of the United Nations. Any amendment adopted by a majority of the States Parties present and voting at the conference shall be submitted to the General Assembly of the United Nations for approval.

2.   Amendments shall come into force when they have been approved by the General Assembly of the United Nations and accepted by a two-thirds majority of the States Parties to the present Covenant in accordance with their respective constitutional processes. 3. When amendments come into force, they shall be binding on those States Parties which have accepted them, other States Parties still being bound by the provisions of the present Covenant and any earlier amendment which they have accepted.

Article 52

1. Irrespective of the notifications made under article 48, paragraph 5, the Secretary-General of the United Nations shall inform all States referred to in paragraph I of the same article of the following particulars:

(a) Signatures, ratifications and accessions under article 48;

(b) The date of the entry into force of the present Covenant under article 49 and the date of the entry into force of any amendments under article 51.

Article 53

1. The present Covenant, of which the Chinese, English, French, Russian and Spanish texts are equally authentic, shall be deposited in the archives of the United Nations.

2. The Secretary-General of the United Nations shall transmit certified copies of the present Covenant to all States referred to in article 48.

Appendix 4:

Universal Islamic Declaration of Human Rights

21 Dhul Qaidah 1401 **19 September 1981**

Contents

Foreword

Preamble

I Right to Life

II Right to Freedom

III Right to Equality and Prohibition Against Impermissible Discrimination

IV Right to Justice

V Right to Fair Trial

VI Right to Protection Against Abuse of Power

VII Right to Protection Against Torture

VIII Right to Protection of Honour and Reputation

IX Right to Asylum

X Rights of Minorities

This is a declaration for mankind, a guidance and instruction to those who fear God. (Al Qur'an, Al-Imran 3:138)

Foreword

Islam gave to mankind an ideal code of human rights fourteen centuries ago. These rights aim at conferring honour and dignity on mankind and eliminating exploitation, oppression and injustice.

Human rights in Islam are firmly rooted in the belief that God, and God alone, is the Law Giver and the Source of all human rights. Due to their Divine origin, no ruler, government, assembly or authority can curtail or violate in any way the human rights conferred by God, nor can they be surrendered.

Human rights in Islam are an integral part of the overall Islamic order and it is obligatory on all Muslim governments and organs of society to implement them in letter and in spirit within the framework of that order.

It is unfortunate that human rights are being trampled upon with impunity in many countries of the world, including some Muslim countries. Such violations are a matter of serious concern and are arousing the conscience of more and more people throughout the world.

I sincerely hope that this *Declaration of Human Rights* will give a powerful impetus to the Muslim peoples to stand firm and defend resolutely and courageously the rights conferred on them by God.

This *Declaration of Human Rights* is the second fundamental document proclaimed by the Islamic Council to mark the beginning of the 15th Century of the Islamic era, the first being the *Universal Islamic Declaration* announced at the International Conference on The Prophet Muhammad (peace and blessings be upon him) and his Message, held in London from 12 to 15 April 1980.

The *Universal Islamic Declaration of Human Rights* is based on the Qur'an and the Sunnah and has been compiled by eminent Muslim scholars, jurists and representatives of Islamic movements and thought. May God reward them all for their efforts and guide us along the right path.

Paris 21 Dhul Qaidah 1401 Salem Azzam

19th September 1981 *Secretary General*

O men! Behold, We have created you all out of a male and a female, and have made you into nations and tribes, so that you might come to know one another. Verily, the noblest of you in the sight of God is the one who is most deeply conscious of Him. Behold, God is all-knowing, all aware. (Al Qur'an, Al-Hujurat 49:13)

Preamble

WHEREAS the age-old human aspiration for a just world order wherein people could live, develop and prosper in an environment free from fear, oppression, exploitation and deprivation, remains largely unfulfilled;

WHEREAS the Divine Mercy unto mankind reflected in its having been endowed with super-abundant economic sustenance is being wasted, or unfairly or unjustly withheld from the inhabitants of the earth;

WHEREAS Allah (God) has given mankind through His revelations in the Holy Qur'an and the Sunnah of His Blessed Prophet Muhammad an abiding legal and moral framework within which to establish and regulate human institutions and relationships;

WHEREAS the human rights decreed by the Divine Law aim at conferring dignity and honour on mankind and are designed to eliminate oppression and injustice;

WHEREAS by virtue of their Divine source and sanction these rights can neither be curtailed, abrogated or disregarded by authorities, assemblies or other institutions, nor can they be surrendered or alienated;

Therefore we, as Muslims, who believe

a) in God, the Beneficent and Merciful, the Creator, the Sustainer, the Sovereign, the sole Guide of mankind and the Source of all Law;

b) in the Vicegerency (Khilafah) of man who has been created to fulfill the Will of God on earth;

c) in the wisdom of Divine guidance brought by the Prophets, whose mission found its culmination in the final Divine message that was conveyed by the Prophet Muhammad (Peace be upon him) to all mankind;

d) that rationality by itself without the light of revelation from God can neither be a sure guide in the affairs of mankind nor provide spiritual nourishment to the human soul, and, knowing that the teachings of Islam represent the quintessence of Divine guidance in its final and perfect form, feel duty-bound to remind man of the high status and dignity bestowed on him by God;

e) in inviting all mankind to the message of Islam;

f) that by the terms of our primeval covenant with God our duties and obligations have priority over our rights, and that each one of us is under a bounden duty to spread the teachings of Islam by word, deed, and indeed in all gentle ways, and to make them effective not only in our individual lives but also in the society around us;

g) in our obligation to establish an Islamic order:

i) wherein all human beings shall be equal and none shall enjoy a privilege or suffer a disadvantage or discrimination by reason of race, colour, sex, origin or language;

ii) wherein all human beings are born free;

iii) wherein slavery and forced labour are abhorred;

iv) wherein conditions shall be established such that the institution of family shall be preserved, protected and honoured as the basis of all social life;

v) wherein the rulers and the ruled alike are subject to, and equal before, the Law;

vi) wherein obedience shall be rendered only to those commands that are in consonance with the Law;

vii) wherein all worldly power shall be considered as a sacred trust, to be exercised within the limits prescribed by the Law and in a manner approved by it, and with due regard for the priorities fixed by it;

viii) wherein all economic resources shall be treated as Divine blessings bestowed upon mankind, to be enjoyed by all in accordance with the rules and the values set out in the Qur'an and the Sunnah;

ix) wherein all public affairs shall be determined and conducted, and the authority to administer them shall be exercised after mutual consultation *(Shura)* between the believers qualified to contribute to a decision which would accord well with the Law and the public good;

x) wherein everyone shall undertake obligations proportionate to his capacity and shall be held responsible pro rata for his deeds;

xi) wherein everyone shall, in case of an infringement of his rights, be assured of appropriate remedial measures in accordance with the Law;

xii) wherein no one shall be deprived of the rights assured to him by the Law except by its authority and to the extent permitted by it;

xiii) wherein every individual shall have the right to bring legal action against anyone who commits a crime against society as a whole or against any of its members;

xiv) wherein every effort shall be made to

(a) secure unto mankind deliverance from every type of exploitation, injustice and oppression,

(b) ensure to everyone security, dignity and liberty in terms set out and by methods approved and within the limits set by the Law;

Do hereby, as servants of Allah and as members of the Universal Brotherhood of Islam, at the beginning of the Fifteenth Century of the Islamic Era, affirm our commitment to uphold the following inviolable and inalienable human rights that we consider are enjoined by Islam.

I Right to Life

a) Human life is sacred and inviolable and every effort shall be made to protect it. In particular no one shall be exposed to injury or death, except under the authority of the Law.

b) Just as in life, so also after death, the sanctity of a person's body shall be inviolable. It is the obligation of believers to see that a deceased person's body is handled with due solemnity.

II Right to Freedom

a) Man is born free. No inroads shall be made on his right to liberty except under the authority and in due process of the Law.

b) Every individual and every people has the inalienable right to freedom in all its forms□ physical, cultural, economic and political — and shall be entitled to struggle by all available means against any infringement or abrogation of this right; and every oppressed individual or people has a legitimate claim to the support of other individuals and/or peoples in such a struggle.

III Right to Equality and Prohibition Against Impermissible Discrimination

a) All persons are equal before the Law and are entitled to equal opportunities and protection of the Law.

b) All persons shall be entitled to equal wage for equal work.

c) No person shall be denied the opportunity to work or be discriminated against in any manner or exposed to greater physical risk by reason of religious belief, colour, race, origin, sex or language.

IV Right to Justice

a) Every person has the right to be treated in accordance with the Law, and only in accordance with the Law.

b) Every person has not only the right but also the obligation to protest against injustice; to recourse to remedies provided by the Law in respect of any unwarranted personal injury or loss; to self-defence against any charges that are preferred against him and to obtain fair adjudication before an independent judicial tribunal in any dispute with public authorities or any other person.

c) It is the right and duty of every person to defend the rights of any other person and the community in general *(Hisbah)*.

d) No person shall be discriminated against while seeking to defend private and public rights.

e) It is the right and duty of every Muslim to refuse to obey any command which is contrary to the Law, no matter by whom it may be issued.

V Right to Fair Trial

a) No person shall be adjudged guilty of an offence and made liable to punishment except after proof of his guilt before an independent judicial tribunal.

b) No person shall be adjudged guilty except after a fair trial and after reasonable opportunity for defence has been provided to him.

c) Punishment shall be awarded in accordance with the Law, in proportion to the seriousness of the offence and with due consideration of the circumstances under which it was committed.

d) No act shall be considered a crime unless it is stipulated as such in the clear wording of the Law.

e) Every individual is responsible for his actions. Responsibility for a crime cannot be vicariously extended to other members of his family or group, who are not otherwise directly or indirectly involved in the commission of the crime in question.

VI Right to Protection Against Abuse of Power

Every person has the right to protection against harassment by official agencies. He is not liable to account for himself except for making a defence to the charges made against him or where he is found in a situation wherein a question regarding suspicion of his involvement in a crime could be *reasonably* raised

VII Right to Protection Against Torture

No person shall be subjected to torture in mind or body, or degraded, or threatened with injury either to himself or to anyone related to or held dear by him, or forcibly made to confess to the commission of a crime, or forced to consent to an act which is injurious to his interests.

VIII Right to Protection of Honour and Reputation

Every person has the right to protect his honour and reputation against calumnies, groundless charges or deliberate attempts at defamation and blackmail.

IX Right to Asylum

a) Every persecuted or oppressed person has the right to seek refuge and asylum. This right is guaranteed to every human being irrespective of race, religion, colour and sex.

b) Al Masjid Al Haram (the sacred house of Allah) in Mecca is a sanctuary for all Muslims.

X Rights of Minorities

a) The Qur'anic principle "There is no compulsion in religion" shall govern the religious rights of non-Muslim minorities.

b) In a Muslim country religious minorities shall have the choice to be governed in respect of their civil and personal matters by Islamic Law, or by their own laws.

XI Right and Obligation to Participate in the Conduct and Management of Public Affairs

a) Subject to the Law, every individual in the community *(Ummah)* is entitled to assume public office.

b) Process of free consultation *(Shura)* is the basis of the administrative relationship between the government and the people. People also have the right to choose and remove their rulers in accordance with this principle.

XII Right to Freedom of Belief, Thought and Speech

a) Every person has the right to express his thoughts and beliefs so long as he remains within the limits prescribed by the Law. No one, however, is entitled to disseminate falsehood or to circulate reports which may outrage public decency, or to indulge in slander, innuendo or to cast defamatory aspersions on other persons.

b) Pursuit of knowledge and search after truth is not only a right but a duty of every Muslim.

c) It is the right and duty of every Muslim to protest and strive (within the limits set out by the Law) against oppression even if it involves challenging the highest authority in the state.

d) There shall be no bar on the dissemination of information provided it does not endanger the security of the society or the state and is confined within the limits imposed by the Law.

e) No one shall hold in contempt or ridicule the religious beliefs of others or incite public hostility against them; respect for the religious feelings of others is obligatory on all Muslims.

XIII Right to Freedom of Religion

Every person has the right to freedom of conscience and worship in accordance with his religious beliefs.

XIV Right to Free Association

a) Every person is entitled to participate individually and collectively in the religious, social, cultural and political life of his community and to establish institutions and agencies meant to enjoin what is right *(ma'roof)* and to prevent what is wrong *(munkar)*.

b) Every person is entitled to strive for the establishment of institutions whereunder an enjoyment of these rights would be made possible. Collectively, the community is obliged to establish conditions so as to allow its members full development of their personalities.

XV The Economic Order and the Rights Evolving Therefrom

a) In their economic pursuits, all persons are entitled to the full benefits of nature and all its resources. These are blessings bestowed by God for the benefit of mankind as a whole.

b) All human beings are entitled to earn their living according to the Law.

c) Every person is entitled to own property individually or in association with others. State ownership of certain economic resources in the public interest is legitimate.

d) The poor have the right to a prescribed share in the wealth of the rich, as fixed by Zakah, levied and collected in accordance with the Law.

e) All means of production shall be utilised in the interest of the community *(Ummah)* as a whole, and may not be neglected or misused.

f) In order to promote the development of a balanced economy and to protect society from exploitation, Islamic Law forbids monopolies, unreasonable restrictive trade practices, usury, the use of coercion in the making of contracts and the publication of misleading advertisements.

g) All economic activities are permitted provided they are not detrimental to the interests of the community *(Ummah)* and do not violate Islamic laws and values.

XVI Right to Protection of Property

No property may be expropriated except in the public interest and on payment of fair and adequate compensation.

XVII Status and Dignity of Workers

Islam honours work and the worker and enjoins Muslims not only to treat the worker justly but also generously. He is not only to be paid his earned wages promptly, but is also entitled to adequate rest and leisure.

XVIII Right to Social Security

Every person has the right to food, shelter, clothing, education and medical care consistent with the resources of the community. This obligation of the community extends in particular to all individuals who cannot take care of themselves due to some temporary or permanent disability.

XIX Right to Found a Family and Related Matters

a) Every person is entitled to marry, to found a family and to bring up children in conformity with his religion, traditions and culture. Every spouse is entitled to such rights and privileges and carries such obligations as are stipulated by the Law.

b) Each of the partners in a marriage is entitled to respect and consideration from the other.

c) Every husband is obligated to maintain his wife and children according to his means.

d) Every child has the right to be maintained and properly brought up by its parents, it being forbidden that children are made to work at an early age or that any burden is put on them which would arrest or harm their natural development.

e) If parents are for some reason unable to discharge their obligations towards a child it becomes the responsibility of the community to fulfill these obligations at public expense.

f) Every person is entitled to material support, as well as care and protection, from his family during his childhood, old age or incapacity. Parents are entitled to material support as well as care and protection from their children.

g) Motherhood is entitled to special respect, care and assistance on the part of the family and the public organs of the community *(Ummah)*.

h) Within the family, men and women are to share in their obligations and responsibilities according to their sex, their natural endowments, talents and inclinations, bearing in mind their common responsibilities toward their progeny and their relatives.

i) No person may be married against his or her will, or lose or suffer dimunition of legal personality on account of marriage.

XX Rights of Married Women

Every married woman is entitled to:

a) live in the house in which her husband lives;

b) receive the means necessary for maintaining a standard of living which is not inferior to that of her spouse, and, in the event of divorce, receive during the statutory period of waiting *(iddah)* means of maintenance commensurate with her husband's resources, for herself as well as for the children she nurses or keeps, irrespective of her own financial status, earnings, or property that she may hold in her own rights;

c) seek and obtain dissolution of marriage (*Khul'a)* in accordance with the terms of the Law. This right is in addition to her right to seek divorce through the courts.

d) inherit from her husband, her parents, her children and other relatives according to the Law;

e) strict confidentiality from her spouse, or ex-spouse if divorced, with regard to any information that he may have obtained about her, the disclosure of which could prove detrimental to her interests. A similar responsibility rests upon her in respect of her spouse or ex-spouse.

XXI Right to Education

a) Every person is entitled to receive education in accordance with his natural capabilities.

b) Every person is entitled to a free choice of profession and career and to the opportunity for the full development of his natural endowments.

XXII Right of Privacy

Every person is entitled to the protection of his privacy.

XXIII Right to Freedom of Movement and Residence

a) In view of the fact that the World of Islam is veritably *Ummah Islamia*, every Muslim shall have the right to freely move in and out of any Muslim country.

b) No one shall be forced to leave the country of his residence, or be arbitrarily deported therefrom without recourse to due process of Law.

Explanatory Notes

1 In the above formulation of Human Rights, unless the context provides otherwise:

a) the term 'person' refers to both the male and female sexes.

b) the term 'Law' denotes the *Shari'ah*, i.e. the totality of ordinances derived from the Qur'an and the Sunnah and any other laws that are deduced from these two sources by methods considered valid in Islamic jurisprudence.

2 Each one of the Human Rights enunciated in this declaration carries a corresponding duty.

3 In the exercise and enjoyment of the rights referred to above every person shall be subject only to such limitations as are enjoined by the Law for the purpose

of securing the due recognition of, and respect for, the rights and the freedom of others and of meeting the just requirements of morality, public order and the general welfare of the Community *(Ummah)*.

The Arabic text of this *Declaration* is the original.

Glossary of Arabic Terms

SUNNAH - The example or way of life of the Prophet (peace be upon him), embracing what he said, did or agreed to.

KHALIFAH - The vicegerency of man on earth or succession to the Prophet, transliterated into English as the Caliphate.

HISBAH- Public vigilance, an institution of the Islamic State enjoined to observe and facilitate the fulfillment of right norms of public behaviour. The "Hisbah" consists in public vigilance as well as an opportunity to private individuals to seek redress through it.

MA'ROOF - Good act.

MUNKAR - Reprehensible deed.

ZAKAH - The 'purifying' tax on wealth, one of the five pillars of Islam obligatory on Muslims.

'IDDAH - The waiting period of a widowed or divorced woman during which she is not to re-marry.

KHUL'A - Divorce a woman obtains at her own request.

UMMAH ISLAMIA - World Muslim community.

SHARI'AH - Islamic law.

References

Note: The Roman numerals refer to the topics in the text. The Arabic numerals refer to the Chapter and the Verse of the Qur'an, i.e. 5:32 means Chapter 5, Verse 32.

I   1 Qur'an Al-Maidah *5:32*

    2   *Hadith narrated by Muslim, Abu Daud,Tirmidhi, Nasai*

    3   *Hadith narrated by Bukhari*

II 4   Hadith narrated by Bukhari, Muslim

    5   Sayings of Caliph Umar

    6   Qur'an As-Shura *42:41*

    7   Qur'an Al-Hajj *22:41*

III 8 From the Prophet's address

    9   Hadith narrated by Bukhari, Muslim, Abu Daud, Tirmidhi, Nasai

    10   From the address of Caliph Abu Bakr

    11   From the Prophet's farewell address

    12   Qur'an Al-Ahqaf *46:19*

    13   Hadith narrated by Ahmad

    14   Qur'an Al-Mulk *67:15*

    15   Qur'an Al-Zalzalah 99:7-8

IV   16   Qur'an An-Nisa *4:59*

    17   Qur 'an Al-Maidah *5:49*

    18   Qur'an An-Nisa *4:148*

    19   Hadith narrated by Bukhari, Muslim, Tirmidhi

    20   Hadith narrated by Bukhari, Muslim

    21   Hadith narrated by Muslim, Abu Daud, Tirmdhi, Nasai

    22   Hadith narrated by Bukhari, Muslim, Abu Daud, Tirmidhi, Nasai

    23   Hadith narrated by Abu Daud, Tirmidhi

    24   Hadith narrated by Bukhari, Muslim, Abu Daud, Tirmidhi, Nasai

    25   Hadith narrated by Bukhari

V 26 Hadith narrated by Bukhari, Muslim

  27 Qur'an Al-Isra *17:15*

  28 Qur'an Al-Ahzab *33:5*

  29 Qur'an Al-Hujurat *49:6*

  30 Qur'an An-Najm *53:28*

  31 Qur'an Al Baqarah *2:229*

  32 Hadith narrated by Al Baihaki, Hakim

  33 Qur'an Al-Isra *17:15*

  34 Qur'an At-Tur *52:21*

  35 Qur'an Yusuf *12:79*

VI *36* *Qur'an Al Ahzab 33:58*

VII 37 Hadith narrated by Bukhari, Muslim, Abu Daud, Tirmidhi, Nasai

  38 Hadith narrated by Ibn Majah

VIII 39 From the Prophet's farewell address

  40 Qur'an Al-Hujurat *49:12*

  41 Qur'an Al-Hujurat *49:11*

IX *42* *Qur'an At-Tawba 9:6*

  43 Qur'an Al-Imran *3:97*

  44 Qur'an Al-Baqarah *2:125*

  45 Qur'an Al-Hajj *22:25*

X *46* *Qur'an Al Baqarah 2:256*

  47 *Qur'an Al-Maidah 5:42*

  48 *Qur'an Al-Maidah 5:43*

  49 *Qur'an Al-Maidah 5:47*

XI *50* *Qur'an As-Shura 42:38*

  51 Hadith narated by Ahmad

  52 From the address of Caliph Abu Bakr

XII 53 Qur'an Al-Ahzab *33:60-61*

  54 Qur'an Saba *34:46*

  55 Hadith narrated by Tirmidhi, Nasai

87   *Hadith narrated by Ibn Majah*

88   *Qur'an Al-Ahqaf 46:19*

89 *Qur'an At-Tawbah 9:105*

90   *Hadith narrated by Tabarani—Majma Al Zawaid*

91   *Hadith narrated by Bukhari*

XVIII 92 Qur'an Al-Ahzab *33:6*

XIX 93 Qur'an An-Nisa *4:1*

94   *Qur'an Al-Baqarah 2:228*

95   *Hadith narrated by Bukhari, Muslim,Abu Daud, Tirmidhi, Nasai*

96   *Qur'an Ar-Rum 30:21*

97 *Qur'an At-Talaq 65:7*

98 *Qur'an Al-Isra 17:24*

99 *Hadith narrated by Bukhari, Muslim,Abu Daud, Tirmidhi*

100   *Hadith narrated by Abu Daud*

101   *Hadith narrated by Bukhari, Muslim*

102   *Hadith narrated by Abu Daud, Tirmidhi*

103   *Hadith narrated by Ahmad, Abu Daud*

XX 104 Qur'an At-Talaq 65:6

105   Qur'an An-Nisa *4:34*

106   Qur'an At-Talaq 65:6

107   Qur'an AtTalaq 65:6

108   Qur'an Al-Baqarah *2:229*

109   Qur'an An-Nisa *4:12*

110   Qur'an Al-Baqarah *2:237*

XXI 111 Qur'an Al-Isra *17:23-24*

112   *Hadith narrated by Ibn Majah*

113   *Qur'an Al-Imran 3:187*

114   *From the Prophet's farewell address*

115   *Hadith narrated by Bukhari, Muslim*

116   *Hadith narrated by Bukhari, Muslim,Abu Daud, Tirmidhi*

Appendix 5:

Cairo Declaration on Human Rights in Islam

The Nineteenth Islamic Conference of Foreign Ministers (Session of Peace, Interdependence and Development), held in Cairo, Arab Republic of Egypt, from 9-14 Muharram 1411H (31 July to 5 August 1990),

Keenly aware of the place of mankind in Islam as vicegerent of Allah on Earth;

Recognizing the importance of issuing a Document on Human Rights in Islam that will serve as a guide for Member states in all aspects of life;

Having examined the stages through which the preparation of this draft Document has so far, passed and the relevant report of the Secretary General;

Having examined the Report of the Meeting of the Committee of Legal Experts held in Tehran from 26 to 28 December, 1989;

Agrees to issue the Cairo Declaration on Human Rights in Islam that will serve as a general guidance for Member States in the Field of human rights.

Reaffirming the civilizing and historical role of the Islamic Ummah which Allah made as the best community and which gave humanity a universal and well-balanced civilization, in which harmony is established between hereunder and the hereafter, knowledge is combined with faith, and to fulfill the expectations from this community to guide all humanity which is confused because of different and conflicting beliefs and ideologies and to provide solutions for all chronic problems of this materialistic civilization.

In contribution to the efforts of mankind to assert human rights, to protect man from exploitation and persecution, and to affirm his freedom and right to a dignified life in accordance with the Islamic Shari'ah.

Convinced that mankind which has reached an advanced stage in materialistic science is still, and shall remain, in dire need of faith to support its civilization as well as a self motivating force to guard its rights;

Believing that fundamental rights and freedoms according to Islam are an integral part of the Islamic religion and that no one shall have the right as a matter of principle to abolish them either in whole or in part or to violate or ignore them in as much as they are binding divine commands, which are contained in the Revealed Books of Allah and which were sent through the last of His Prophets to complete the preceding divine messages and that safeguarding those fundamental rights and freedoms is an act of worship whereas the neglect or violation thereof is an abominable sin, and that the safeguarding of those fundamental rights and freedom is an individual responsibility of every person and a collective responsibility of the entire Ummah;

Do hereby and on the basis of the above-mentioned principles declare as follows:

ARTICLE 1:

(a) All human beings form one family whose members are united by their subordination to Allah and descent from Adam. All men are equal in terms of basic human dignity and basic obligations and responsibilities, without any discrimination on the basis of race, colour, language, belief, sex, religion, political affiliation, social status or other considerations. The true religion is the guarantee for enhancing such dignity along the path to human integrity.

(b) All human beings are Allah's subjects, and the most loved by Him are those who are most beneficial to His subjects, and no one has superiority over another except on the basis of piety and good deeds.

ARTICLE 2:

(a) Life is a God-given gift and the right to life is guaranteed to every human being. It is the duty of individuals, societies and states to safeguard this right against any violation, and it is prohibited to take away life except for a shari'ah prescribed reason.

(b) It is forbidden to resort to any means which could result in the genocidal annihilation of mankind.

(c) The preservation of human life throughout the term of time willed by Allah is a duty prescribed by Shari'ah.

(d) Safety from bodily harm is a guaranteed right. It is the duty of the state to safeguard it, and it is prohibited to breach it without a Shari'ah-prescribed reason.

ARTICLE 3:

(a) In the event of the use of force and in case of armed conflict, it is not permissible to kill non-belligerents such as old men, women and children. The wounded and the sick shall have the right to medical treatment; and prisoners of war shall have the right to be fed, sheltered and clothed. It is prohibited to mutilate or dismember dead bodies. It is required to exchange prisoners of war and to arrange visits or reunions of families separated by circumstances of war.

(b) It is prohibited to cut down trees, to destroy crops or livestock, to destroy the enemy's civilian buildings and installations by shelling, blasting or any other means.

ARTICLE 4:

Every human being is entitled to human sanctity and the protection of one's good name and honour during one's life and after one's death. The state and the society shall protect one's body and burial place from desecration.

ARTICLE 5:

(a) The family is the foundation of society, and marriage is the basis of making a family. Men and women have the right to marriage, and no restrictions stemming from race, colour or nationality shall prevent them from exercising this right.

(b) The society and the State shall remove all obstacles to marriage and facilitate it, and shall protect the family and safeguard its welfare.

ARTICLE 6:

(a) Woman is equal to man in human dignity, and has her own rights to enjoy as well as duties to perform, and has her own civil entity and financial independence, and the right to retain her name and lineage.

(b) The husband is responsible for the maintenance and welfare of the family.

ARTICLE 7:

(a) As of the moment of birth, every child has rights due from the parents, the society and the state to be accorded proper nursing, education and material, hygienic and moral care. Both the fetus and the mother must be safeguarded and accorded special care.

(b) Parents and those in such like capacity have the right to choose the type of education they desire for their children, provided they take into consideration the interest and future of the children in accordance with ethical values and the principles of the Shari'ah.

(c) Both parents are entitled to certain rights from their children, and relatives are entitled to rights from their kin, in accordance with the tenets of the shari'ah.

ARTCLE 8:

Every human being has the right to enjoy a legitimate eligibility with all its prerogatives and obligations in case such eligibility is lost or impaired, the person shall have the right to be represented by his/her guardian.

ARTICLE 9:

(a) The seeking of knowledge is an obligation and provision of education is the duty of the society and the State. The State shall ensure the availability of ways and means to acquire education and shall guarantee its diversity in the interest of the society so as to enable man to be acquainted with the religion of Islam and uncover the secrets of the Universe for the benefit of mankind.

(b) Every human being has a right to receive both religious and worldly education from the various institutions of teaching, education and guidance, including the family, the school, the university, the media, etc., and in such an integrated and balanced manner that would develop human personality, strengthen man's faith in Allah and promote man's respect to and defence of both rights and obligations.

ARTICLE 10:

Islam is the religion of true unspoiled nature. It is prohibited to exercise any form of pressure on man or to exploit his poverty or ignorance in order to force him to change his religion to another religion or to atheism.

ARTICLE 11:

(a) Human beings are born free, and no one has the right to enslave, humiliate, oppress or exploit them, and there can be no subjugation but to Allah the Almighty.

(b) Colonialism of all types being one of the most evil forms of enslavement is totally prohibited. Peoples suffering from colonialism have the full right to freedom and self-determination. It is the duty of all States peoples to support the struggle of colonized peoples for the liquidation of all forms of and occupation, and all States and peoples have the right to preserve their independent identity and econtrol over their wealth and natural resources.

ARTICLE 12:

Every man shall have the right, within the framework of the Shari'ah, to free movement and to select his place of residence whether within or outside his country and if persecuted, is entitled to seek asylum in another country. The country of refuge shall be obliged to provide protection to the asylum-seeker until his safety has been attained, unless asylum is motivated by committing an act regarded by the Shari'ah as a crime.

ARTICLE 13:

Work is a right guaranteed by the State and the Society for each person with capability to work. Everyone shall be free to choose the work that suits him best and which serves his interests as well as those of the society. The employee shall have the right to enjoy safety and security as well as all other social guarantees. He may not be assigned work beyond his capacity nor shall he be subjected to compulsion or exploited or harmed in any way. He shall be entitled - without any discrimination between males and females - to fair wages for his work without delay, as well as to the holidays allowances and promotions which he deserves. On his part, he shall be required to be dedicated and meticulous in his work. Should workers and employers disagree on any matter, the State shall intervene to settle the dispute and have the grievances redressed, the rights confirmed and justice enforced without bias.

ARTICLE 14:

Everyone shall have the right to earn a legitimate living without monopolization, deceit or causing harm to oneself or to others. Usury (riba) is explicitly prohibited.

ARTICLE 15:

(a) Everyone shall have the right to own property acquired in a legitimate way, and shall be entitled to the rights of ownership without prejudice to oneself, others or the society in general. Expropriation is not permissible except for requirements of public interest and upon payment of prompt and fair compensation.

(b) Confiscation and seizure of property is prohibited except for a necessity dictated by law.

ARTICLE 16:

Everyone shall have the right to enjoy the fruits of his scientific, literary, artistic or technical labour of which he is the author; and he shall have the right to the protection of his moral and material interests stemming therefrom, provided it is not contrary to the principles of the Shari'ah.

ARTICLE 17:

(a) Everyone shall have the right to live in a clean environment, away from vice and moral corruption, that would favour a healthy ethical development of his person and it is incumbent upon the State and society in general to afford that right.

(b) Everyone shall have the right to medical and social care, and to all public amenities provided by society and the State within the limits of their available resources.

(c) The States shall ensure the right of the individual to a decent living that may enable him to meet his requirements and those of his dependents, including food, clothing, housing, education, medical care and all other basic needs.

ARTICLE 18:

(a) Everyone shall have the right to live in security for himself, his religion, his dependents, his honour and his property.

(b) Everyone shall have the right to privacy in the conduct of his private affairs, in his home, among his family, with regard to his property and his relationships. It is not permitted to spy on him, to place him under surveillance or to besmirch his good name. The State shall protect him from arbitrary interference.

(c) A private residence is inviolable in all cases. It will not be entered without permission from its inhabitants or in any unlawful manner, nor shall it be demolished or confiscated and its dwellers evicted.

ARTICLE 19:

(a) All individuals are equal before the law, without distinction between the ruler and the ruled.

(b) The right to resort to justice is guaranteed to everyone.

(c) Liability is in essence personal.

(d) There shall be no crime or punishment except as provided for in the Shari'ah.

(e) A defendant is innocent until his guilt is proven in a fast trial in which he shall be given all the guarantees of defence.

ARTICLE 20:

It is not permitted without legitimate reason to arrest an individual, or restrict his freedom, to exile or to punish him. It is not permitted to subject him to physical or psychological torture or to any form of maltreatment, cruelty or indignity. Nor is it permitted to subject an individual to medical or scientific experiments without hisconsent or at the risk of his health or of his life. Nor is it permitted to promulgate emergency laws that would provide executive authority for such actions.

ARTICLE 21:

Taking hostages under any form or for any purpose is expressly forbidden.

ARTICLE 22:

(a) Everyone shall have the right to express his opinion freely in such manner as would not be contrary to the principles of the Shari'ah.

1.. Everyone shall have the right to advocate what is right, and propagate what is good, and warn against what is wrong and evil according to the norms of Islamic Shari'ah.

(c) Information is a vital necessity to society. It may not be exploited or misused in such a way as may violate sanctities and the dignity of Prophets, undermine moral and ethical Values or disintegrate, corrupt or harm society or weaken its faith.

(d) It is not permitted to excite nationalistic or doctrinal hatred or to do anything that may be an incitement to any form or racial discrimination.

ARTICLE 23:

(a) Authority is a trust; and abuse or malicious exploitation thereof is explicitly prohibited, in order to guarantee fundamental human rights.

(b) Everyone shall have the right to participate, directly or indirectly in the administration of his country's public affairs. He shall also have the right to assume public office in accordance with the provisions of Shari'ah.

ARTICLE 24:

All the rights and freedoms stipulated in this Declaration are subject to the Islamic Shari'ah.

ARTICLE 25:

The Islamic Shari'ah is the only source of reference for the explanation or clarification of any of the articles of this Declaration.

Bibliography

"'There is no such thing as free speech': an interview with Stanley Fish" (http://www.australianhumanitiesreview.org/archive/Issue-February-1998/fish.html.

Abdul Baaqi, Muhammad Fuad. *al-Mujam al-Mufahras li-Alfaadh al-Quran al-Kareem.* Cairo, Egypt: Daar al-Hadeeth. 1364 A.H.

Abou El Fadhl, Khalid. "The Human Rights Commitment in Modern Islam," in Joseph Runzo, Nancy M. Martin and Arvind Sharma, eds. *Human Rights and Responsibilities in the World Religions.* Oxford, England: One World. 2003.

Abou El Fadl, Khaled, et al. *Islam and the Challenge of Democracy.* Princeton: Princeton University Press. 2004.

Abou El Fadl, Khaled. "Islam and the Challenge of Democratic Commitment." In Elizabeth M. Bucar and Barbra Barnett, eds. *Does Human Rights Need God?* Grand Rapids, Michigan: William B. Eerdmans Publishing Company. 2005.

Abu Zahrah, Muhammad. *Maalik: Hayaatuhu wa Asruhu Araauhu wa Fiqhuhu.* Daar al-Fikr al-Arabi. N.d.

Afkhami, Mahnaz. "Gender Apartheid and the Discourse of Relativity of Rights in Muslim Societies." In Courtney W. Howland. *Religious Fundamentalisms and the Human Rights of Women.* New York, NY: Palgrave. 2001.

Ahmad, S. Maqbul. "Ibn Rushd." In B. Lewis, et al. *The Encyclopaedia of Islam.* Leiden: E. J. Brill. 1986.

Ajalooni, Ismaaeel al-. *Kashf al-Khafaa.* Beirut, Lebanon: Muasassah al-Risaalah. 1405 A.H.

al-Albaani, Muhammad Naasir al-Deen. *Irwaa al-Ghaleel fi Takhreej Ahaadeeth Manaar al-Sabeel.* Beirut, Lebanon: al-Maktab al-Islaami. 1985.

Alexander, Larry. *Is There a Right of Freedom of Expression?* New York: Cambridge University Press. 2005.

Ali, Shaheen Sardar. *Gender and Human Rights in Islam and International Law: Equal Before Allah, Unequal Before Man?* The Hague, Netherlands: Kluwer Law International. 2000.

al-Nabraawi, Khadeejah. *Mausooah Huqooq al-Insaan fi al-Islaam.* Cairo, Egypt: Dar al-Salaam. 2006.

al-Shareef, Kaamil. "Huqooq al-Insaan fi Saheefah al-Madeenah." In *Huqooq al-Insaan bain al-Shareeah al-Islaamiyyah wa al-Qaanoon al-Widhiee.* Riyadh, Saudi Arabia: Naif Arab Academy for Security Sciences. 2001.

An-Na'im, Abdullahi Ahmed. *Toward an Islamic Reformation: Civil Liberties, Human Rights, and International Law.* Syracuse, NY: Syracuse University Press. 1990.

An-Na'im, Abdullahi. "The Synergy and Interdependence of Human Rights, Religion and Secularism," in Runzo, et al.

Aql, Naasir al-. *Sharh al-Aqeedah al-Tahaawiyyah.* Riyadh, Saudi Arabia: Markaz al-Najaashi.

Asbahaani, Abu Nuaim al-. *Hilyah al-Auliyaa.* Beirut, Lebanon: Daar al-Kitaab al-Arabi. 1405 A.H.

Baderin, Mashood. *International Human Rights and Islamic Law.* Oxford, England: Oxford University Press. 2003.

Badri, Abdul Azeez al-. *al-Islaam bain al-Ulamaa wa al-Hukkaam.* Madinah, Saudi Arabia: al-Maktabah al-Ilmiyyah. n.d.

Bahi, Muhammad al-. *al-Tafriqah al-Unsiriyyah wa al-Islaam.* Cairo: Maktabah Wahba. 1979.

Bainton, Roland H. *Christian Attitudes Toward War & Peace: A Historical Survey and Critical Re-Evaluation.* Nashville, TN: Abingdon Press. 1990.

Bauman, Richard A. *Human Rights in Ancient Rome.* Routledge: London. 2000.

Bell, Daniel A. *East Meets West: Human Rights and Democracy in East Asia.* Princeton, NJ: Princeton University Press. 2000.

bin Taib, Nasseri. "Islam and Eradication of Poverty: An Ethical Dimension of Development with Special Reference to Malaysia's Five Year Plans." Ph.D. Dissertation. Temple University. 1989.

Bloom, Allan. *The Closing of the American Mind.* New York: Simon and Schuster. 1987.

Bricmont, Jean, *Humanitarian Imperialism: Using Human Rights to Sell War* New York: Monthly Review Press. 2006.

Bucar, Elizabeth M. and Barbra Barnett. "Introduction: The 'Why' of Human Rights." In Elizabeth M. Bucar and Barbra Barnett, eds. *Does Human Rights Need God?* Grand Rapids, Michigan: William B. Eerdmans Publishing Company. 2005.

Bumiraaf, Saeedah. "Al-Taleel al-Maslahi li-Tasarrufaat al-Haakim." Master's Thesis. University of Baatinah. Algeria. 2008.

Caner, Ergun Mehmet, and Emir Fethi Caner. *Christian Jihad.* Grand Rapids, MI: Kregel Publications. 2004.

Chandler, David. *From Kosovo to Kabul: Human Rights and International Intervention.* Sterling, VA: Pluto Press. 2002.

Charney, Jonathan I. "Universal International Law." 87 *American J. International L.* 529. 1993.

Clapham, Andrew. *Human Rights: A Very Short Introduction.* Oxford, England: Oxford University Press. 2007.

Conferences of Riyad, Paris, Vatican City, Geneva and Strassbourg on Moslem Doctrine and Human Rights in Islam between Saudi Canonists and Eminent European Jurists and Intellectuals. Riyadh, Saudi Arabia: Ministry of Justice. n.d.

D'Amato, Anthony. "Is International Law Really 'Law'?" 79 *Northwestern University Law Review.* 1293 (1985).

Denniston, George, Frederick Hodges and Marylin F. Milos. *Circumcision and Human Rights*. Springer. 2009.

Desai, Manisha. "Women's Rights." In James R. Lewis and Carl Skutsch. *The Human Rights Encyclopedia*. Armonk, New York: Sharpe Reference. 2001.

Donnelly, Jack. "An Overview," in David P. Forsythe, ed. *Human Rights and Comparative Foreign Policy*. Tokyo, Japan: United Nations University Press. 2000.

Donnelly, Jack. *Universal Human Rights in Theory & Practice*. Ithaca: Cornell University Press. 2003.

Elshtain, Jean Bethke. "Afterword," in Bucar and Barnett.

Encyclopædia Britannica: Ultimate Reference Suite. Chicago: Encyclopædia Britannica. 2009.

Feldman, Noah. "The Best Hope." In Khaled Abou El Fadl, et al. *Islam and the Challenge of Democracy*. Princeton: Princeton University Press. 2004.

Freeman, Michael. *Human Rights*. Cambridge, England: Polity Press. 2002.

George, Robert P. "Natural Law and Human Rights: A Conversation," in Bucar and Barnett.

Ghaamidi, Abdul Lateef al-. *Huqooq al-Insaan fi al-Islaam*. Riyadh, Saudi Arabia: Naif Arab Academy for Security Sciences. 2000.

Ghaamidi, Naasir al-. "Qaaidah al-Tasarruf ala al-Raiyyah Manoot bi-l-Maslahah: Diraasah Taseeliyyah Tabqeeqiyyah Fiqhiyyah." *Majallah Jaamiat Umm al-Qura li-Uloom al-Shareeah wa al-Diraasaat al-Islaamiyyah*. No.46. Muharram 1430.

Gokal, Alison Swicker. "Human Rights and Shari'a: An Essay on the development and use of Shari'a in Islamic States and its meaning for Women in Iran, a country with a history of criticism from Human Rights groups and the United Nations." *Hertfordshire Law Journal* 5(1), 86-106.

Goldhaber, Michael. *A People's History of the European Court of Human Rights*. New Brunswick, NJ: Rutgers University Press. 2007.

Gray, John. *Men are from Mars, Women are from Venus.* New York, New York: Harpers Paperback. 2004.

Green, Jonathon and Nicholas J. Karolides, *Encyclopedia of Censorship.* New York, NY: Facts on File, Inc. 2005.

Gregorian, Vartan Gregorian. "Islam: A Mosaic, not a Monolith." www. drsoroush/E-CMO-20021100-Islam-A_Mosaic-Not_a_Monolith.html.

Griffin, James. *On Human Rights.* Oxford, England: Oxford University Press. 2008.

Guroian, Vigen. "Human Rights and Modern Western Faith: An Orthodox Christian Assessment," in Bucar and Barnett.

Gustafson, Carrie and Peter Juviler, eds. *Religion and Human Rights: Competing Claims.* Armonk, New York: M. E. Sharpe. 1999.

Gustafson, Carrie and Peter Juviler. "Foreword." In Carrie Gustafson and Peter Juviler, eds. *Religion and Human Rights: Competing Claims.* Armonk, New York: M. E. Sharpe. 1999.

Gutmann, Amy. "Introduction." In Michael Ignatieff, *Human Rights as Politics and Religion.* Princeton, NJ: Princeton University Press. 2001.

Halsell , Grace. *Forcing God's Hand: Why Millions Pray for a Quick Rapture ... and Destruction of Planet Earth.* Amana Publications. 2002.

Hathout, Maher with Uzma Jamil, Gasser Hathout and Nayyer Ali. *In Pursuit of Justice: The Jurisprudence of Human Rights in Islam.* Los Angeles, CA: Muslim Public Affairs Council. 2006.

Hawley, John Stratton. "Fundamentalism." In Courtney W. Howland. *Religious Fundamentalisms and the Human Rights of Women.* New York, NY: Palgrave. 2001.

Helaoui, Sarah. "Cultural Relativism and Reservations to Human Rights Treaties: The Legal Effects of the Saudi Reservation to CEDAW." Master's Thesis. Faculty of Law. University of Lund. 2004.

Henkin, Louis. "Religion, Religions, and Human Rights," in Bucar and Barnett.

Henry J. Steiner and Philip Alston, *International Human Rights in Context: Law, Politics, Morals.* Oxford, England: Oxford University Press. 1996.

Hertz, Noreena. *The Debt Threat.* New York: HarperBusiness. 2004.

Human Rights Watch, "Questions and Answers on the Danish Cartoons and Freedom of Expression," at

http://www.hrw.org/legacy/english/docs/2006/02/15/denmar12676.htm.

Huqail, Sulaiman al-. *Huqooq al-Insaan fi al-Islaam wa al-Radd ala al-Shubuhaat al-Mathaarah Haulahaa.* self-published. 2003.

Hussain, Amir. "'This tremor of Western wisdom': A Muslim response to human rights and the declaration." In Joseph Runzo, Nancy M. Martin and Arvind Sharma, eds. *Human Rights and Responsibilities in the World Religions.* Oxford, England: One World. 2003.

ibn al-Qayyim, Muhammad. *Al-Turuq al-Hukumiyyah.* Cairo, Egypt: Matbaah al-Madani. n.d.

ibn Asaakeer, Ali ibn al-Hasan. *Tareekh Madeenah Dimashq.* Beirut, Lebanon: Daar al-Fikr. 1995.

ibn Baih, Abdullah. *Hawaar an Bu'd Haul Huqooq al-Insaan fi al-Islaam.* Riyadh: Maktabah al-Ubaikaan. 2007.

ibn Hajar, Ahmad. *Fath al-Baari fi Sharh Sahih al-Bukhari.* Beirut, Lebanon: Daar al-Marifah. n.d.

ibn Katheer, Ismaaeel. *al-Bidaayah wa al-Nihaayah.* Beirut, Lebanon: Maktabah al-Maarif. n.d.

ibn Katheer, Ismaaeel. *Al-Bidaayah wa al-Nihaayah.* Beirut: Dar al-Kutub al-Ilmiyya. n.d.

ibn Mujaahid, Ahmad. *Kitaab al-Saba fi al-Qiraat.* Cairo, Egypt: Daar al-Maarif. n.d.

ibn Taimiyyah, Ahmad. *Majmooah Fataawa ibn Taimiyyah*. Riyadh: collected by Abdul Rahmaan ibn al-Qaasim and his son Muhammad.

Ignatieff, Michael. *Human Rights as Politics and Religion* (with commentary by K. Anthony Appiah, David A. Hollinger, Thomas W. Laqueur, Diane F. Orentlicher). Princeton, NJ: Princeton University Press, 2001.

Ishay, Micheline R. *The History of Human Rights: From Ancient Times to the Globalization Era*. Berkeley, CA: University of California Press. 2004.

Jaarid, Faatimah al-. *Inaayah al-Sunnah al-Nabawiyyah bi-Huqooq al-Insaan*. Riyadh, Saudi Arabia: Naif Prize. 2005.

Jackson, Sherman. "Concretizing the Maqaasid: Islam in the Modern World." *International Conference on Islamic Jurisprudence and the Challenges of the 21st Century: Maqasid al-Shari'ah and its Realization in Contemporary Societies*. Kuala Lumpur, Malaysia: International Islamic University Malaysia. 2006.

Johnson, James Turner. *The Holy War Idea in Western and Islamic Traditions*. University Park, PA: The Pennsylvania State University Press. 1997.

Johnson, James Turner. "Historical Roots and Sources of the Just War Tradition in Western Culture," in John Kelsay and James Turner Johnson, *Historical and Theoretical Perspectives On War And Peace In Western And Islamic Traditions*. New York: Greenwood Press. 1991.

Judai, Abdullah al-. *Taiseer Ilm Usool al-Fiqh*. Beirut: Muassasah al-Rayyaan. 1997.

Kausar, Zeenath. *Woman's Empowerment and Islam: The UN Beijing Document Platform for Action*. Selangor, Malaysia: Ilmiah Publishers. 2002.

Khoder, Mohammad. *Human Rights in Islam*. Beirut: Dar Khoder. N.d.

Kotb, Sayed. *Social Justice in Islam*. New York, New York: Octagon Books. 1970.

Kung, Hans and Jurgen Moltmann. *The Ethics of World Religions and Human Rights*. London, England: SCM Press. 1990.

Larry Rasmussen. "Human Environmental Rights and/or Biotic Rights," in Gustafson and Juviler.

Luwaihiq, Abdul Rahmaan al-. *Religious Extremism in the Lives of Contemporary Muslims.* Denver, CO: Al-Basheer Company for Publications and Translations. 2001.

M. Bucar, Elizabeth and Barbra Barnett, eds. *Does Human Rights Need God?* Grand Rapids, Michigan: William B. Eerdmans Publishing Company. 2005.

Majallah Majma al-Fiqh al-Islaami. No. 13. 2001.

Mamdani, Mahmood. *Good Muslim, Bad Muslim: America, the Cold War, and the Roots of Terror.* New York: Pantheon Books. 2004.

Martin, Richard C. Martin, editor in chief. *Encyclopedia of Islam and the Muslim World.* New York: MacMillan Reference USA. 2004.

Mawdudi, Abu Ala. *Human Rights in Islam.* Leicester, England: the Islamic Foundation. 1976.

Mayer, Ann Elizabeth *Islam and Human Rights: Tradition and Politics.* Boulder, CO: Westview Press. 4th Edition. 2007.

Mayer, Ann Elizabeth. "Cultural Particularism as a Bar to Women's Rights: Reflections on the Middle Eastern Experience." In Julie Peters and Andrea Wolper, eds., *Women's Rights Human Rights: International Feminist Perspectives.* New York: Routledge. 1995.

Mayer, Ann Elizabeth. "Reconsidering the Human Rights Framework for Applying Islamic Criminal Law," http://lgst.wharton.upenn.edu/mayera/Documents/mayerislamabad05.pdf.

Mayer, Ann Elizabeth. *Islam and Human Rights.* Boulder, CO: Westview Press. 1999.

McGoldrick, Dominic. *Human Rights and Religion: The Islamic Headscarf Debate in Europe.* Portland, OR: Hart Publishing. 2006.

Meulders-Klein, Marie-Therese, Ruth Deech and Paul Vlaardingerbroek, *Biomedicine, the Family and Human Rights*. The Hague: Kluwer Law International. 2002.

Microsoft Encarta. 1993-2003 Microsoft Corporation.

Mittal, Anuradha and Peter Rosset. *America* Needs *Human Rights*. Oakland, CA: Food First Books. 1999.

Mohammadi, Ali and Muhammad Ahsan. *Globalisation or Reconolisation? The Muslim World in the 21st Century*. London: Ta-Ha Publishers, Ltd. 2002.

Nacos , Brigitte L., and Oscar Torres-Reyna. "Framing Muslim-Americans Before and After 9/11." In Pippa Norris, Montague Kern and Marion Just, eds. *Framing Terrorism: The News Media, the Government and the Public*. New York: Routledge. 2003.

Nadwah Huqooq al-Insaan fi al-Islaam. Makkah, Saudi Arabia: Raabitah al-Aalim al-Islaami. 2000.

Nakhoori, Sayid Thaur al-. *Inaayah al-Sunnah al-Nabawiyyah bi-Huqooq al-Insaan*. 2007.

Oh, Irene. *The Rights of God: Islam, Human Rights, and Comparative Ethics*. Washington, D.C.: Georgetown University Press. 2007.

Orend, Brian. *Human Rights: Concept and Context*. Ontario, Canada: Broadview Press. 2002.

Pease, Barbara and Allan Pease. *Why Men Don't Listen & Women Can't Read Maps*. Broadway. 2001.

Perry, Michael J. *The Idea of Human Rights: Four Inquiries*. New York: Oxford University Press. 1998.

Pinker, Steven. "The Mystery of Consciousness." *Time Magazine*. Friday, Jan. 19, 2007.

Qaisi, Marwaan al-. *Mausooah Huqooq al-Insaan fi al-Islaam*. http://www.scribd.com/doc/970694/1-.

Qurtubi, Muhammad ibn Ahmad al-. *al-Jaami li-Ahkaam al-Quraan*. Riyadh, Saudi Arabia: Daar Aalim al-Kutub.

Reeves, Minou. *Muhammad in Europe: A Thousand Years of Western Myth-Making*. Washington Square, New York: New York University Press. 2000.

Runza, Joseph, Nancy M. Martin and Arvind Sharma, eds. *Human Rights and Responsibilities in the World Religions*. Oxford, England: Oneworld Publications. 2003.

Ryn, Claes G. *America the Virtuous: The Crisis of Democracy and the Quest for Empire*. New Brunswick, New Jersey: Transaction Publishers. 2004.

Sallaabee, Ali al-. *The Biography of Abu Bakr As-Siddeeq*. Riyadh, Saudi Arabia: Daar al-Salaam. 2007.

Sallabi, Ali Muhammad al-. *Umar ibn al-Khattab: His Life & Times*. Riyadh, Saudi Arabia: International Islamic Publishing House. 2007.

Saloom, Rachel. "You Dropped a Bomb on Me, Denmark—A Legal Examination of the Cartoon Controversy and Response as it Relates to the Prophet Muhammad and Islamic Law." *Rutgers Journal of Law and Religion*. Volume 8. Fall 2006.

Schwartz, Stephen. *The Two Faces of Islam: The House of Sa'ud from Tradition to Terror.* New York: Doubleday, 2002.

Sheha, Abdul Rahman al-. *Misconceptions on Human Rights in Islam*. Riyadh, Saudi Arabia: Islamic Propagation Office. 2001.

Shue, Henry. *Basic Rights: Subsistence, Affluence and U.S. Foreign Policy*. Princeton University Press. 1980.

Soage, Ana Belen. "The Danish Caricatures Seen from the Arab World." *Totalitarian Movements and Political Regimes*. Vol. 7. No. 3. September 2006.

Sommers, Christina Hoff. *Who Stole Feminism?* New York, Simon and Schuster. 1994.

Spectrum. IEEE. June 2008.

Stackhouse, Max. "Why Human Rights Needs God: A Christian Perspective," in Bucar and Barnett,

The Bible Suite Collection. ValuSoft. 2006.

Voll, John. "Republican Brothers." In Richard C. Martin, ed. *Encyclopedia of Islam and the Muslim World.* New York, New York: MacMillan Reference. 2004.

Waldron, J. ed., *"Nonsense Upon Stilts": Bentham, Burke and Marx on the Rights of Men.* London, England: Methuen. 1987.

Witte, Jr., John and Johan D. van der Vyver, eds. *Religious Human Rights in Global Perspective* The Hague, Holland: Martinus Nijhoff Publishers. 1996.

Wolfrum, Rudiger and Ulrike Deutsch, eds. *The European Court of Human Rights Overwhelmed by Applications: Problems and Possible Solutions.* Berlin, Germany: Springer. 2009.

Yaaseen, Hikmat. *Inaayah al-Sunnah al-Nabawiyyah bi-Huqooq al-Insaan.* Riyadh, Saudi Arabia: Naif Prize. 2005.

Yu, Anthony C. "Enduring Change:Confucianism and the Prospect of Human Rights," in Elizabeth M. Bucar and Barbra Barnett, eds. *Does Human Rights Need God?* Grand Rapids, Michigan: William B. Eerdmans Publishing Company. 2005.

Zarabozo, Jamaal al-Din. *The Authority and Importance of the Sunnah.* Denver, CO: Al-Basheer Company. 2000.

Zarabozo, Jamaal. *What is Islam.* Riyadh, Saudi Arabia: Ministry of Religious Affairs. 2005.

Table of Contents